BAGGARA ARABS

Humrawi horseman

(Frontispiece)

BAGGARA ARABS

Power and the Lineage in a Sudanese Nomad Tribe

By
IAN CUNNISON

CLARENDON PRESS
OXFORD
1966

Oxford University Press, Ely House, London W. 1

GLASGOW NEW YORK TORONTO MELBOURNE WELLINGTON
CAPE TOWN SALISBURY IBADAN NAIROBI LUSAKA ADDIS ABABA
BOMBAY CALCUTTA MADRAS KARACHI LAHORE DACCA
KUALA LUMPUR HONG KONG

PRINTED IN GREAT BRITAIN IN THE CITY OF OXFORD AT THE ALDEN PRESS

PREFACE

In spite of the recognized place of Sudanese studies in the literature of social anthropology, it is only recently that anthropologists have taken a sustained interest in the predominantly Arab and Muslim north of the country. Indeed, up to the time of independence only Professor and Mrs. Seligman had produced—on the Kababish—anything approaching a tribal monograph, and this was as long ago as the First World War. Occasional short articles by Government officials and others have appeared since then, but until the considerable research which is now being undertaken, largely from the University of Khartoum, has been published, our information on the social forms of the region will remain rudimentary.

When the Sudan Government offered in 1951 to finance a full study of one of the nomadic, cattle-owning Baggara tribes it was an opportunity to be welcomed. Among these tribes the Humr of Kordofan Province are, with the Rizeygat of Darfur, the most renowned, the most numerous, and probably the most conservative. But they are unlikely to retain for much longer their present way of life. Fortunately this could be recorded while it flourished in its pre-development era: fortunately not only because of its academic interest but also because, as I hope, the publication of the data will enable the Humr to be developed in a way consistent with their social organization and values, and will help planners to envisage a successful scheme for them.

Various articles on this research, which are listed in the Bibliography, were written in response to a lively interest by Sudanese civil servants with responsibilities for development, and paid particular attention to problems which the economic development of the territory, and in particular the settlement of the nomads, might give rise to.

But radical change is mostly in the future. Change has nevertheless been proceeding, notably in the administrative field. In the nineteenth century, the period of Turkish rule in the Sudan followed by the years of the Sudanese Mahdist state, many events affected the relation of the Humr with their neighbours, including the governments of the country. The twentieth century saw the establishment of the Anglo-Egyptian

Condominium in which even the most independent of Sudanese tribes came under some kind of control, and the warfare and raiding which had characterized their relations with their neighbours were brought to an end. With the development of new institutions of administrative control, the internal politics of the Humr also took on new forms.

This book is a general account of Humr social organization centring on these changes in the political field. The Humr have always had some men occupying positions of leadership and having power at their disposal. Last century these leaders often changed, the range of their following altered swiftly with passing events, and the distribution of leadership throughout the tribe was irregular. The Condominium Government in contrast established positions of power at the head of the larger lineages, and, since it administered the tribe through these positions, saw to it that they were filled at all times. These new and relatively stabilized positions of power came to co-exist with the traditional segmentary lineage system, and it is to the resulting problems that this account gives most attention. These problems could not be considered without reference to the way leaders arise from the milieu of camp, lineage, and family, and this in turn depends upon an appreciation of men's economic responsibilities and the means of fulfilling them. These considerations have set the plan of the book.

I spent in all about twenty-five months in the field, between August 1952 and January 1955. In the middle, I went to England for about three months. I had my home in the camp of Ḥurgaṣ Merida, one of the eleven omdas of the tribe, and I lived and fed as a member of this camp.

It was by no means easy to collect research material. The contrast in this respect with my previous experience in what is now Zambia was marked. There, I could hardly keep pace with the transcription of notes, material was so readily obtainable. Here, I found few people in the camps who were prepared to spend time in question-and-answer sessions, or in producing 'texts', although I found towards the end of my second year that this was becoming possible. My work depends far more upon observation and participation than is usual, and far less upon regular informants and ethnographic texts. This difference from normal fieldwork practice should be noted, as it presumably affects the value of the findings.

Using Ḥurgaṣ's shifting camp as home I took trips to see most of the parts of Dar Humr which are used in the different seasons, and to visit all the omodiyas. It was possible to make such tours without jeopardizing relations with my camp mates, but it was less easy to spend long periods aways from camp in administrative centres, partly because the cattlemen have suspicions about the administration in general, and partly because I could be suspected of tiring of camp life and finding excuses to revert to despised urban ways. I did spend some time at Muglad visiting the courts, usually when Ḥurgaṣ himself was there on some official errand, but I only once visited the Rural Council at El Fula, and there is a gap here in my fieldwork. Yet for the sake of my position in the camps, which I regarded as most important, I was always glad to return to them.

The account which follows is a third main draft. Within a few months of leaving the field I prepared a short report for the Ministry of the Interior. This was later expanded in an attempt to clothe a structural account in the detail of old style ethnography. The result was unsatisfactory, and inordinately long, but the work of distilling that draft into this one helped to clarify the issues which did in fact exist.

Humr speak a dialect of Arabic which is quite distinct from any written Arabic, whether the classical or the language of Sudanese literature and newspapers. I have chosen to transliterate from the dialect rather than from the classical or standard Arabic words with which the dialect would seem to be connected; but I have kept familiar words in their standardized English usage: for example El Obeid, Muglad, Bahr, Humr, Nazir, Omda, Sheikh.

Full bibliographical references to titles cited in the text are given at the end of the book.

POSTSCRIPT

The Sudan became independent shortly after I left the field. There was a Parliamentary régime for the first three years, and for most of this time the Umma party shared in a coalition Government. In November 1958 the country came under a fairly mild military dictatorship. In October 1964 a popular, almost bloodless revolution dismissed the military, and at the time of writing a caretaker civilian Government is preparing for elections.

During the military régime the local councils were abolished but later reopened with largely nominated members. They will no doubt reappear in their old form. During that period also the long-planned railway to the west and south was completed, so that a new town, 'Babanusa', has emerged at the junction of the two lines from Nyala and from Wau. The Wau line cuts south through western Dar Humr.

At the new town of Babanusa a milk-processing factory is being built.

One of the first acts of the caretaker Government was to reconsider the position of tribal nazirs. At first it was proposed to do away with their magisterial powers, but later it appeared that the nazirs should retain them for the time being, to keep their disciplinary roles intact. A committee is now examining the whole question of their positions.

Another important recent development has been the outbreak of hostilities between the Humr and the Ngok Dinka, who for twenty-five years had been fellow members of Dar Messiriya Rural Council. I have so far only heard the Humr side of the dispute; but it is so serious that the Humr are going less far south during the present dry season and are marketing not at Abyei, but at Antila, about twenty miles north. The hostilities have resulted in numerous deaths. The trouble dates from the rains of 1964, and is said to be connected with the activities of the southern Sudanese rebels. They are particularly tragic because Dar Messiriya Rural Council had been a sphere of apparently friendly and fruitful co-operation between the north and south of the country.

ACKNOWLEDGEMENTS

I am grateful to the Sudan Government for financing field-work and a writing period. During my research I had the fullest co-operation from Mr. G. Hawkesworth and Sayed Mekkawi Suliman Akrat, Governors of Kordofan, and from Mr. G. M. G. Tibbs and Sayed Muḥammad Ibrahim 'Abd el Ḥafiz, District Commissioners of Dar Messiriya. A previous Commissioner, Dr. P. P. Howell, had left copious anthropological notes in the files; he also drafted a manuscript about the Humr, but, on learning that I was to make a full study, decided not to publish and instead allowed me to use his material. I am grateful for this generosity.

In Dar Humr, Nazir Babo Nimr, Nazir 'Ali Nimr, and Nazir Sereyr el Ḥaj gave me the facilities I wanted. Sayed Abu Jabr el Ḥaj made many arrangements for me, and gave much initial help with the Humr dialect. I was very fortunate in having the services of Sayed Muḥammad Kubr Menawwir. He worked with me throughout. Although he had no English he interpreted into Arabic at a speed I could understand, and he was also largely responsible for my progressive fluency in it. He was patient, tactful, and popular, and altogether a most satisfying colleague and friend.

In preparing the book for publication I had the benefit of what Max Gluckman and my colleagues at Manchester had to say about a first draft; I had detailed critiques from Neville Dyson-Hudson on the second draft and from Fredrik Barth and Talal Asad on the third. I thank them for their work; it is only fair to them to say that I did not succeed in meeting all their objections.

Khartoum, February 1965

CONTENTS

Preface v

Acknowledgements viii

1. INTRODUCTION 1
   - The position of the Humr among the Baggara 1
   - The sections of the tribe 8

2. LAND AND MOVEMENT 13
   - Types of land 13
   - Cattle movements 19
   - Cultivation 22
   - Movements of the main sections of the tribe 24

3. MEN AND CATTLE 28
   - The material uses of cattle 29
   - The cattle urge 31
   - Building and maintaining a herd 34
   - Cattle policy 36
   - The effect of administrative action 39

4. HOUSEHOLD AND EXTENDED FAMILY 42
   - The tent and the household goods 42
   - The maintenance of dependants 45
   - Examples of household organization 49

5. CAMP AND SURRA 59
   - Composition and residence of ‘Iyal Ganiṣ 59
   - The camp: physical 64
   - Co-operation in cattle management 66
   - The influence of cattle numbers on surra organization 68
   - Leadership and social co-operation within the surra 71
   - Co-operative aspects of cultivation 74
   - Modes of co-operation among ‘Iyal Ganiṣ 77
   - Non-Arab descent 80
   - The extension of personal followings 84

6. SOME FEATURES OF HUMR MARRIAGE 86
Distribution of marriage partners 86
The ideal and the practice 90
Marriage and political relations 94

7. A SEGMENTARY LINEAGE 97
Symbols of segmentation 97
Administration through agnatic groups 103
The brotherhood of the closest 110

8. SOME HUMR IDEAS ABOUT POWER 114
Women's role in the struggle for power 116
Power and the Government 118
Power and the Baramka association 122

9. TRIBAL POLITICS 129
Fights and alliances in the nineteenth century 129
Tribal politics since the Reoccupation 134
Power, alliances, and administrative action 143

10. THE OMODIYA 149
The omodiya as a lineage 149
The tribute sheikhs 151
Leaders of intermediate lineages 153
The course of disputes 154
Blood-money 157
Shifting alliances in the Mezaghna omodiya 162

11. RECENT POWER RELATIONS IN ONE OMODIYA 165
Mezaghna groups 165
Intrigue and the omdaship 170
The course of a blood feud 173

12. CONCLUSION: POWER AND THE AGNATIC SEGMENTARY MODEL 187

Appendix 1. Omodiya areas 195
2. Distribution of cattle through inheritance 198
3. Drum calls 201
4. Cattle brands 205
5. Details of a blood-money transaction 209
6. Speeches made at a peace-making ceremony 211
7. The omodiyas and their sections 213

Bibliography 223

Index 225

FIGURES

1. Administrative divisions of the Humr 10
2. Main camp of ʻIyal Ganiṣ, April 1954 50
3. Extended family of I. Merida 51
4. Extended family of I. Ḥamid 54
5. Extended family of I. Adim 54
6. Extended family of I. Jedid, with I. Bokur 55
7. Relationships of founders of I. Ganiṣ extended families 60
8. Nucleus of the splinter camp of I. Ganiṣ 62
9. Some possible types of camp formation 70
10. Non-Arab descent in I. Ganiṣ 81
11. Comparison of certain units of the ʻAjaira in about 1905 and in 1955 106
12. Usual version of relationships between groups descended from Muḥammad el Messir 112
13. Felaita bedanas during the Turkiya 130
14. ʻAjaira bedanas and sections mentioned in the Turkiya and Mahdiya episodes 132
15. The ruling families of ʻAjaira and Felaita 135
16. The division of the Humr into omodiyas 138
17. Some alliances within the Mezaghna omodiya 166

The agnatic segments of the Humr are shown, by omodiyas, in Appendix 7.

TABLES

1. Omodiya populations 9
2. Cattle moves 22
3. The Humr year 24
4. Distribution of marriage partners in two Mezaghna surras 87
5. Distribution of marriage partners in a surra of A. Kamil 87
6. Distribution of marriage partners in intra-surra marriages for three surras 89
7. Intra-surra marriages as first and subsequent marriages 89
8. Proportion of surra marriages ending in divorce compared with proportion of outside marriages ending in divorce 90
9. Proportion of divorces to total completed marriages in two surras 90
10. Tribute divisions of the 'Ajaira in 1905 104
11. Comparison between actual and legal distributions of cattle on inheritance 199

MAPS

1. The position of Dar Humr 5
2. Dar Humr in relation to the soil and vegetation types of the Sudan 14
3. Distribution of Humr omodiyas *facing p.* 224

LIST OF PLATES

Humrawi horseman *Frontispiece*

I. Migrating south through the Goz in December *facing p.* 20

II. Autumn camp in the Muglad 21

III. Men's tree at a hot dry season camp on the Bahr 64

IV. Omda Ḥurgaṣ with his elders on the way to peace-making ceremony 179

V. The end of the feud: saying the opening of the Koran 183

I

INTRODUCTION

THE POSITION OF THE HUMR AMONG THE BAGGARA

FOR generations the belt of savanna between Lake Chad and the White Nile has been the home of the Baggara Arab tribes. History and environment together throw light on their distribution.

The Arab nomads of the Sudan and Chad republics are of two kinds: camelmen and cattlemen. 'Baggara' means simply 'cattlemen' but Sudanese apply the word particularly to the nomadic cattlemen of this belt of country. The camelmen occupy the semi-desert southern fringes of the Sahara. The cattlemen live well to the south of them, away from the semi-desert, and in the Sudan they approach, and sometimes enter, the flood plains of the White Nile basin. They are Arabs who have been 'forced by circumstances to live in a country which will support the cow and not the camel',[1] for which their land is too wet and in places too muddy.

To judge from the few available accounts the Baggara tribes, who all keep cattle, are culturally similar in other ways as well, and most of them claim distant kinship with one another.[2] In the reckoning of their genealogists they span centuries to connect with the Guheyna, a section of the Himyarites of southern Arabia from the days before the Prophet Muḥammad. We do not know how the Baggara reached their present belt. Some say that after the Arab invasion of Egypt groups which later became Baggara continued their march along the north African coast to the present Tunisia, and then struck south across the desert. Others say that they formed a part of an invasion up the Nile valley at the end of the fourteenth century which is known to have consisted largely of Guheyna. In any event, they seem to have settled many centuries ago in the regions of Bagirmi and Wadai.[3]

[1] Henderson, 'The migration of the Messiria tribe into South West Kordofan', p. 49.

[2] The easternmost Baggara tribes, generically known as the 'White Nile Baggara', alone appear to have a different origin and markedly different customs; see Reid, 'Some notes on the tribes of the White Nile Province'.

[3] For these theories see Macmichael, *A History of the Arabs in the Sudan*, vol. I, pp. 276–8; and Henderson, op. cit., p. 52. The Humr make mention of *Tunis el*

Darfur. In 1822 it was conquered by Turco-Egyptian forces, and it remained under their control until 1883. In that year the Mahdist revolution broke out; it prevailed, and had political control of most of the Sudan until 1898, when the country was conquered by Britain and Egypt. Subsequently the Sudan came under the Anglo-Egyptian Condominium, and from 1899 this administration was effective in Kordofan.[12] Thus, throughout, Kordofan has been subject to rulers from elsewhere; and to the Baggara the rulers have always been settled peoples, different from themselves.[13]

Although Kordofan was under the Turkiya for sixty years, it is doubtful if the administration had firmer control over the nomads than the sultans had before them. There is little mention of the Humr in the literature of the Turkiya. Ignatius Pallme, writing of El Obeid, the capital of Kordofan, in 1837–8, speaks of

> Kordofan, one of the most southern provinces under the government of the viceroy of Egypt. . . . Towards the south, no definite confines can be described, as the extent of these dominions increases or decreases accordingly as the inhabitants of this part of the country become tributary either by their own free will or are rendered subjects by force as occasionally occurs and subsequently free themselves from the yoke.

He says of the Baggara of Kordofan that their tribute had generally to be collected by force, and that they were 'not reckoned among the other inhabitants of the five districts' into which the province was divided administratively. 'With the commencement of the hot season, they wander into distant regions, unknown to the governor of Kordofan, into which he dare not venture to penetrate.'[14] While the northern parts of Kordofan and Darfur were long in contact with the outside world by trade as well as through administration, much of the south, and Humr country in particular, remained unfamiliar.[15]

In consequence of the lateral movement which has been taking place for centuries, former Baggara groups have become widely scattered; they did not always move as complete units. Thus the Messiriya and Humr of Kordofan claim that they once formed a single group with those Messiriya who now live in Chad and others who now live in

[12] The Turkiya, the Mahdiya, and the Condominium denote these periods. The reconquest of 1898 is known as the Reoccupation. The Sudan has been independent since 1 January 1956.

[13] Macmichael has a useful summary of the history of Kordofan in Chapter I of *The Tribes of Northern and Central Kordofan.*

[14] Pallme, op. cit., pp. 1, 118.

[15] Catholic missionaries left some accounts of the pagan Nuba among whom they were working to the east of Humr country.

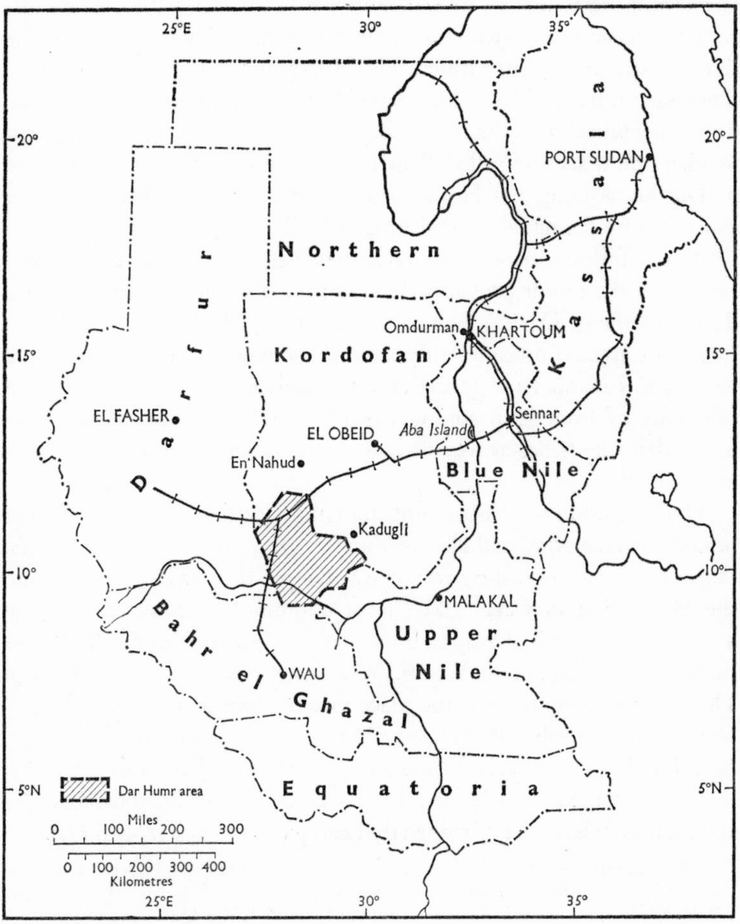

MAP 1. The Position of Dar Humr

Darfur. Today there is no significant contact between these three 'Messiriya' groups.[16]

The lateral movement had another result. From time to time small parts of tribes have moved and sought refuge with other tribes. The Humr and the Rizeygat, their neighbours in Darfur, which were both widely known to be wealthy and strong, came to harbour many fugitive sections from other tribes. The Humr, for example, have among them a section called Salamat, reputed to be from the tribe of that name near Lake Chad; a section called Ziyud, from the tribe of that name in Wadai; and a section called Beni Helba, from the tribe of that name in Darfur. Among the Humr also are 'stranger' sections which are called not by the names of their original tribes but by the names of the sections of those tribes to which they belonged. Thus the Jubarat section of the Humr probably derived from the Jubarat section of the Ta'esha tribe of Darfur. Sections of this kind which are not Humr in origin are treated no differently from those which are, and indeed the 'stranger' Jubarat have gained for themselves one of the two main positions of leadership among the Humr. Henderson has correctly noted that 'the tribes as we know them today are fortuitous conglomerations'.[17]

The migration which brought the Humr to their present homeland is said to have consisted also of the Messiriya, the Rizeygat, and the Hawazma, and, according to some versions, the Awlad Ḥimeyd and the Habbaniya as well.[18] The most commonly recounted tradition among the Humr is that they undertook the journey to evade the demands of the Sultan of Wadai. When they reached the land called Denga, whose centre was the place now known as the Muglad, they found pagan people called Dajo and Shatt in possession and drove them out. The Humr quarrelled successively with the other Arab tribes that had accompanied them, battled them all away, and retained the place for themselves. It has since remained the headquarters (the *dar*) of the tribe.[19]

[16] For the distribution of Baggara groups in the Sudan, see Harrison, op. cit., App. VI, which is the fullest account. Barbour, *The Republic of the Sudan*, Chap. XI, is more accessible. For Chad, see Lebeuf, J. P., 'Die Stämme zwischen Schari und Nil'; Lebeuf, A. M. D., *Les Populations du Tchad*, p. 92; and Gilg, 'Mobilité pastorale au Tchad occidental et central'.

[17] Op. cit., p. 52.

[18] Henderson, op. cit. This is a very full account of Messiriya and Humr traditional history.

[19] The word *dar* has a number of uses. In the phrase *Dar el Ḥumr* it means the centre, headquarters, and main cultivating area of the tribe. In the phrase *Dar Ḥumr*, it means the whole of their territory, and Humr speak similarly of *Dar Riẓeygat*, *Dar Nuer*, *Dar Jengy* (Dinka), etc. The word is also a component of the names of many sections of the tribe, *Dar Salim*, for example, having the meaning of 'house of Salim'.

The Messiriya, Humr, Hawazma, and Rizeygat now form a block of Baggara in south-western Kordofan and south-eastern Darfur. Together they are known as 'Aṭaya, and Humr say of the 'Aṭaya that they are the best of the Baggara nomads, and are alone in enjoying the full sweets of the nomadic life.[20] But the four tribes together seem not to constitute a unit of any political or other significance.

Within the 'Aṭaya the Humr and the Messiriya are related specially closely. The tribes now known as Messiriya and Humr were once two sections of one tribe, the Messiriya. The two sections were the Messiriya Zurg (the present Messiriya) and the Messiriya Humr (the present Humr).[21] According to a tradition which Henderson collected, it was Sultan Kharif Teyman of Wadai (who came to office about 1745) who first made the Humr independent of the Zurg.[22] Today the Sudan Government regards the Messiriya and Humr of Kordofan as forming one tribe. They share (along with the Ngok Dinka and a few Dajo of the western Nuba hills) a single local council. But in sentiment, and to go by certain indicators like the way in which they treat blood-money payments, they are distinct tribes. The Humr are called Humr by both of them, and the Zurg are called Messiriya. Although they could properly do so, since the Humr as well as the Messiriya trace their descent from Muḥammad el Messir, Humr never, outside administrative circles, refer to themselves as Messiriya. The Humr are continually intermingling among themselves, but except for a few places in the east of the country they have little opportunity of meeting Messiriya. Generally they prefer to avoid one another.[23]

[20] A much-loved poem, *Mesarna 'izz el 'Aṭaya*—literally 'Our migration is the glory of the 'Aṭaya'—expresses this.

[21] The words *zurg* and *ḥumr* applied to people mean dark and fair of complexion. There is no reason to suppose that these terms, applied to tribal sections, refer to differences in colouring of their members or their ancestors; for among the Humr, where a section is divided into two sub-sections, these are usually given contrasting names of this sort: fair and dark, right and left, tall and short, all exist. Where a section is divided into more than two sub-sections these are given names deriving from the personal names of their respective founders. The existence of a pair of such names in a trio indicates that the third refers to a stranger group.

[22] Henderson, op. cit., p. 52. Barth, op. cit, vol. III, p. 549, indicates that the Messiriya Humr and the Messiriya Zurg were in different administrative districts of Wadai in the nineteenth century. A note in the Kordofan Province files (CR/66/E.13, p. 3, 1925) states of the Messiriya of Darfur that the two sections live under one name only, the Messiriya, but that they are comparatively few in number.

[23] Important Humr and Messiriya meet in the Rural Council. A certain amount of trade exists between them: Humr buy clay pots and grindstones from Messiriya women who bring their wares to Muglad market.

THE SECTIONS OF THE TRIBE

The Arabic word which I have translated as 'tribe' in distinguishing Humr from Messiriya is *gabily*. To Humr, the largest group to which the word is applicable is the Humr themselves. It is one of a number of words in use to designate the tribe and tribal sections of various sizes. In a sense to be explained in later chapters, the Humr tribe consists of an agnatic lineage whose founder was Ḥeymir.[24] This lineage is in turn part of that founded by Muḥammad el Messir; which is in turn a part of that founded by 'Aṭiya; and so on. Ḥeymir himself is reckoned at some ten to twelve generations back from the living.

The tribe subdivides as follows. It comprises two main sections, the 'Ajaira and the Felaita, each under a *naẓir*. These are also called *gabily*. The 'Ajaira and Felaita are each divided, secondarily, into five sections. Humr call these, again, *gabily*, but they are the units known to the administration as 'omodiyas'. This is an administrative term, the *'omodiya* being a group under one *'omda*. The word has been in use among the Humr since 1911, the date of the first appointment of omdas.[25]

The Sudan census of 1955 indicates that the omodiyas vary in population from about two thousand to about nine thousand.[26] Each is subdivided, but there is no relation between the size and the number of the main divisions; the Fayyarin, Faḍliya, Awlad 'Umran,[27]

[24] The name of the alleged founder is given by some Humr as Ḥamid el Aḥmer.

[25] The words *'omda* and *naẓir* were introduced into the Sudan during the Turkiya. Under the present administrative system most rural populations, settled and nomadic alike, are divided into nazirates and omodiyas. Before 1911 some of the larger groups among the Humr were known by the word *bedana*, implying agnatic kinship.

[26] Ministry of Social Affairs, *First Population Census of Sudan, First Interim Report*, p. 10. In the report the omodiyas are listed not by name but under the names of their omdas. The enumeration district included also the Ngok Dinka and Muglad town and surrounding settlements. Some Humr, number unknown, residing in Muglad town at the time of the census would be included in its 2,820 inhabitants. At all times a number of people are absent from their country, working in towns. Perhaps accordingly we may safely say that the number of Humr approaches sixty thousand.

With one exception, the census figures tally with the impression that I had, and that the Humr have, regarding the relative size of the omodiyas: it looks as if the figure for A. Kamil, listed under their omda, Ḥammad 'Abd el Jelil, and the Fayyarin, listed under their omda, Abu el Gasim Musa, have been accidentally reversed. A. Kamil are almost certainly by far the largest omodiya (although exceeded by the two sections of A. 'Umran combined), and the Fayyarin seem to be an omodiya of about medium size. See Table 1.

[27] The two main divisions of A. 'Umran (itself often called an omodiya), the Menama and the 'Addal, both have omdas and are omodiyas. There is no overall omda of A. 'Umran.

and Jubarat each have two main divisions; the Mezaghna have three, the Metanin have five, Awlad Kamil, Awlad Serur, and the Salamat have six, and the Ziyud have eight.[28]

Each primary division of an omodiya is called *khashm beyt*,[29] which I shall translate as 'lineage'. Nearly every lineage is subdivided

TABLE 1. *Table of omodiya populations adapted from the census of* 1955

	Fayyarin	8,944*	
	A. Kamil	4,456*	
	Mezaghna	3,096	
	Faḍliya	2,590	
	Menama	7,288	A. 'Umran
	'Addal	4,573	A. 'Umran
Total	'Ajaira	30,947	
	Metanin	6,230	
	Ziyud	6,878	
	A. Serur	6,754	
	Jubarat	2,096	
	Salamat	2,092	
Total	Felaita	24,050	
Total	Humr	54,997	

* See p. 8, note 26.

further, sometimes twice more, sometimes thrice more, and each of these subdivisions, except for the smallest, is again *khashm beyt*. The smallest of the subdivisions is called *surra*;[30] and this is a group of agnates whose common ancestor is said to have been five or six generations back from the living. The *surra* is also, in a sense to be defined later, the basis of a single camp. Within the surra the only named divisions are extended families of one, two, or three generations, which the Humr call *'iyal rajl*, literally 'children of a man'.

In this account I shall use the following terms to distinguish these various groups: extended family, surra, lineage (distinguishing where

[28] 'Awlad' means sons, or descendants; this is, like 'Dar', a part of the names of many large sections. Names of other large lineages are derived from the names of their founders: e.g. Faḍliya from Faḍl, Mezaghna from Muzghan, Metanin from Mutnan, etc. In tables and footnotes the abbreviation 'A'. denotes Awlad.

[29] Literally, entrance or threshold of a house or tent. The word strongly implies that its members have common agnatic descent.

[30] This word means also 'navel'.

necessary between minor, medium, and major lineages), omodiya. The two main divisions of the tribe will be so described, or else their names, 'Ajaira and Felaita, will be used. The Humr as a whole I shall refer to as 'tribe'.

A Humrawi,[31] then, belongs to a series of lineages extending from his own surra and including minor and major lineage, omodiya, one of the two main sections of the tribe, and the tribe itself. Although the lineage extends further to embrace the Messiriya as a whole, the

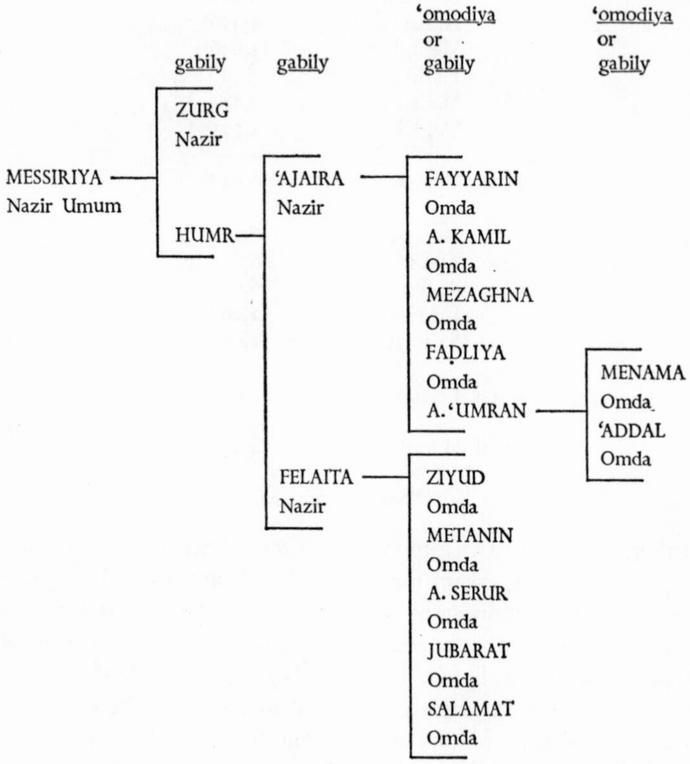

FIG. 1. The administrative divisions of the Humr, with the kind of political officer in charge of each.

'Aṭaya, and so on, he does not describe himself as belonging to any wider agnatic group (except that for certain restricted purposes he would mention the 'Aṭaya). For further identification he would say he belonged to Kordofan Province, or else that he was a Baggari, or an

[31] The singular form of 'Humr'.

'Arab', signifying neither a sedentary farmer nor a townsman, but a nomad.

Fig. 1 represents the way in which Humr most commonly represent the relations of the omodiyas to one another. At this level the administrative divisions assume the aspect of segments of an agnatic lineage. This tribal mode of segmentation takes account of many 'stranger' elements incorporated as full members of the body of agnatic kinsmen. In a broad sense the component groups of the Humr behave to one another in terms of it. Strangerhood has no drawbacks. Indeed, it must remain highly doubtful whether at any time even a bare framework of the presently accepted lineage has ever been a reality. Macmichael, for instance, has collected a genealogy which shows the founders of the 'Ajaira and the Felaita not as brothers but as second cousins, and which gives no common ancestor closer than 'Aṭiya.[32] Whatever may have been the actuality, Humr recognize certain of their present-day omodiyas as 'genuine' descendants of Ḥeymir, and others as strangers. Those they regard as genuine are Awlad Kamil, the Mezaghna, the Faḍliya, and Awlad 'Umran within the 'Ajaira; and the Metanin and Awlad Serur within the Felaita. The founders of the other omodiyas, though not descendants of Ḥeymir, are yet held to be fairly closely related in the genealogies of the Guheyna of the Sudan. The Fayyarin are said to be descended through Muḥammad el Far (hence their name) from Ḥeymad, a brother of 'Aṭiya; and the Ziyud from Rashid, another brother. The Jubarat and the Salamat are perhaps not so close, but all are Guheyna.

The process of splitting, migrating, and resettling which has given rise to the present distribution of Baggara groups is active also within

[32] *The Tribes of Northern and Central Kordofan*, p. 147, extract:

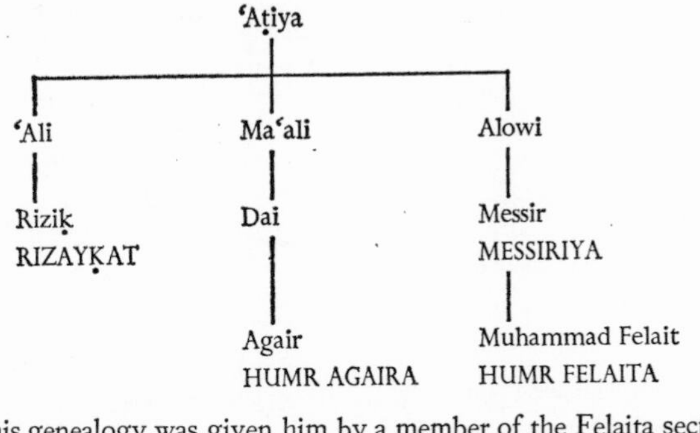

Fig. 1a. This genealogy was given him by a member of the Felaita section, who may be interested to show their especially close relationship to Muḥammad el Messir because of the present internal politics of the tribe.

single tribes. Sections secede, move to a new part of the tribal territory, and make brotherhood with distantly related sections; and they are at once considered close kinsmen of their new neighbours. Lineages move in dissatisfaction from one omodiya to another; surras move to join some other omodiya or some other lineage within their own omodiya. Finally, individuals occasionally go and join other surras.

The arrangement of Humr groups given here will be treated more fully later in relation to other arrangements which they recognize. In the meantime this mode of segmentation will serve as a convenient reference for the next chapter, which deals with the way the tribe is distributed over the land.

2

LAND AND MOVEMENT

TYPES OF LAND

HUMR move in a regular seasonal cycle through the four distinct types of country into which Dar Humr is naturally divided.

Almost the entire country utilized by the Humr is one or other of the subdivisions of Low Rainfall Woodland Savannah,[1] a belt of which lies east and west across the central Sudan. Throughout this belt, rainfall is less towards the north and greater towards the south; Dar Humr is in the south, with a precipitation ranging from about 450 to about 900 millimetres—about eighteen to thirty-six inches—a year. The rainfall collects in depressions of different kinds in different parts of the country, and Humr move about largely in order at every season to be within reach of drinking supplies for men and cattle. The details of these moves are also related to the various types of soil and vegetation, to the presence or absence of flies, and to the demands of the dominant activities: cattle husbandry, the cultivation of millet, and the increasing cultivation of cotton.

The country is flat, and largely tree-covered. The 1500-foot contour runs east and west across it, but the slope down to the river system in the south is scarcely perceptible to the traveller. There are exceptions to the general flatness. The district near the new administrative town of El Fula has hills and valleys; the Muglad area is criss-crossed with sand ridges; and all over the south and east is a network of wide and shallow watercourses. In the south a few low sand mounds rise out of the clay plain.

The main regions of Dar Humr are, to give them their local names, the Babanusa, the Muglad, the Goz, and the Bahr. A fifth region sometimes used is called the Sahaly. These regions correspond to divisions

[1] Harrison defines Woodland Savannah as 'any mixed type of vegetation composed of grass with bushes and/or trees in which the very variable proportion of grass to bushes and/or trees is determined by the frequency and intensity of forest fires. It is the type of vegetation characteristic of the dryish tropics with a monsoon rainfall confined to a few months followed by a long dry hot season.' Op. cit., Part I, p. 5.

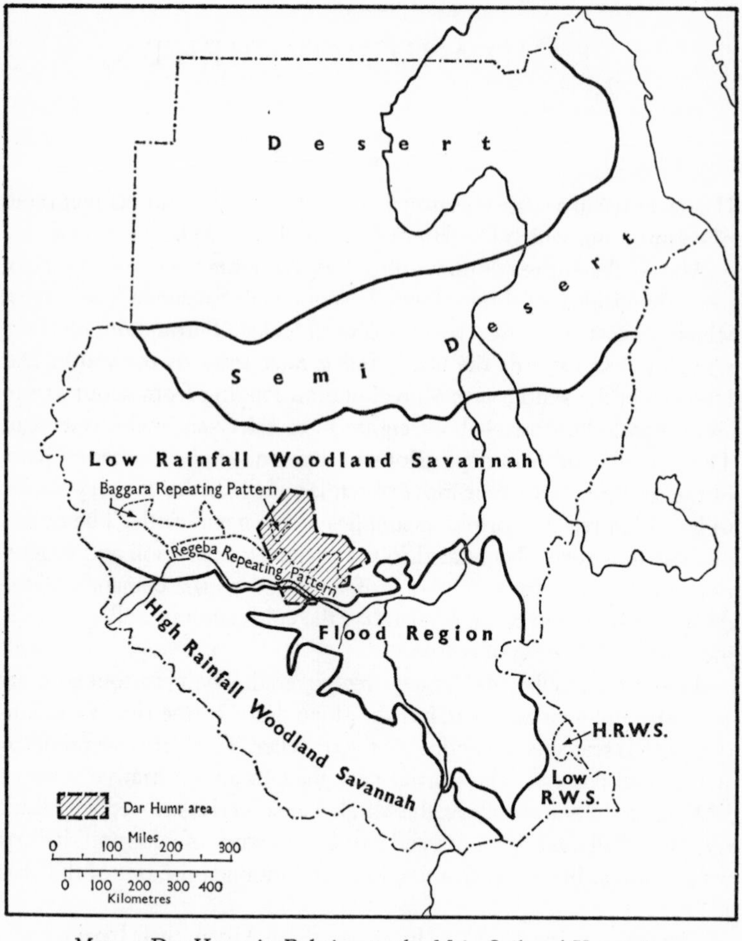

MAP 2. Dar Humr in Relation to the Main Soil and Vegetation Types of the Sudan

which Harrison established on the basis of soils and vegetation, and to which reference is made in footnotes.[2]

(1) *The Babanusa.* This is the sandy area in the north and north-west of the country, which is used for grazing during the rains. It takes its name from the prevalence of *babanus*, a kind of ebony.[3] In many respects it is like the third area, the Goz, from which it is separated by the Muglad and the Wadi el Ghalla. Rainfall is from eighteen to twenty-five inches a year, and collects in scattered clay-bottomed pools. In the dry season this district lacks water and verdure completely, but it becomes a pleasant place in the rains. It is very thickly wooded with low trees and shrubs, one of which, the *ghubeysha*, makes direction-finding and even penetration difficult in places.

The Humr distinguish four different soil and vegetation types in the Babanusa. There is (i) pure soft sand with thick scrub and good grazing. This rises out of a second which is characteristic of most of the Babanusa. This is (ii) less thickly wooded, but contains ebony and other larger trees: the sand is mixed with some soil, which makes it firmer. The vegetation it supports is mainly a herb (*liseyg*), which is good grazing, although at some stages of its growth it bloats cattle dangerously. Here and there are (iii) small thickets with clay in the soil. The larger of these contain water after heavy rain, and are valuable since shallow wells may be dug in them. Finally (iv) the land around the rain pools supports good grazing.[4] The best part of the Babanusa lies in the north-west corner of the country; towards the north-east it degenerates, and much of the land is stony with poor vegetation.

[2] A detailed comparison of the Humr classification of land and vegetation with that of Harrison is given in my paper 'Subsidiary nomadic movements of the Humr'. See the map at the end of the book for the main regions.

[3] *Dalbergia melanoxylon.* Harrison classifies this vegetation as a type of Low Rainfall Woodland Savannah on sand, to which he gives the generic name of *goz*. From the dominant trees he names it '*Combretum cordofanum—Dalbergia—Albizzia scericocephela* Savannah Woodland'.

The word '*goz*' is the Arabic for sand-dune country. The Humr give it this general meaning, but to them it is especially the Goz, the third area to be considered. Harrison states, in respect to his generic use of it, that 'in a long past drier geological age these gozes were moving blown sand dunes.... Subsequently, in a moister period the dunes were stabilized by vegetation. At the present day the undulations vary greatly in steepness and size, and in places they have almost disappeared to form a flat sand plain. Goz soil ... is low in mineral nutrients and deficient in organic matter but is high in moisture availability ... the vegetation is therefore better than would be expected from the chemical composition.' Op. cit., App. I, p. 1.

[4] Humr call these soil and vegetation types respectively *atul*, *jengaba*, *kub'*, and *khashm el raḥad*. Harrison distinguishes harder and softer sands, and sands having a hard red layer due to iron salts. Op. cit., Part II, p. 8.

The relevant features of the Babanusa are as follows. It is a relatively small area which can be used only in the rains. Although rainfall may start in April it is not until July, or perhaps even August, that adequate water can be guaranteed in all the pools. In most years it is entirely free of harmful insects. The grazing is in general good, though the grasses lack important salts. The bush is thick and direction-finding difficult. It is suitable land for the cultivation of groundnuts and bulrush millet, which is increasing.

(2) *The Muglad.* The border of the Babanusa with the Muglad is well marked by a watercourse, the Hajiz, which curves in the arc of a circle round the Muglad's northern half. To the south the Muglad extends in places over the Wadi el Ghalla and in turn breaks more gradually into the Goz beyond. In all, the region is about three hundred square miles, and contains near its north-west corner the administrative capital of the same name, which was established there during the first decade of the Condominium.[5]

Here most Humr gardens are situated, including nearly all the gardens of the ʻAjaira section; but many Felaita gardens lie along the Wadi el Ghalla, specially near Kijeyra and El Fula. Cattle sojourn in the Muglad for two short periods of the year, in June and after the end of the rains. This is the area of good water supply, good 'salty' grazing, and land suitable for cultivation; these characteristics are common to the headquarter areas of all the Baggara tribes of the Sudan.[6]

The Muglad is a well-watered plain with red, non-cracking clay which is gluey and slippery when wet, and from which it takes its name.[7] It supports five different soil and vegetation types. Much of the

[5] To distinguish between the town and the district, I call the district 'the Muglad' and the town simply 'Muglad', although the same name, more accurately transliterated as El Mujlad, is in use for both. Baggara usually call the town 'El Deym' (i.e. 'the town'), or 'Ghereygy', the name of its biggest rain pool.

[6] Harrison names this type of land 'Baggara Repeating Pattern'. It consists of 'frequently alternating patches of two contrasting types of soil, namely flats of Non-cracking Clay (nagaʻa) and slightly higher areas of Stabilized Sand Dune. The smooth hard-surfaced nagaʻa, almost impenetrable to water, generally has a scanty grass cover while some areas are completely bare of vegetation, and other areas have poorly developed trees and bushes. The large run-off from the nagaʻa stands on the surface and then collects in shallow rain pools . . . which are a feature of the area. . . . On the transitional zone between the nagaʻa and atmur is a characteristic group of grasses which are said to be "salty" ' (op. cit., App. II, p. 19). The non-cracking clays of the nagaʻa 'owe their characteristic to certain mixtures of sand and clay which cement to produce a non-cracking surface which is impermeable. Consequently there is high surface run-off, very little moisture is available for plant growth, and the vegetation is far scantier than on any other soil type under the same rainfall.' (App. I, p. 3.) The 'Baggara Catena' of some other areas has similar characteristics.

[7] *Mujlad* is the name of this clay.

area is taken up by (i) the smooth red clay flats which support only short grass. The flats are cut through by (ii) long winding sand ridges, upon which millet is cultivated. Land consisting of (iii) black clay supporting thorny shrubs and trees is often found by rain pools. There are (iv) thickets, generally larger than those of the Babanusa, which, being in depressions, may afford water from time to time. Lastly, (v) the rain pools in the Muglad differ in structure from those of the Babanusa (and also from those of the Goz further south), and they go by a different name. Generally they are much larger, one or two of them being nearly a mile across; many are perennial; and in addition they afford grazing as well as water.[8]

This area has a plentiful water supply, which could probably support the men and cattle for much of the year. The grazing is excellent, though somewhat scanty, being usually finished by December. It has cultivable soil. In the rains it has troublesome insects, which do not spread north to the Babanusa. It is relatively small in extent. It is open country in comparison with the Goz and the Babanusa; going is smooth, direction-finding is easy.

(3) *The Goz*. The vast Goz, lying between the Muglad and the Wadi el Ghalla in the north and the river system in the south, is seldom used for camps of long duration, but it is the means of getting from the rains areas to the dry-season areas and back again. Cattle graze in it also, just before and during harvest. It is like the Babanusa, but wetter (twenty-four inches of rainfall and upwards in a year); it supports larger trees, and rather coarse grasses.[9] The rain pools are similar but somewhat further apart.

Humr recognize various distinctive features of the Goz. There is (i) soft sand; there is (ii) ground with varying thicknesses of sand covering red clay, where vegetation is often scant; there are (iii) long strips of slightly depressed ground with thicker trees, affording green grass late into the dry season; and (iv) the land around rain pools, as in the Babanusa.[10] The tussocky grasses of the soft sands and the depressions yield regrowth after burning, which is put to good use in November and during the southward migration later.

The Goz is a large area with some good grazing. It has insects in the rains, and it lacks the plentiful water of the Muglad to the north and

[8] These soil and vegetation types are respectively *naga'a*, *'atmur*, *umm ḥataba*, *kub'*, and *boṭa*.

[9] Harrison calls it '*Sclerocaryea–Anogeissus–Prosopis* Savannah Woodland', and describes it as the 'best developed type of vegetation on Low Rainfall Woodland Savannah'. Op. cit., App. II, p. 13.

[10] Respectively *goz*, *dandana*, *shagg*, and *khashm el raḥad*.

the Bahr to the south, and the insect-free condition of the Babanusa.

(4) *The Bahr*. The southern part of the country, the Bahr (the word means 'river' in Arabic), is the area in which the Humr spend the latter half of the dry season. It is characterized by dark, deeply cracking clays and numerous winding watercourses all connected eventually with the Bahr el Arab, a tributary of the White Nile. It contains also two almost permanent lakes, Keylak (which lies slightly south of east from the Muglad) and Abyad, in the south-east corner of the country.

The Bahr is the name which the Humr give to the whole of this dry-season watering country. Within it they recognize different districts: 'the Regeba'[11] is the northern part of the Bahr, where the Humr make their earliest dry-season camps. Some early camps are to the north of this, even, in a kind of island of meadowland in the Goz, which is called 'the Firshai'. The 'Bahr' proper is the region where the camps are made towards the end of the dry season, mainly around the largest watercourses, the Regeba Umm Bioro and the Regeba Zerga. Finally the 'Sahaly', or 'toich' of the Nilotic region, is the area of treeless flood plain towards the south-east, which is occasionally used for cattle camps and for giraffe-hunting.

The Bahr region is, like the Muglad, another 'repeating pattern' type of country.[12] The Humr recognize the following components in it: (i) the watercourses; (ii) higher, non-cracking clay areas, on which Dinka build permanent homesteads; (iii) high, non-cracking clay with small muddy saucers that fill in the early rains; (iv) cracking clays, covered with the red acacia from which it takes its name; (v) very rough clumpy land; and (vi) low-lying meadowland.[13]

The Bahr provides ample water throughout the dry season. As the watercourses dry out, water collects in pools (*daḥal*, pl. *duḥul*) in the deeper parts of them. Meadowland is also flooded at first. As all surface water disappears, wells can be dug in the watercourse beds. The Bahr

[11] *Regeba* is the Arabic name for a watercourse of the type found here.

[12] Harrison calls it 'Regeba Repeating Pattern'. It has a floor of dark cracking clays, which 'occur in huge monotonous flat uniform plains . . . and carry a poorer vegetation than does stabilized sand dune under the same rainfall. Mineral status is good. . . . The clay shrinks considerably in drying, causing the soil to crack widely and deeply in the dry season. Water penetration is confined almost entirely to cracks' (op. cit., App. I, p. 2). According to his account, the repeating elements consist of *gardud*, which occupies the biggest areas and consists of non-cracking flat clay with a big run-off; *ṭalḥa* or dark cracking clay, which is typical of *Acacia seyal–Balanites* Savannah; and *fau* (which the Humr call *feyḍ*), open grassland of tussocky perennial grasses. He describes how the run-off from the *gardud* floods the *fau* and collects also into a network of water channels connected with the Bahr el Arab (App. II, p. 21).

[13] Respectively *regeba, ga'a, gardud, ṭalḥa* (= *Acacia seyal*), *bug, feyḍ*.

also supplies good grazing: the succulent *birdi* grass (*Echinochloa* sp.) fills the watercourses, and after being grazed away it shoots up again and can be grazed a second time. The meadowland provides excellent grazing. Towards the end of the season the position becomes more difficult, and cattle have to survive on standing hay. Other features of importance in the Bahr lands are: rain falls early—in April—and at once attracts numerous insects;[14] and the land has clay underfoot, which makes going difficult after the rains have started. The area which can be utilized for grazing is comparatively large. Finally, much of the Bahr has permanent Dinka settlements, although during most of the time that the Humr occupy it the Dinka are with their cattle south of the Bahr el Arab.

The use of these regions is seasonal, and the seasons are as follows. 'Spring' (*rushash*) begins about May and continues until the end of July or until the water supplies in rain pools become certain. Although rain usually falls before May—particularly in the south, where the Humr are at the time—the earlier rains are sporadic and uncertain, and the beginning of spring is acknowledged only when cattle are able regularly to eat new grass. Late July, August, and early September are the 'rains' (*kharif*),[15] which one can be fairly sure of having rainstorms every two or three days. The 'autumn' (*chelawy*), when there is still much cloud but rain falls only as comparatively light sunshowers, covers the end of September and the first half of October. Next is the 'harvest' (*deret*), until the middle of December, when it gradually gets cooler. The cold dry season (*shity*) lasts until the beginning of February; the start of this season is marked by a strong cold north wind (*gerwa*) that blows night and day. Gradually the weather becomes warmer (*seyf*) and very hot (*seyf hannan*),[16] particularly in a year which has little early rain. The end of the hot dry season is marked by intermittent showers in April and early May.

CATTLE MOVEMENTS

Movements through these four regions are dictated by four main needs. These concern the condition of grass, water, and ground underfoot, and the presence or absence of annoying flies. Clearly cattle cannot

[14] Mainly mosquitoes, a kind of midge (*Tebanid*; *gim* in Arabic), and a kind of horsefly (*Stomoxis*; *teyr el bagar* or *serut* in Arabic). The ordinary housefly is abundant at most times. The tsetse does not occur in Dar Humr.

[15] The height of the rains is *kharif bukli*; within the rainy season a period of continued drought is *ṣabny* and a particularly wet season is *'eyny*.

[16] In the dry season, if there is little surface water the condition is known as *suwaḥ*; if it is abundant the condition is known as *wokhery*.

thrive where water is short or grazing bad. They can exist where there are biting flies, but these are better avoided, since they disturb the grazing and may be carriers of disease. They can exist on wet clay, but they are inclined to develop hoof trouble, and travel badly with loads through mud.

These considerations force the Humr to take their cattle to certain broad areas at certain seasons, but within these areas there is usually a wide choice of places to camp, and the cattleman or the camp leader uses his own judgement to find the best combination of all the factors for his cattle. The major moves, now established by long usage, are south in winter, north in spring, north again in the rains, and south at the end of the rains. Within this broad outline the cattle-owner may choose his camp site as he will.

In the middle of December the cattle pour out of the Muglad, go south through the Goz, and reach the Bahr about the beginning of January. They are fleeing from the brown, dried-up grass of the Muglad, although that area still has plenty of water and for the time being is free of flies. At this season there are still horseflies on the Bahr, and the water in the watercourses may be too deep to allow grazing in them; but the call of the green grass is strong. The cattle may dally for some time in the Goz. This stretch of country has not been entirely empty since the rains, for parties of Humr honey-gatherers have gone there and fired the land for their own purposes; and after the burning of the grass ample regrowth appears. As soon as the cattle approach the Bahr, scouts go forward; if the Bahr is in suitable condition the cattle are taken there immediately; if not, they wait by rain pools north of the first watercourses until the Bahr insects have lessened, but scarcity of water in the Goz may compel an early move into the Bahr.

On the Bahr the usual camp sites are beside watercourses and meadows. The meadows have both water and grazing; the watercourses have water, grazing, and, later on, regrowth grazing; and when all the surface water has died, well water is obtained from their beds. The other parts of the Bahr sustain standing hay, which is also suitable grazing for grown animals. An exceptionally dry season with little surface water is bad for cattle, for they may have to be driven many miles through great heat to reach grazing, and it is specially bad for the calves, which require green grass.[17]

[17] Harrison claims this season to be the most difficult for Baggara: op. cit., Pt. II, pp. 18–19 and App. V, p. 17. I consider that the cramped position in the Babanusa with the enforced early return to the Muglad is an equal drawback. Harrison does, however, point out that the Humr are better off than other Baggara tribes in respect of dry-season grazing. Recent provision of deep bores

Migrating south through the Goz in December

(*Facing p.* 20)

PLATE II

Autumn camp in the Muglad

After the first few showers the Humr take the cattle back to the higher *gardud* land, to let them eat the first green shoots and to be able to water them without the tedious labour of using wells; moreover the rain may well have spoiled the wells themselves. It is the little saucers (*kelgeya*, pl. *kelage*) in the *gardud* which allow them to do this, for these hold any rain that falls. Horseflies come with the first rains, and the move to the *gardud* land is the first of the moves northward to the Muglad. At this period the Humr have to balance the dangers of the horseflies against the possibility of not finding enough water in the Goz for transit.

The long northward migration varies in duration according to the amount and condition of water in the rain pools of the Goz; it may take up to a month. On the arrival in the Muglad, the cattle separate, each owner taking his beasts to manure his garden. But the rain spreads in greater intensity northwards and soon brings mosquitoes; and these, combined with the sticky mud of the Muglad flats after rain, force the cattle north to the Babanusa after barely a fortnight.

The cattle spend July, August, and most of September in the Babanusa. At the end of this time the beasts, which had been in good condition at the height of the rains, deteriorate, because the Babanusa grasses are saltless.[18] They can stand saltless grasses for only a short time, and a herd that has gone to the Babanusa early may have to return for a few days in the middle of the rains to recuperate. Cattle that have been long in the Babanusa sometimes dash southwards on their own accord: they know their country.

Back in the Muglad in October the cattle are kraaled on the sand ridges while there is still likelihood of rain, then descend to the flats. They graze much in the grass-bearing rain pools of the Muglad. When favourable reports come from people who have visited the Goz, the cattle are taken to the northern rain pools there to be away from the ripe millet gardens, for they will break the strongly built thorn

[18] Humr recognize this quality. They call Babanusa grasses '*masikh*', as compared with the grasses on the Muglad sand-ridges, which are '*ṭa'im*'.

---

in the Bananusa has, while improving the water supply, had an adverse effect on the grazing situation. With the guarantee of good water at all seasons, cultivations have increased, thus lessening the amount of land available for grazing in the already cramped area. The cultivators are not only Ma'alia and others who have been settled in the area in small numbers for a long time, but also Humr themselves, some of whom have begun to farm near traditional rains grazings. The establishment of 'Babanusa' (Gubba on the map) as an important railway junction will no doubt enhance this effect. The latest development here is the preparation of a milk-processing factory at Babanusa under the supervision of Russian technicians.

fences to gain entry to the crops. After harvest they return once again to eat the stover, each beast in its owner's garden, then reunite in their herds for the southward migration.

The annual cycle thus comprises four main moves and a number of subsidiary ones,[19] and it is within this general plan that the cattle-owner exercises judgement in choosing where and when to take his stock.

TABLE 2. *Cattle moves*

No. of nights in	Bahr	Goz	Muglad	Babanusa
Jan. 1–May 22	142			
May 23–June 6		15		
June 7–18			12	
June 19–21				3
June 22–July 15			24	
July 16–Sept. 22				69
Sept. 23–Oct. 19			27	
Oct. 20–Nov. 3		15		
Nov. 4–Dec. 12			39	
Dec. 13–31		19		
	142	49	102	72

The table shows the number of nights spent by the cattle of I. Ganiṣ of the Mezaghna omodiya in the various areas during the course of 1954. The cattle reached the first watercourses on 1 January 1955. In all, camp was moved 61 times during 1954. Unusual shortage of water forced the return to the Muglad on June 22.

CULTIVATION

Although Humr are not great farmers, millet cultivation is part of their life. They prefer cattle husbandry to crop husbandry and claim to dislike the periods of settled life and hard, monotonous work that agriculture entails. But agriculture, which demands weeks of settlement, is not really compatible with nomadic pastoralism. In the circumstances, it is a wonder that Humr cultivate as much as they do. Special arrangements for large-scale co-operation, to which reference will be made later, allow them to carry out both activities simultaneously.

[19] The names of the main ones are: southwards from the Muglad to the Bahr: *woṭy*; northwards from the Bahr to the Muglad: *munshagh*; northwards from the Muglad to the Babanusa: *ṭal'y*; southwards from the Babanusa to the Muglad: *kabby*. Of the move from the watercourses to the *gardud* at the first rains, it is said *el bagar gillan fog*, or . . . *gogan fog*. Of short moves within the same region, it is said *el bagar kissan*.

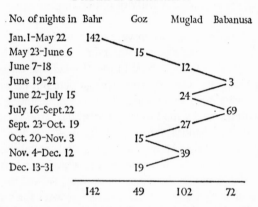

Bulrush millet, which is grown almost to the exclusion of other crops,[20] does best on sand, and Humr use the sand ridges in the Muglad for this purpose. The Muglad has the advantage over other areas in having not only sand ridges but also an abundance of water at the time of harvest in November. Other areas used are parts of the Goz and the Babanusa near Muglad, and the land which lies close to the Wadi el Ghalla eastwards.

The time-table is as follows. If a garden in current use is to be worked again the following year, it is manured by the owner's cattle after harvest, just before the southward move. It is then abandoned until the caravan returns to the Muglad in the early rains.[21] If the growth is not too heavy, the gardener plants the seed and then removes the weeds, but if the grass is long, the process is reversed. This first weeding is followed some weeks later by a second one, perhaps in early August, and only then does the gardener rejoin his cattle. Thereafter he simply lets the grain grow, and does not see it until shortly before harvest. From the end of October he is engaged in harvesting; he has the grain threshed and packed in sacks or leather containers for removal to granaries in the close neighbourhood. Most people are ready to move by the end of December, but those who cultivate more intensively may not be ready to move away until mid-January. A man intending to start a new garden, or to reopen a garden that has been long fallow, takes steps about it a year or six months in advance. He cuts down the trees, and piles them to be burnt just before planting.

In recent years, cotton has also been cultivated. This requires clay, as distinct from the sand required by millet, and so the cotton gardens are far from the millet gardens. The main centres of cultivation are Lakes Keylak and Abyad; the Firshai, a district midway between Muglad and Keylak; and—more recently—the south centre of the country near Abyei. By no means everyone cultivates cotton, and those in the west of the country do so hardly at all; there is no cotton west of the Muglad-Abyei road.

The cotton time-table is much the same as the millet time-table, but in addition the cotton has to be taken to the weighing machines,[22] and

[20] They grow small amounts of maize, groundnuts, and cucurbits, and intensive cultivators grow watermelons to water themselves and the few cattle that remain with them late into the dry season. The grains growing on the Muglad clays are the sorghum crops of Muglad townsmen.

[21] Sometimes an early cultivator will go north before the main body; he is then known as *tabbary*.

[22] The Government provides buying centres and weighing machines at a few convenient places. The transport of cotton by bull to these centres is a major undertaking.

the garden has to be scrupulously cleaned of every stalk before the next planting.

Table 3 gives the annual economic cycle.

TABLE 3. *The Humr year*

Month	*Season*	*Weather*	*Activities*
Jan.	Cold dry	Cold; dry; north wind	Arrival and establishment on Bahr; camps on northern regebas
Feb.	Cold dry/ warm dry	Dry; getting hot	Bahr. Camps going to late dry-season positions
Mar.	Warm dry/ hot dry	Dry; hot; dust devils	As surface water disappears, wells are reopened
Apr.	Hot dry	First few rains; still very hot	Bahr; move from watercourses to *gardud*
May	Spring	Dust laid; fresh grass	Cattle move north with approach of insects; cotton cultivators remain on Bahr
June	Spring	Rain more frequent	Migration northward completed; cattle to gardens, thence to Babanusa; preparing gardens for millet and cotton; sowing and first weeding
July	Spring/rains	Rain more frequent	Cattle move to Bananusa; millet and cotton cultivation
Aug.	Rains	Heavy rain	Cattle and camps reunited in Babanusa; cotton people come north
Sept.	Rains/ autumn	Rain, much reduced at end of month	Southwards to Muglad at end of month; cattle and camps still together; some cotton people return south
Oct.	Autumn	End of rains	Cattle in the Muglad; first millet cultivators back to gardens
Nov.	Harvest	Dry; getting cold; north wind	Cattle in Goz; millet harvest; cotton harvest
Dec.	Harvest/ cold dry	Cold; dry; north wind	Cattle eat remains of gardens and go south; cotton harvest; end of millet harvest and stacking grain

MOVEMENTS OF THE MAIN SECTIONS OF THE TRIBE[23]

The usable land of Dar Humr fans out from the cramped north and west to an extensive area in the south and east; consequently the tribe

[23] See Appendix 1 for further details. The map at the end indicates the omodiya areas.

tends to be concentrated in the rains and harvest, and dispersed in the winter and summer.

The way in which the component parts of the tribe move and distribute themselves over the land is influenced by the need for access to land of each type, and the nature of water, grazing, and cultivation rights. There is a joint estate of grazing and surface-water rights, and individual ownership of gardens and wells.

Since each cattleman has, for the sake of his cattle, to exploit the four main areas, his annual moves take him right through the country. In satisfying the needs of his cattle he is free to use any part of Dar Humr, without let or hindrance, so long as he avoids land at the time under cultivation.[24] In practice, however, he limits his choice of camp sites to small areas: from the Muglad in most years he will take the same path to the Babanusa in the rains, and the same path, or at least the same general direction, to the Bahr in winter. In the Babanusa and the Bahr, he will then select, within the general area to which he has gone, camp sites which for the time being appear to offer the best conditions for his cattle. He will return to some of the sites year after year. His annual movements are in the same general directions, but they vary in detail according to conditions of weather, insects, and vegetation. He allows himself at the same time to be influenced in his choice of site by his current relationships with those who usually accompany him.

Those who travel near him happen usually to be closer rather than more distant kinsmen. The camp, which is the unit of movement, has a nucleus of close agnates. Camps of one lineage, though intermingled with those of others, are usually fairly near one another. Yet at all levels there is a great deal of intermingling, and it is the exception rather than the rule for close agnates to travel as a block unmixed with

[24] Since the administrative amalgamation with the Messiriya, the country of the Messiriya Zurg also is open to grazing for Humr and vice versa. Humr seldom use the far more cramped Messiriya country, although the Salamat migrate each year through a part of it. Some Messiriya, on the other hand, camp annually in Dar Humr near Lake Keylak. The country, centred on Abyei, of the Ngok Dinka is traditional grazing ground of the Humr in the dry season, and it forms a part of the Dar Messiriya administrative district. Ngok Dinka are free to migrate north with the Humr, but only a handful of cattlemen do so in company with the Humr camps. By mutual agreement between the tribes concerned some Humr (Fayyarin) regularly graze in summer in the south-east of Rizeygat country; some others (Salamat) graze in Nuba country. Humr of many omodiyas enter the Sahaly type of country in Bahr el Ghazal and Upper Nile Provinces, the land of the Twij Dinka, the Rweng Dinka, and the Bul Nuer. During the dry season Ngok Dinka move into Bahr el Ghazal Province; while in the rains Bul Nuer and Rweng Dinka sometimes camp in Humr country along the Regeba Zerga, and Twij Dinka along the Regeba Umm Bioro.

others more distant. All the same, the Humr themselves view their land as being occupied by omodiyas in a particular order from west to east, although they have no legal title to these strips.[25] If one asks about the tribal distribution, one learns that the ʻAjaira are to the west and the Felaita are to the east; and further that the omodiyas are arranged from west to east in this way: Fayyarin, Awlad Kamil, Mezaghna, Faḍliya, Awlad ʻUmran (ʻAjaira); Metanin, Ziyud, Awlad Serur, Jubarat, and Salamat (Felaita). Women selling their wares in Muglad market-place dispose themselves in the same order; women of the Rizeygat tribe, when they are present, sit to the west of the Fayyarin; women from the Messiriya sit to the east of the Salamat. (In the cattle market Dinka cattle are sold to the south of Humr cattle, whoever the sellers may be.)

The map at the end of the book indicates the nature of this distribution by omodiyas.[26] The amount of overlap is striking, but the general axes of migration routes and camp sites of the various omodiyas are disposed in this order. The same is true for garden areas. Indeed, people like to have their gardens in a direct line between their Bahr and their Babanusa sites, and gardens, being stable, may in turn help stabilize the movements made by individuals and camps. People have two or three different garden sites which they cultivate in sequence, reopening one as the garden in use loses fertility after a few years: but all are within a few miles of a central line of march. In the same way, wells in the south may be a stabilizing element, for although most of the watercourse beds produce water, a man prefers to clear out a well which he had previously dug, rather than to dig a new one which he cannot be sure will produce water; and wells are private property. Most years, towards the end of the summer, he is thus advised to be camped within reach of his traditional wells.

The way in which the tribal sections move seems not to have varied much since the Reoccupation. Before that, dangers of raids from the Rizeygat made the Regeba Umm Bioro unsuitable and the Fayyarin and Awlad Kamil spent the dry season further east in the district now used by Mezaghna, who, in turn, were further east along

[25] Although some sections smaller than omodiyas are traditionally associated with certain places for their grazing, they cannot be placed in any order so clearly. Humr themselves mention the west-east order with reference only to the ʻAjaira and Felaita, and the omodiyas.

[26] The names of sites require explanation. Humr name their camp sites after the watercourses or rain pools from which they get water. A camp site near a rain pool would be named after the rain pool, but the same name could imply a site at any place within easy reach of it: thus many camps can be at the 'same place'. Some watercourses have the same name for the whole of their course; others are divided into reaches, each with a separate name.

the Regeba Zerga. Today, also, Humr have less hesitation than they had about camping in Dinka and Nuer country. One of the few ways in which Humr constantly praise the Government is in respect of the freedom which they now have to graze in distant parts; this suggests that they previously kept to a more rigid pattern of migration. In Humr theory there are no individual or sectional rights, within Dar Humr, to grazing land and surface water 'because the land belongs to the Government'.

It was not, of course, Government action which caused the lack of territorial divisions among the Humr: as far as we know they always lacked them, and 'Government' has been effective only from the time of the Reoccupation. The lack of sectional rights in specific stretches of land is likely, rather, to be connected with the situation in the early rains, when the cattle are forced by flies out of the Muglad into the Babanusa at a time when water supplies there may be very difficult. Rain pools fill irregularly at the whim of passing storms; in one year the western pools may fill earliest, in another year the eastern ones. Wherever the rain has fallen, the people go, and sectional land rights here would create an unworkable situation. Throughout the year Humr exploit their joint rights to grazing and surface water and tolerate the exercise of these rights by others. Significantly, the only disputes over the use of grazing which came to my attention were not amongst Humr, but were between Humr and various other groups that use their country.[27]

[27] Disputes arose between Humr and Twij Dinka, who used the Regeba Umm Bioro in the early dry season, spoiling the land before the Humr reached it; between Humr and Fellata nomads from Nigeria, who did the same in the Goz; between Humr and Messiriya, when the latter camped at L. Keylak in usually large numbers; and between Humr and settled cultivators over the rights of cattle versus crops in the Babanusa.

3

MEN AND CATTLE

AMONG the Humr, as elsewhere, wealth is one road to prestige, power, and political position. Here it is perhaps the main road. Humr keep most of their wealth in cattle: a man is wealthy only when he has cattle in camp to prove it. The drive to obtain cattle, and to keep them once he has them, dominates his life.

While a man who aspires to positions of leadership must have cattle,[1] in building his herd and maintaining it he has regard to other considerations, for the uses of cattle are numerous; and in formulating a cattle policy he has to take account of them all. Accordingly these uses have a bearing on political life; a man must meet economic obligations to household and kin before undertaking political commitments towards a larger body of men. This is not to say that all Humr seek political position, but that some do; and for the most part those who achieve it are among those who have sought it. With few exceptions Humr want cattle; those who gain cattle have power thrust upon them; and those who so desire may achieve political office on the basis of that power.

Before the Mahdiya, the Humr could rely on livestock for most of their requirements and commitments: they made purchases from settled peoples by means of cattle, dairy produce, and small stock; they paid tribute, when they had to, in cattle and liquid butter; they married with small stock or cattle (though only a few). But since the Reoccupation they have been progressively drawn into the cash economy. They pay taxes in cash and no longer in kind. They marry with cash. In the new markets which have attracted merchants from other parts of the northern Sudan they deal in cash only. But many kinds of transactions within the tribe are still often made in kind or a mixture of cash and kind. A horse was purchased for a cow, a three-year calf, a two-year calf, thirteen reals, and one khairiya.[2] Cattle are handed over

[1] In the past some holy men (such as 'Ali bu Gurun: cf. p. 130) were leaders, although they were not rich, but recently no one whose claim has lain in holiness rather than wealth has emerged as a leader.

[2] About £20. 14*s*.: the *riyal* is the 20-piastre coin (in other parts of Sudan it is

as blood compensation, but some are sold and the minor recipients receive their dues in cash.

The fact that most wealth is kept in livestock and especially in cattle, and not in other kinds of goods, cash or securities, relates to the nomadic pastoral way of life. The tribesmen are continually on the move, and do not have permanent houses anywhere, and so they are obliged to carry all their household possessions about with them.[3] Their home is where they happen to be. This prevents them from accumulating material possessions, and what they have is mostly of practical use. The tent is a light and simple structure made of local products, and its components are cheaply replaced; it has no accoutrements of expensive luxury, like the carpets of many Bedouin tents. Household possessions are limited to what can be carried on the backs of two or three bulls—and bulls carry much smaller loads than camels. Luxury items are mainly the silver (and increasingly gold) ornaments worn by women. The cash value of cattle thus exceeds that of other property.[4]

THE MATERIAL USES OF CATTLE

Cattle are a form of capital which can be highly productive. They also constitute wealth of a kind that can be put to practical uses without intermediate transactions. These uses, mainly as a source of food and a means of transport, are mandatory in the Baggara way of life. While the staple food is bulrush millet, few families cultivate enough of this to last them for a year, and milk and its products are a necessary addition to the diet. Members of some omodiyas even make a practice of doing without grain for a few weeks on the Bahr when they are far from their granaries and from markets; then they rely wholly on milk.[5]

[3] People with kinsmen in Muglad town, or who have made close friends with Dinka in the south, from time to time leave some possessions with them in their permanent houses.

[4] This statement excludes consideration of the acre or two of agricultural land that a man may have. But land is not for sale, and there is no cash value on it.

In two previous papers, 'The social role of cattle' and 'Some social aspects of nomadism in a Baggara tribe', I discussed these and other points in this chapter. See also Barth *et al.*, 'The settlement of nomads as a development policy'.

[5] A. 'Umran, the Ziyud, and A. Serur, who camp furthest from markets in the late dry season, are notorious for this.

---

10 piastres), and the *khairiya* is the 10-piastre coin. Humr normally use the *riyal* as their unit of cash measurement for large values, and not the pound.

The word *mal*, wealth, is commonly used to mean cattle, which are proverbially described as 'silver with hair' (*faḍḍ umm suf*); sheep and goats are 'the small change of the market-place' (*karabish el sug*).

Cows provide four main dairy products: milk, curdled milk, whey, and liquid butter.[6] Milk is drunk at any time; curdled milk is prepared overnight and drunk in the morning; whey is a thirst-quencher for the heat of the day. Liquid butter is made in large quantities; it is used as a cooking fat, as a component in the usual sauce eaten with grain, as a part of other millet and wild-rice dishes and as an oil for anointing the body and girls' hair. Furthermore, it is the main source from which women get cash at market, where they sell it to other Humr, to sedentary farmers, and to dwellers of the towns.

Humr do not normally slaughter cattle as food: for fresh meat they keep sheep, goats, and chickens; some hunt game birds and animals with gun or spear. But they occasionally slaughter cattle, and will do so in honour of an important guest. Sometimes a young bull falls victim to a sacrifice, but sacrifices involving cattle are rare. For large gatherings, such as peace-making ceremonies at which a group acts as host, bulls may be butchered. Yet beef is eaten nearly every day, for animals which are on the point of death are slaughtered, and most of the meat is dried and kept to be pounded down as a component of the sauce which accompanies the staple millet polenta. The only other part of the animal used is the hide, from which women make articles of various kinds; each tent has as part of its furniture a complete hide which provides a smooth surface for the bed, a covering if the roof leaks, and a seat and a covering for the baggage when a bull is loaded in a certain way.

All the baggage and nearly all the people of a household are transported from place to place on bulls. For an average household two beasts can carry wife, children, tent, and household goods. Men move on horses when they have them, sometimes on donkeys, sometimes on foot or on bull back. It is considered a right for a wife or a divorcee to migrate on a bull, and there is some hire of baggage bulls for this purpose on the major moves.[7]

Cattle, then, are essential for the maintenance of the domestic family, and it is for the man who is supporting a family to provide them. Up to four baggage bulls is a reasonable requirement for most households, including allowance for spares; but a reasonable requirement for milch cows cannot be so easily measured, for there is no limit to the amount of liquid butter which a woman may think it reasonable to make and sell.

[6] Respectively, *laban*, *rob*, *nesiya*, and *dihn*.

[7] The cost of such hire between the Muglad and the Bahr is about a pound.

THE CATTLE URGE

Strong pressures exist on all men to acquire and maintain a herd. Balancing the belief that God is the ultimate dispenser of all things and that if one has no cattle then God has willed it so, there is the precept that initiative, careful husbanding of resources, and puritan thrift as regards expenditure on women, tea, sugar, and cloth are the requisites for building a herd.[8] The poor man who is a spendthrift with what cash he finds is castigated by his richer relatives whose wealth he is eating and drinking. By being industrious and thrifty, anyone, with God's will, can own cattle. A single calf is the promise of a herd. 'A wife and a donkey is capital enough'; 'The eye of the owner brings increase'; 'Wealth is better than its owner'; 'Wealth lies between the upper and nether millstone'; these are all well-known proverbs stressing the importance of hard work and the opportunities which even a small herd can afford.[9] Physical bravery used, in cattle-raiding days, to be another necessary quality; along with quickness of mind it is still important in the defence of herds against lions, leopards, and hyenas, and finds expression in the lines:

> The tailed one that lows
> When she strays she is not soon found
> A fine lad plants his sand-ridge to the edge of the plain
> A fine lad is ready to die by the spear.[10]

In part, the drive for cattle exists because these provide food at all seasons, because a family can subsist solely on them in times of hunger, and because they provide, through the sale of liquid butter, the cash required for everyday purchases in the market. These are important reasons. There is a great difference between the quality of life of a man who has many cattle, and that of a man who has few. If he has enough cattle to satisfy the material demands of himself and his household, he can live in remarkable comfort; if not, it can be hard for him. Humr day-dream about the life of ease and comfort that cattle can bring them. Cattle attract women and enable a man to marry more than one wife. The women feed him and bring tea to him as he lies under his tree,

[8] I have described some Humr notions about the relation between God and material success in 'Giraffe hunting among the Humr tribe' at pp. 56–58.

[9] *Ras el mal, mara' wa ḥumar; 'eyn el sid teẓid; el mal akheyr min sida; el mal beyn el murḥaka wa beyna bitta.*

[10] Umm danab umm bah
Kin raḥat ma mteleggy bisra'
Au ṣabeyn zeyn bekammil el 'atmur fil naga'a
Au ṣabeyn zeyn fil ḥadid waga'.

content in the knowledge that his numerous sons are taking their turns at herding. All he has to do is to wait until evening, sleeping or talking to the guests who honour him with their presence, and whom he can treat generously by bringing them milk, sour milk, and one of the flock of sheep or goats that his ample cattle have enabled him to establish. Evening is the best time of day, for then the cattle return, filled with the finest grazing his sons could find; they come lowing into camp and cluster round the wood and dung fires his dependants and his Dinka servants have built. He wanders in among his herd and inspects them as his wives release the calves at milking. Perhaps he milks one or two himself. At night there is plenty of liquid butter for a wife to massage his legs; he sleeps in peace, to be wakened only by the churning of the sour milk calabash outside the door of his scent-filled tent.[11]

This idyllic picture of cattle bringing rest and contentment is seldom real. Cattle can bring these various delights and many more, but with the possession of cattle goes much hard work, and also responsibility, not only towards the herd, but to other Humr. Whether he wants it or not, a man with cattle attracts followers to him—poorer kin who have perhaps no other camp in which they can drink milk (Humr say that the owner of many cattle has a large number of female relatives); so by the very fact of ownership he is involved in more intensive manipulation of personal relations: his family grows. As his herd increases so do his responsibilities. Those who live off his bounty help him in the work of managing his herd and become his followers. Their dependence starts as an economic one, but this leads eventually to dependence in other spheres. As they listen to the rich man's commands in respect of the herding of the cattle, so they listen to him on other matters; they go to him for advice, ask him to arbitrate in quarrels, and give him moral support when he is in difficulties. The cattle-owner finds himself in a position which, on a small scale, resembles the position of the leaders of the more important groups. He can use his ownership of cattle and his embryonic following as a springboard for making a name for himself, and kinsmen may put pressure on him to reap, from his wealth, some political advantage from which indirectly further benefits will accrue to them. For the urge to have a name and renown (*ism*) vies with the pastoral ideal of the 'Aṭaya; and with many cattle it is easier for a man to gain a name than to be rewarded with peace and quiet.

[11] Cattle are *dereja bela bughḍ*, rank without hatred, referring to the position of the cattleman who cares to limit his use of wealth to domestic purposes in this manner.

So a man with more cattle than his kinsmen cannot help assuming a position of leadership, and he has achieved a useful base for the beginnings of a political career. The 'name' is achieved not solely through the ownership of cattle, but by attaining a reputation for generosity. Generosity takes two main forms: the loan, or gift even, of a milch cow to a poor relative; and liberal hospitality to guests. The loan or gift of a milch cow attaches a kinsman to the donor in perpetuity, and the recipient will stand by him in all circumstances. But name and fame spread largely with hospitality, and so it is important to be hospitable, not only towards acquaintances and kinsmen, but also, and especially, to complete strangers who seek a meal or a night's rest at camp, for afterwards they will discuss with their own people the kind of reception they had. Every Humrawi has the duty of providing travellers with such food as he can reasonably afford. Ability to provide lavish entertainment rests on the foundation of cattle, for it is mainly from the proceeds of cattle that he can buy tea, sugar, and sheep. The man of generosity is praised in song by minstrels who go from camp to camp singing in honour of famous men, for cash: as for cash they also deride the stingy ones. Women have their own songs, on similar themes, which spread fast. Here again there is a circular process, because the more generous a man is known to be, the more casual guests he receives, and the more cattle he has to have in order to keep up his reputation. The eventual achievement of political position brings even more guests, and the drive for more cattle continues.[12]

Possession of cattle plays an important part also in the relations of men and women. The ideal husband has plenty of cattle: for he is a good provider, and this means providing milk. Women delight in milk: they make it into the various kinds of drink; they drink it themselves, serve it to their children, their family, and their guests, and the more they can spare to make into liquid butter, the more will they, personally, have to spend in the market on tea, sugar, and scents. But—and this is perhaps more important—the possession of cattle implies that a man is endowed with those qualities that Baggara men and women alike regard as most admirable. They say that without piety, bravery, industry, physical hardiness, asceticism, and pastoral skill a man will be unable either to build a herd or to keep one. A herd, too, enables a man to be obviously generous, which women like. In consequence a lover

[12] I reserve until later discussion of the distinction between positions of leadership which are recognized by the Government and those which are not. Possession of cattle is a prerequisite for both.

or a suitor readily gains access to a girl's tent if he has cattle,[13] or even if his father has, for the qualities of a father, they consider, are likely to reveal themselves in the son. So herd-building has the added incentive that it makes easier the accession of wives and mistresses, and in general brings favour from women who play a positive part in spreading, by song, the word of a man's virtues. In Humr life the possession of cattle, the attraction of women, and the accession to prestige and power form a complex of closely related elements.

BUILDING AND MAINTAINING A HERD

Most cattle belong to men, but women do own some. Of those which women own, some come from inheritance and some from calves which they have received as young girls. Many older women in addition hold cattle in trust for their daughter's children. That women have fewer cattle than men is due mainly to their disadvantage in inheritance. Moreover, they have less time at their disposal to keep personal watch over their animals and to apply themselves to trading ventures. They may also have rather more incidental expenditure than men. But, owing to the system of maintenance, a woman needs no assets of her own.

Soon after birth, the father gives a cow or a cow-calf to his child of either sex. This is the 'cow of the navel' (*bart el surra*), for the navel-string is cut and tied to the animal's tail. A girl has no other customary gifts of cattle in childhood, but a boy is given a cow or cow-calf, the cow of the hair (*bart el suf*), the first time the hair of his head is shaved, and sometimes a beast or two when he is circumcised at about the age of nine. If the cows survive, natural increase follows, and the grown child may find himself the owner of a substantial herd.

In inheritance men have the advantage over women. Islamic law accords the advantage and Humr custom enhances it. If the case of inheritance should be heard in one of the courts, the distribution is made in accordance with Islamic law. While a case of inheritance, as such, is unlikely to be taken to court, questions relating to inheritance sometimes arise in the course of other suits. Some months after the death, a family council discusses the distribution of the cattle, and it may decide on a distribution markedly different from the legal one.

[13] A third phrase applied to cattle is *ashawwar aya*. It means 'let me ask my mother': implying that a girl accepts at once the advances of a suitor with cattle, but has only to get her mother's permission for him to enter the tent; and in the circumstances, this permission will be readily given.

I think that some sections of the tribe hold more strongly to Islamic practice than others, inviting a holy man to interpret the law. Humr state categorically that they go by the Book; but the few cases of inheritance whose details I heard suggest that they may only think they do.

These details are given in Appendix 2, where there is also a table contrasting the actual with the ideal Islamic distribution. While all those who inherited cattle were entitled to inherit according to Islamic law, their shares were not the legal shares, and not everyone entitled by Islamic law to inherit did so. Where parents were alive and were offered shares they sometimes declined. Widows never had their full eighth of the property, their share—however large the herd—being limited to a bull and a milch cow or a cow-calf to give the promise of increase.[14] Some sisters and daughters were neglected entirely. As far as it is possible to find a common pattern in these few distributions, it seems to be this: that after provision was made for the widow men were given shares which were considered to be equitable in view of the holdings of cattle they had already, while women were admitted only in respect of great personal need.[15]

Women have fewer cattle and so leave fewer to be inherited. I have no reliable evidence about the way in which a dead woman's cattle were distributed; I was told they would go primarily to her children, failing whom to her father, her brothers, and her sisters.

From these modes of inheritance, two important consequences ensue. First, cattle stay for the most part within the close agnatic group, for most go from males to male agnates. Second, men have far more cattle than women. In the distributions listed in Appendix 2 (with the exception of two cases in which the size of the herd was not remembered) about ninety per cent. of the cattle went to males and about ten per cent. to females.[16] The extent to which the Humr system, even more than Islamic law, favours men is clearly shown, for by the latter men would have inherited only fifty-seven per cent. of the cattle of these distributions. The preponderance of cattle going to men tallies

[14] A bull and a milch cow is the minimum (and usual) rate of maintenance of a divorced wife, if she has children and until she remarries.

[15] In inheritance cattle are always kept whole and never turned into cash to allow subtler divisions, as is done with blood-money cattle. Of other property, a man's clothes, spear, knife, and similar objects go to the holy man who conducted the burial. Garden land either goes to the eldest son or is divided between sons. A horse is either shared by sons as co-owners, or sold and the money divided between them. The same applies to guns, although the unlicensed muzzle-loading guns (known as *kiri*) are prized heirlooms and seldom sold. From a big herd of cattle one beast may be set aside as a sacrifice at the time of burial.

[16] All the distributions involved property of males who had died.

with the Humr custom whereby no woman is expected to be economically independent, each, whether married or not, having assigned to her one man to afford her material support.

A herd may be increased by purchase as well as by inheritance. Weekly cattle markets are held at Muglad, Abyei, and other smaller centres according to the season. Here cattle are sold to other Humr, and to merchants who then transport them on the hoof to sell them further east. Humr themselves sometimes take part in this export trade, driving their animals to El Obeid, Nahud, Kadugli, or Malakal. There is a good market for butcher meat in all the large towns of Sudan, and most of this is supplied from Baggara herds. Still other cattle are sold by private deals in the camps.

The cattle which Humr prefer to sell are bull-calves of two or three years old,[17] beasts which are old or which straggle on the march, and sterile cows. With the proceeds of these, they buy young cows sold by people who are forced by temporary financial straits to put them on the market. The proceeds of the sale of labour and of surplus grain and cotton are also frequently devoted to the purchase of cattle.

CATTLE POLICY

The element of chance is always present to account in some measure for the size, composition, and quality of a herd: changes resulting from cattle sickness, from inheritance, and heavy financial commitments like the payment of blood-money, are largely outside the owner's control. But to the extent that he is able (and this is limited by various social obligations, and by his variable access to markets and market intelligence), a cattleman controls the size and make-up of his herd. He bases decisions about his herd on the various uses of cattle, material and social, as well as on the peculiar conditions of cattle husbandry in his country.

Baggara cattle are those of the short-horned zebu type, with hump and dewlap. They are distinct from the cattle of their southern neighbours, the Dinka, which are available to Humr if they wish to buy them. But the qualities of stock which Humr most admire are to be found in their own animals, and of these the most important is the ability to walk fast, to keep up with the herd, and not to straggle.

[17] According to their stage of development, bull-calves are respectively *munṣalab*, *kartot*, *holy*, *maḍmun*, *jeḍa*ʿ, *teni*, *raba*ʿ, and *tor* (bull). Cow-calves are called by the feminine forms of these names, as far as *rabaʿya*, then *bikr*—a cow that has calved once. Marketable bulls are particularly those of *jeḍa*ʿ grade and upwards.

The nature of the country they move through accounts for this: slow cattle are left behind, or wander away from the grazing herd or the caravan, and it may take many days of search to find them once they are lost in the forest.[18] It is the restricted visibility of the forest land that makes this quality so important. For cows, two other points are sought: plenty of milk and regular calving. Bulls should be strong, swift, and broad-backed for comfort and efficiency as transport animals. Since Humr do not slaughter their animals for beef, the quality and quantity of meat is not of great importance: the typical beast is tall, long-legged, and broad-backed, and Humr say that leanness makes them swift. Bulls kept for stud purposes are those which are fast and good carriers, and whose dams have been good milkers and regular calvers. Humr have also welcomed stud bulls provided by the Government, as they admit that well-built animals may be more resistant to disease.

Because of the special qualities they seek, Humr do not invest much in Dinka cattle, which were, during my stay, some ten per cent. cheaper than Humr cattle age for age. Dinka cattle are to some extent the negation of what Humr deem good in stock: they are small,[19] they are not fast, they wander from the herd, they give less milk, they are attuned to clay and not sand beneath their feet, they are not trained for transport. Their advantages, that (according to Humr) they can stand mud better, they mature sooner, and they are more prolific, are outweighed by the disadvantages, and Humr buy them occasionally only because they are cheap. In the herds I knew, about a tenth of the cattle were clearly Dinka beasts or offspring of Dinka and Baggara beasts.[20]

Thus Humr prefer for convenience a quality in their cattle which is not directly productive. They do not breed primarily for milk, or primarily for beef, although the milk-giving aspect is always taken into

[18] Even although Humr select their animals largely for swiftness, I estimate that from three to four per cent. of the cattle are missing from their herds at any one time.

[19] In general they are smaller than Humr cattle, but Dinka herds contain some exceptionally large bulls and oxen, which Humr sometimes buy with the express purpose of making a quick profit by selling them at a northern market. They buy Dinka cattle of all kinds, especially in times of crop failure in Dinka country, when they exchange them for grain at a very favourable rate. A few indulge in a specialized trade: they buy young white cows from Dinka and march them to Nuer, who give a big bull in exchange for a small cow of this colour. The bull is then sold at great profit to merchants in Muglad or elsewhere.

[20] Dinka cattle are *jenage*, the plural of *jengayi*, Dinka, as distinct from Baggara cattle, which are *bagar hurrat*, a term used to express the superiority of Baggara cattle in Humr eyes.

account. They could, by a different kind of selective breeding, have greater cash profits from their cattle. No doubt they have a more mercenary attitude to their beasts than many other pastoral people of Africa, including their Nilotic neighbours,[21] but cash profits as such are of little interest to them.

Other facts support this view. Humr could sell more bulls and oxen and buy more young cows, but they prefer to have a number of spare bulls to lend out for riding and transport; they could sell more old cows instead of waiting to slaughter them until they are on the point of death, but men and women grow sentimentally attached to cows that have been long with them, and which have calved well—I have seen families reduced to sadness when they have at last had to put to death a prolific cow. Men with herds of a comfortable size have the practice of gelding one or two of their bulls and keeping them in an unproductive capacity, specifically for show. By itself, an ox treated in this way, so that it grows fat and sleek, and lopes along in front of the herd, announces that its owner is rich enough to have it, and a fine ox draws generous comment.

From the point of view of his dependants' welfare and of his own prestige and status, the cattleman is interested in maintaining not his cash profits but the number of head of his cattle. The advantage of numbers is that the more he has, so he reasonably believes, the more are likely to survive an epidemic; and the more cows he has, the more are likely to be in milk at any one time, and the less likely is his family to be completely deprived of milk. In making gifts and loans to poor relatives, again, it is the number and not the quality that counts. The prized gift or loan is not milk, but a milch cow or a riding bull. For prestige also it is the size of the herd, with possibly the presence of a few unproductive oxen, which counts. And it is numbers of cattle which the Humrawi seeks and by which he measures his wealth, and the wealth (and to some extent the worthiness) of others. Cattle are better than cash savings or material goods, for they usually increase and they are always useful, while cash, though necessary at times, is of little value if a man is short of grain and far from a market.

To maintain a large herd, the cattleman has to avoid as far as possible

[21] There is none of the identification of a man with a favourite beast, of the Nilotic kind. Quality of service is what counts, and Humr are not interested in horn-shape, and little interested in colour pattern, except for identifying lost animals (although a red cow with white legs—very rare—is considered to be a particularly lucky beast to have). A very few youths sharpen the horns of their wilder bulls so that they can boast of the damage they do: it is commoner for horn-tips to be filed round, to prevent damage.

selling cattle for reasons other than the purchase of animals more productive than those he has sold. The relation between cash needs and holdings of livestock is thus important. The continuous sources of small cash are the sale of liquid butter and various small manufactures and local products made or collected by women. Here the more cattle one has the better, for then more milk is available to turn into the saleable liquid butter. Larger commitments, however, like taxes, marriage costs, blood-money payments, and perhaps the hire of agricultural labour, have to be financed from other sources. Some people have sheep or goats which they sell readily for these purposes. Some cultivate cotton, or cultivate millet above their immediate requirements, or sell their labour for short periods. They do so to avoid having to sell cattle, or to have enough cash to buy more cattle than they could from the sale of young bulls and unproductive cows.[22]

Cattle-keeping is more than simply one element in the economic life. It is the overriding interest, and absorbs people from childhood. All that is sweet in life stems from the possession of cattle, and without them Humr cannot enjoy life to the full. To start a herd men without cattle leave and seek work; or they concentrate on millet or cotton cultivation for a year or two with the same end. They live in the hope that they will be rich in cattle, for the fortunes of cattle-rearing are variable. There is much difference in the size of herds: there are men whose last cow has died; there are those with a cow and a bull which they are trying devotedly, and with trust in God, to turn into a worthwhile herd; there are those with comfortable herds of fifty head, there are those few with cattle numbering hundreds, and a handful with over a thousand. By hard work, skill, an abstemious life, and divine favour anyone can build a herd; economic opportunities, and political ones likewise, are open to all.

THE EFFECT OF ADMINISTRATIVE ACTION

Since the Reoccupation there have been innovations of various kinds in Dar Humr, some of them affecting the economy. Cotton has been introduced, and the Government has facilitated its sale by taking weighing machines to the tribe. Given the expectancy of a good price, it is a popular crop. The veterinary services have provided inoculation

[22] There are other sources of income. Hunting, especially giraffe hunting, the hire of baggage bulls, horses, and donkeys, driving other people's cattle to a distant market (the drover receives ten per cent. of the proceeds), and the sale of wild honey, are among the most important.

against various epidemic diseases, and have established a veterinary clinic in the country. After initial difficulties, their services are now welcomed. They have also brought in stud bulls to improve the quality of the herds. The use of cash is increasing. Humr sell their labour, travelling perhaps as far as Omdurman to do so. Slavery has been abolished, and the many who do not care to pay for Dinka labour for their fields work in them themselves.

In spite of these changes the economic and social uses of cattle seem not to have changed, and men still have the same policy towards their cattle. For it is clear that Humr have accepted those innovations which enable them to be more prosperous in terms of their traditional way of life. The innovations have not brought about an economic revolution. On the contrary, Humr have been selective and have adapted to their own purposes those which are capable of enhancing rather than altering the way of life of their forefathers. Increase in cash has not brought a greatly increased demand for market goods: cash from cotton and sale of labour is used for the purpose of adding to, or avoiding the sale of, holdings of stock; veterinary measures accepted so far have helped the traditional way of life rather than led to a change. Cattle retain their customary social value.

One aspect of development which the Humr have notably rejected is the opportunity for education. The Sudan census found in 1955 that 91.5 per cent. of the boys and 98.5 per cent. of the girls in the census district had had no education, and that 94.4 per cent. of the men and 99.5 per cent. of the women had had no education;[23] the illiteracy figures for the Humr themselves are actually higher than these, because the same census area included the merchants and white-collar workers in Muglad town who normally send their children to school.

The difference between education, which has been resisted, and the other innovations which have been accepted is that education on a large scale would at once mark a revolutionary change. Pastoral nomadism is a full-time activity of a high degree of skill, and this skill is learned by children of school-going age. It is then that they go out herding regularly; they learn through this experience the lore of the grasses, waters, soils, and insects, and acquaint themselves with the geography of their country. This is the pastoral education, with which formal education would interfere. Men are reluctant to send their children to school because they would lose their services as herders, and also because a child who spends more than about two years away from the

[23] Ministry of Social Affairs, *First Population Census of the Sudan*, First Interim Report, pp, 18–19.

cattle and the nomadic life becomes softened by urban manners and unable to readapt himself to the demands of nomadic cattle-husbandry; for he does not learn the skills, and loses the hardiness required of him. In the same way, girls who are educated are not acceptable as nomad wives. The skills and the hardiness required of them are just as great. So far, those children who have been to school have been for the most part children of nazirs and omdas of the tribe.[24]

Accordingly Humr fear the results of education, from which, they clearly see, cattle herding, and hence the family stock, would suffer. Their aim is still to own cattle and increase their herds, and to gain through the possession of cattle the opportunity of leading a life of material comfort and of winning influence and power among their own people.

The work of pasture research officers suggests that the country has absorbed as many cattle as it can.[25] The official view is that the land is already well overstocked. Humr themselves can see growing difficulties, especially in the rains period in the Babanusa, where the introduction of deep bores has attracted cultivators (both Humr and others) to increase the agricultural land in this already cramped grazing area. Nevertheless, an expanding cattle ownership remains a purpose firmly embedded in the aspirations of all the Humr. In this respect administrative control has not so far given rise to significant change, for although innovations have been offered, Humr have rejected some, and incorporated others in such a way as to make them serve the purposes of the traditional values and the traditional structure of their society.

[24] In discussion with Humr recently (1962) I learned that there is a growing tendency to send the last-born son to school, the older sons being reserved to ensure continuity in cattle herding.

[25] For 1951, the tax lists (a notoriously inaccurate source) gave the following numbers of grown cattle for omodiyas:

Fayyarin	14,742	Metanin	11,091
A. Kamil	11,822	Ziyud	12,534
Mezaghna	8,366	A. Serur	10,966
Faḍliya	2,021	Jubarat	2,661
A. 'Umran	27,240	Salamat	1,899
Total 'Ajaira	64,191	Total Felaita	39,150

Grand total 103,341

4
HOUSEHOLD AND EXTENDED FAMILY

THROUGH control of cattle, men come to control people. Ownership of cattle links domestic interests with political ones, for the ability to fulfil political aspirations starts in the ability to control and maintain a family. But domestic organization has another and different kind of relevance in a description of political life. While the Humr are outwardly a society based on the principles of a segmentary lineage system, informal positions of leadership have always existed, and latterly formal ones have been instituted by the Sudan Government. Neither class distinction nor heredity determines who are going to fill these positions, which are open to anyone in the groups which the positions represent. A political leader can emerge from any household, and once he has emerged his domestic arrangements, including his commitments, continue to be much as they always had been: unless he is a nazir he remains with the camps, and his tent is indistinguishable from others. As he goes higher he takes on responsibilities which are not only wider but also more numerous, since he retains all those which he has contracted on the way up. I turn now to discuss the commitments and responsibilities which men have in household, camp, and lineage, as they relate to their chances of political emergence.

THE TENT AND THE HOUSEHOLD GOODS

Humr camps consist for the most part of groups of up to about twenty tents arranged in circles. The camps, considered as units, shift frequently and independently of one another and pitch in ever-changing patterns. But each camp also is constantly changing in its size and composition, according to the needs of the season, its members' outside interests, and their relations of harmony or conflict with one another. At some seasons, notably sowing and harvest, camps of the usual kind cease to exist, for they break up into small groups, or single tents. In this nomadic society there is a kind of secondary nomadism; no one has a fixed set of people with whom he continually and exclusively resides; individuals and households move within the primary framework of the nomadism of the camps. To arrive at a structure which, though itself mobile, constitutes a durable physical centre of residence we have to come down to the tent. But the people who associate themselves with a single tent change also. Even the tent itself is not an irreducible unit, for it is a structure of a kind that can be divided up, and the pieces amalgamated into other tents. Moreover, all the component parts have to be replaced more or less frequently: the supple sticks of the framework are cut fresh at most sites, to save carrying them around; the bark of the roof may last for about a year, the mats rather longer. The tent has no major, durable part, such as a canvas, which stamps it with its own permanence and individuality. Flux and instability thus characterize even the smallest residence group, and its physical framework, the tent.

The tent (*beyt*) consists of a hemispherical framework of strips of shredded bark, which make it more or less windproof. These in turn are covered by mats, firmly roped in position. When the tent is being erected, the first thing to be put up is the bed (*diringil*), which is across it, opposite the entrance, and takes up much of the space inside. Supported on short tripods, it consists of layers of sticks and split cane criss-crossed, a cowhide, and mats. To the left of this bed facing the entrance is a large tripod, associated with the women, which supports the household goods; to the right is another support for the few possessions of the men. Outside the doorway a forked stick is planted to hold calabashes and pots and pans. Sometimes in the dry weather, when a camp is to be on one site for a week or two, a square grass building is put up facing the doorway as a shelter and kitchen; at other times cooking is done inside the tent or at the threshold.[1]

Although we can distinguish the tent structure from the household goods, the items of property concerned are, as property, all of the same status: to the Humr, tent and household property are classified together under the same generic term, *el khuman*. This is not surprising, since many of the items can be used as parts of the tent or as household goods interchangeably. Mats which at one site are used on the roof of the tent may at others be used on the bed, or as part of the shelter, or for sitting on. The shredded bark is used not only for the tent roof but also as padding between the bull's back and the bull saddle

[1] The shelter is known as *rakuba*. Tents of different styles are made at different seasons: for example, the tents to withstand the heavy early rains of the Bahr sometimes have conical lids of thatch over the bark: in the rains waterproof papyrus mats are used for the roof, there being little thatching grass at this season; in the dry season decorated mats of finer quality, but not rainproof, are put up.

in transport. The rope for tying the roof may be used in transport for tying loads.

Moreover, the tent and the household goods are obtained, kept up, and disposed of in the same manner. A woman first obtains this equipment on her first marriage. Most of it is paid for by her husband-to-be, although some of the leatherwork and basketry has been made slowly over the years by her mother and other women of her household, and may have been used in the mother's tent.[2]

The tent and household goods remain in the woman's possession. She looks after them and replaces items when necessary, but if these have to be bought the husband provides the money. On divorce she retains the tent and household goods and continues to use them. Under certain limited circumstances Humr custom clearly allows a man who divorces his wife at her instigation to keep the equipment, but he seldom in fact does so. When her husband dies she retains tent and household goods. If she remarries she uses the same stuff, but her husband before marriage gives her some money to refurnish a bit. On the woman's own death the equipment is taken to market and sold;[3] the proceeds are divided amongst her nearest female kin, her mother, if she is still alive, taking the largest share. Out of courtesy these women ask the husband's advice about the disposal of the money; he usually waives any claim to it.

Humr custom does not indicate clearly who, between husband and wife, owns this equipment. Apparently, unless he predeceases his wife or divorces her against her will, the husband has an opportunity to exercise some control over its disposal. But normally the only way in which he avails himself of it is to the extent that his wife uses it on his, or on their joint, behalf during his marriage to her. Humr custom differs from the practice of Humr courts over the disposal of this pro-

[2] The money handed over to the bride's mother at marriage is commonly in the region of twenty pounds. The amount she spends on camp and household equipment varies, but is often about half of this.

The main items of tent and household goods are: bark, mats, rope, a cowhide, tripods, clay and metal cooking utensils, wood or calabash serving-bowls, footed and lidded metal bowls of Czech manufacture, kettles, tea-glasses, grindstones, censers, leather grain-bags (sometimes replaced by sacks); small leather or basketry containers for the transport of light items like prepared meal, foodstuffs, cloth, and scents; wooden pestles and mortars; leather straps, often finely braided and decorated, for the transport of small items on bulls. Wealthier households have great quantities of braided leather to decorate tent and bull, kidney-shaped leather pillows with brass rings attached, and, for the bulls, ostrich feathers, leather bands with cowries or beads sewn in, and bells.

[3] It is considered unsuitable to use the tent and household goods of a deceased kinswoman.

perty. In 1954 when a man sued his mother-in-law for a share in the proceeds of the equipment she had sold on his wife's death, the nazir upheld his claim and divided the money in the way that, in Islamic law, it would have been divided if the goods had been the woman's own property: the husband got a half, her brother a third, and her daughter a sixth. By Humr customs none of this would have gone to her brother; the property is entirely women's business, and any male, even the husband, who wants to share in the proceeds is held in poor esteem.[4]

THE MAINTENANCE OF DEPENDANTS

With only occasional exceptions, members of Humr society are resident at tents. I refer to people resident at one tent as a 'household', and will distinguish two main categories—the married and the unmarried household. The composition of a household is determined mainly by two things: first, the Humr system of economic maintenance; and second, the wealth, marital status and personal relationships of a group of close kin. The group of kin from which the members of one household come is largely, though not entirely, the extended family; in some circumstances people may become a charge on a family other than their own. But each household, at any time, is clearly associated with one extended family, in whose arc of a camp circle it lives.

The tent is the only focus for domestic life. The only tents which exist belong to women who are, or who have been, married. Other people are attached for various reasons and for longer or shorter periods to such women and their tents. The resultant households either include a married couple, or do not. Neither 'married' nor 'unmarried' households can be said to be typical or normal. The married household is the more stable and usually consists of man, wife, and children, the composition changing only through death or as children are born or leave to marry; while the unmarried household receives members from outside the nuclear family more readily. But the difference is one of degree only, for married households may also include members who are not of the nuclear family.

Two offices exist in relation to every woman and minor: that of

[4] This was an unusual suit. The woman had lied to the man when she told him how much the sale had brought; this had annoyed him, and he brought the case in consequence.

The only items of household property which a man can claim or take without giving rise to adverse comment are a drinking bowl and a kettle.

guardian, and that of provider.[5] These offices may or may not be filled by the same person. The provider is usually, and the guardian seldom, a member of the household of the woman concerned. For a married woman, the provider is her husband, the guardian a member of her own extended family, and thus often residing in another camp. It is the provider's duty to furnish reasonable material support. The husband is the only provider for a married woman: he relieves her extended family of the responsibility of maintaining her. If he fails she can compel him in court; if he still fails after a warning she can insist on a divorce from the court if she wants it. With an unmarried woman, however, if one relative fails, then some other relative is at hand to provide. Widows and divorcees, unless they have grown-up sons, fall back on their own agnates.

What is reasonable support for a wife depends to some extent on the man's circumstances and the number of dependent children. For a wife basic provision should be made of a bull to ride and a cow to milk and a set of cheap blue clothing once a year; if there is not enough grain from the family cultivations for the year's use, the husband should get it by purchase or barter; he should provide money for tea, sugar, and scents unless the woman can find it herself by selling liquid butter, leatherwork, basketry, or woodland scents. In insisting upon the basic minimum and in not requiring maintenance according to ability, the courts of the Humr are consciously upholding Humr custom and not Islamic law. In 1954 the nazir's court was confronted by a woman whose husband had many cattle and who, exceptionally, was wearing big gold earrings. She complained that her husband refused to provide her with a fairly good kind of clothing that a number of Humr women wear. The nazir said that if all husbands gave their wives everything they demanded there would soon be no cattle left in the country; and he rejected the claim. It cuts at the root of Humr values to be liberal in the sphere of 'luxuries' to one's wife. But, through the threat of being taken to court, men give their wives more than they give to unmarried women dependent on them.

Some simple rules exist to determine who should maintain whom. Wives, unmarried daughters, and minors are looked after by the hus-

[5] The guardian is *wali* and the provider is *mukellif*. The woman or minor provided for is called *'ar*.

The Arabic *wali* is often translated as 'marriage guardian', but this rendering would only lead to misunderstanding of the position among the Humr. More often the word is used in the plural (*ulyan*), for close male agnates generally share the responsibility for the woman's morals, although one of them is regarded as having the main responsibility.

band and father. A divorced woman, or a widow, without a grown son, is looked after by her oldest unmarried brother, a young full brother taking precedence over an older half-brother. If all her brothers are married they jointly provide maintenance. A widow or divorcee with a son over the age of about fourteen[6] is looked after by that son, and usually she lives in the camp of her former husband (for there her son is at home) rather than with her brothers. But while these rules are widely recognized, the situation in any extended family varies in practice according to its size and composition and the wealth and temperament of individual members.

The males on the one side of the relationship and the females on the other provide mutual support. The tent is the home of a self-contained domestic unit. That of a married man belongs to his wife, and it is she who lives in and around it, but the husband sleeps in it, keeps his belongings in it, and ties his horse outside it. It is to this tent that the milk from his cattle goes, as well as any food which he may bring to camp; and the women of this tent send a meal out to the men of the camp on those occasions when he himself is present. Around this tent his children play when they are small. A son sleeps in it until he is about eleven; at this age he starts sleeping outside, and he continues to do so until he marries. A daughter sleeps in the tent until she marries. The husband with a grown-up unmarried daughter no longer uses his tent regularly. When he wants to sleep with his wife, either the daughter may be sent to the tent of some relative or else husband and wife may sleep in the grass shelter, if one has been built.

A bachelor looking after his unmarried sister treats her and her tent as a married man treats his wife and her tent, except that he seldom sleeps in it. In heavy rain he may drag his *'angereyb*[7] inside the doorway for shelter: the bachelor's proper place, however cold it may be, is in the open. But a man who is resident at an unmarried household spends more of the waking hours at the tent than a husband does at his tent, and it is a common sight to see a man drinking tea, even with relatives from outside the camp, at the tent of his sister. Otherwise the arrangements are the same: his cattle are milked by himself and the women of this tent, who take the milk; he brings food here; the women send a meal to the tree for him if he is in camp; and he keeps his belongings in this tent.

[6] It is at about this age that a lad is said to have 'rolled up his sleeves' (to use an almost literal translation of *rafa' el kimm*). He is then adult and responsible.

[7] Portable Sudanese bedstead of wood and rope or leather strips, quite different from the *diringil* mentioned earlier.

However, men and women in camp are seldom paired off evenly for the purpose of mutual support. A man may have no woman whom he maintains and in consequence have no tent to use as if it were his own; he therefore joins a household by 'living on'[8] some woman who is being maintained by another man. If he contributes to the larder, so much the better; but if he is unable, or too lazy, to provide anything, this is no matter: no one will ever require it of him. Living on a woman in this sense is common: by reason of the frequent splitting and regrouping of members of an extended family or of a wider group, a man may be away from the woman for whom he provides. He simply joins for the time being the household of a suitable close relative who can afford the extra mouth to feed.

Each household has to be provided in some manner with the necessities of life: shelter, grain, milk, and transport. With the married household, the wife has the proceeds of any cattle which she has in her keeping, whether they are her own or she is holding them in trust for her children. In addition she has all the milk from her husband's herd, or, if she is a co-wife, from those cattle which her husband has specifically allotted to her. Milk from a cow goes directly to the tent, and then it is for the wife to do with it as she likes, including, of course, answering the demands of her husband to provide hospitality for his guests. It is the husband's annual duty to prepare a garden for each wife; in addition he sometimes prepares one of his own. While he relies on the wife's grain in the ordinary course of events, he supplements this with grain from his own garden if he has heavy obligations of hospitality; or he may sell the proceeds of his own garden to buy cattle or to save selling cattle. Although a husband has to provide and prepare a garden for each wife, he need not sow, weed, or harvest it. If a divorce takes place before the grain is used, the husband takes two shares to the wife's one share.

Outside the conjugal family, the people who actually share in the harvest from one field, and to some extent in its cultivation as well, depend largely on the kinship configuration. A woman without a husband, whether widow or divorcee, may cultivate alone, but if her provider is himself unmarried, they may cultivate together. Thus a woman often cultivates along with her grown-up unmarried son. This does not necessarily mean that the son does more than a token stint of garden labour; he may be away with the cattle, engaged on production which benefits the household in other ways. Other combinations are possible, and according to the situation a mother and son, or

[8] The Arabic expression is *gaʿid fog*.

a brother and sister, or a mother and daughter cultivate together; should the male marry in the meantime, he would take two out of three shares of the produce. Males sometimes combine: two unmarried brothers, or mother's brother and sister's son. Usually the pair thus cultivating belong to the same household, and usually the male partner is the provider for the woman.

EXAMPLES OF HOUSEHOLD ORGANIZATION

The details of the arrangement of households connected with a single extended family are flexible, and this flexibility in turn gives men the opportunity, without transgressing norms of kinship, to gather people about them as personal followers. In this section I give details of the households of one camp in order to show some of the variety of residential arrangements and indicate some possibilities of acceptable manipulation.

The examples are taken from the surra of 'Iyal Ganiṣ[9] as they were arranged in camp at the end of the dry season of 1954. The camp which a part of them formed is sketched in Fig. 2, and the tent numbers refer to the positions on that sketch. Tents 3 to 7 were all associated with the extended family of *'Iyal Merida*, whose kinship connexions are shown in Fig. 3. The late Merida had been omda of the Mezaghna omodiya, and this position was now held by his son Ḥurgaṣ, who was also the leader of this extended family.

Tents 6 and 7 belonged to two of Ḥurgaṣ's wives.[10] In tent 6, Jidya was childless; the household consisted of herself and Ḥurgaṣ. In tent 7 Simeyḥa had five young children, and the household comprised the nuclear family. Tent 5 belonged to Ḥurgaṣ's widowed mother, who, although herself from a different omodiya, chose to live as was customary with her son who maintained her. She lived alone. Ḥurgaṣ had the direct responsibility for maintaining these three women and Simeyḥa's five children. He could afford to do this. As an omda he had a small salary. He had a good herd of cattle, at a guess about sixty head. Each woman had certain cattle allotted to her for milk and transport. Each of the wives cultivated a garden, but the mother, being very old, was simply provided with grain. Each household did its own

[9] The names of surras, usually, and of extended families always, are in this form: '*Iyal* means children or descendants, and is used in the smaller lineages in the same way as *Awlad* is used in the larger lineages. 'I.' in footnotes and tables denotes '*Iyal*.

[10] A third lived in Muglad. Some previous wives had died or been divorced, and some young children lived with the divorced wives in other camps.

cooking every day: the wives took day about in sending a dish to the men's tree if Ḥurgaṣ was in camp. Ḥurgaṣ himself grew cotton, and either he or one of his wives was there when work on it was required.

These households, two married and one unmarried, were all straightforward. The responsibilities which Ḥurgaṣ had towards these

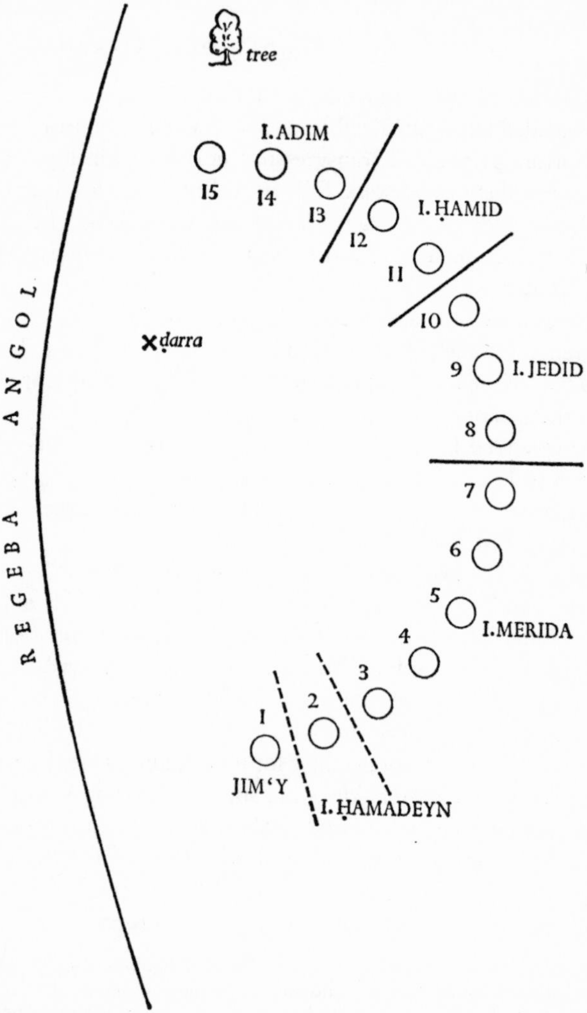

FIG. 2. Diagram of main camp of I. Ganiṣ at Regeba Angol, in April 1954, with extended families. (For discussion of tents 1 and 2, see p. 82.)

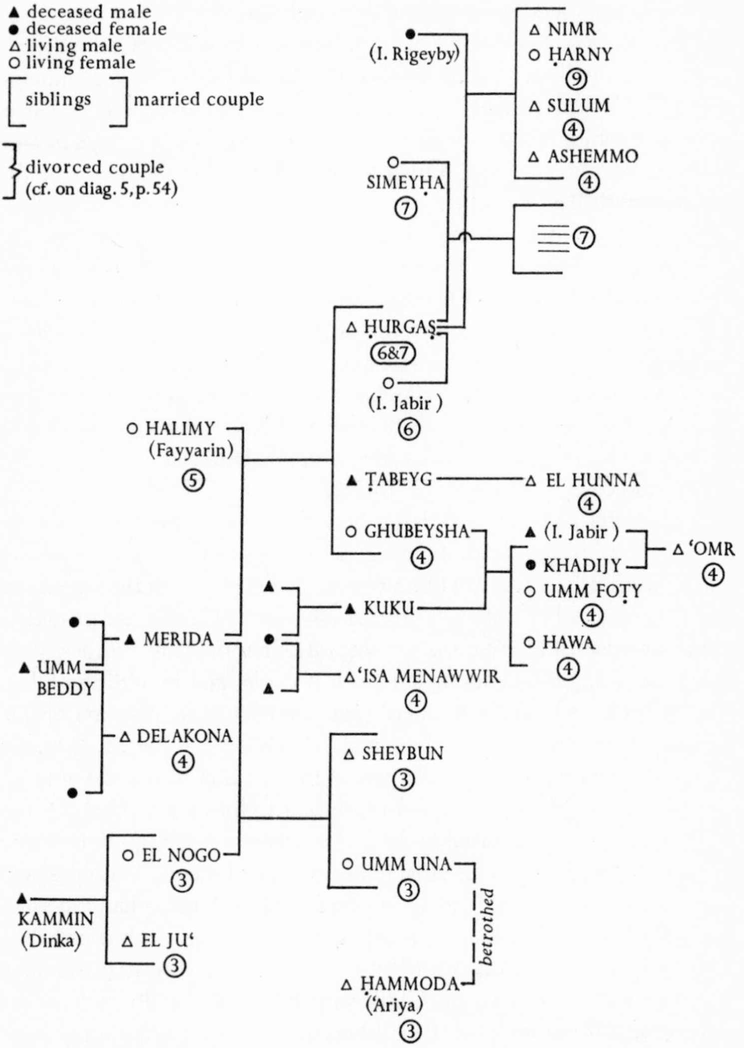

FIG. 3. Extended family of I. Merida, with some dependants. The numbers indicate the tents (Fig. 2) to which people are attached. For other relationships within I. Ganiṣ see subsequent Figures.

women were self-evident. Tent 4, however, which belonged to Ḥurgaṣ's widowed full sister, was the home of a more complex household. She was perhaps about sixty; had married first a man of her own surra, had three daughters, and was then divorced. Her ex-husband then died. She married again, this time without issue, and was again divorced. She returned to live in her brother's camp, bringing her three daughters with her. Her eldest daughter married a man of a closely related surra and had a son; but she and her husband died within a few days of one another, leaving the infant 'Omar an orphan. Ghubeysha now lived in this tent with her two other daughters, one unmarried and the other divorced,[11] and with young 'Omar. Two men were continually attached to her household, and two others sporadically. El Hunna, the son of Ḥurgaṣ's dead full brother, and Delakona, old Merida's senile half-brother, were permanent; a son of Ḥurgaṣ, who had been at school and usually had a job in the towns, lived on Ghubeysha when he visited camp. The other man was 'Isa Menawwir, a married man from another lineage, who was maternal half-brother to Ghubeysha's first husband; her daughters treated him as a paternal uncle. He often left his family behind and came as a kinsman to this camp.

Ghubeysha managed this large household very ably. She had the reputation of sound wisdom and great strength of character—people said of her that she was not like a woman at all because of this: she was a man. Ḥurgaṣ as her only full brother alive was officially her provider, but in practice El Hunna, the grown son of another full brother, provided for her. He had about ten head of cattle, and in addition Ghubeysha held cattle, from the herd that young 'Omar inherited on his father's death, in trust for him and to use on his behalf. 'Omar's mother's mother was the proper person to look after him in the unusual circumstances. These cattle and those of El Hunna provided for the whole household, and Ghubeysha had no need to insist upon maintenance from Ḥurgaṣ with his already heavy commitments. With the help of her daughters she cultivated a big garden which Ḥurgaṣ had inherited from his father. Sulum, who as a grown son whose mother had died had no special claim on or obligation to his father or step-mothers, found it suitable to live on Ghubeysha and occasionally helped her household with grain when he cultivated. 'Isa Menawwir simply lived there, and provided nothing.

Tent 3 belonged to a young widow of Merida named El Nogo. She was with her daughter Umm Una, who, though she had gone

[11] The divorced daughter was chronically unwell and for this reason had amalgamated her tent with Ghubeysha's.

through the marriage ceremony, was waiting for her husband to finish the marriage payments before moving to his camp. Two bachelors completed this household: Sheybun, a son of Merida and a full brother of Umm Una, and El Juʿ, a full brother of El Nogo. Sheybun as El Nogo's son was the official provider. He had been married and had a daughter; he had divorced his wife, who now had the daughter with her. He provided her with the loan of a cow and a bull, but as he had only one or two other beasts he was not in a position to provide much for this household. El Juʿ was looking after my horses at the time, in return for which he had a wage; much of this money went to his sister's son Sheybun to help him in his aspirations to remarry his former wife,[12] and he also contributed to his young daughter's upkeep. The money which Sheybun made from cotton largely went to provide the household with grain in addition to that which came from the garden that Sheybun and his mother jointly cultivated. El Juʿ himself cultivated, sold some grain, and helped the household with the remainder.

These two households show the pragmatic way in which Humr go about interpreting their own rules of maintenance. El Nogo and her son Sheybun were respectively *ʿar* and *mukellif.* El Juʿ had no other close relatives, and he had no *ʿar*, since his widowed sister had a grown son; but he contributed to the household's maintenance directly and indirectly. In Ghubeysha's household Delakona was too old to do anything, but he had to live somewhere. Sulum contributed when he could; the infant ʿOmar had cattle from his late father, and he would continue to live there with his cattle, at least until he was seven; his paternal kin, his official providers, gave Ghubeysha money from time to time. El Hunna, who also had cattle, had grown up in Ghubeysha's household, although he was strictly a charge on Ḥurgaṣ, as Ghubeysha herself was; but since the household as composed could look after itself, the official maintenance was inoperative. These five tents centred on five women, of whom only one belonged to ʿIyal Merida—Ghubeysha. Of the others one was Merida's widow, two were wives of Ḥurgaṣ, and one was his mother. But they were all where they were in virtue of their connexions with the men of ʿIyal Merida.

Tents 11 and 12 were associated with the extended family of *ʿIyal Ḥamid* (Fig. 4). Ḥamid, who had died, had two sons and one daughter. Of the sons, Abu Dik was at the time married to Ḥurgaṣ's daughter

[12] This would be expensive, because the woman had re-married in the meantime; her husband then divorced her, at her instigation, and put a price on her back; no one could marry her without first making him a substantial payment.

Rabha; but as a poor man he had managed to marry only through his elder brother Adim's abnegation. Adim had married twice and divorced

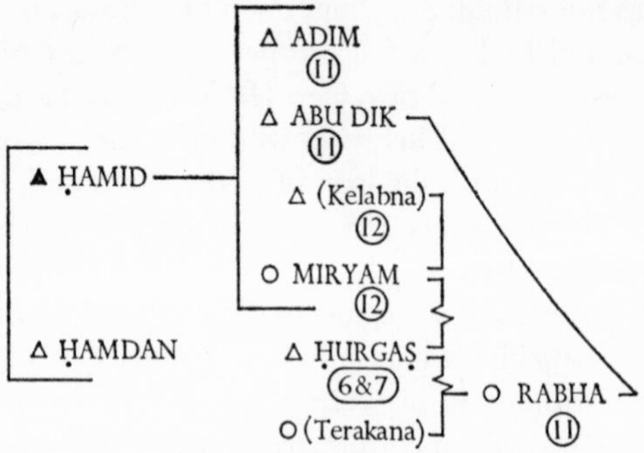

FIG. 4. Extended family of I. Hamid.

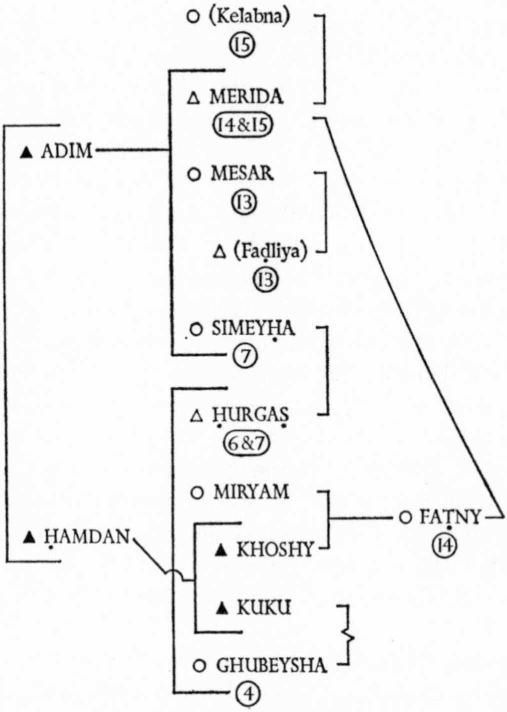

FIG. 5. Extended family of I. Adim.

twice after he saw that the wives were not bearing him children. He then devoted all his wealth to obtaining a wife for his young brother in the hope that he would he more successful, which he was. Now Adim lived on Abu Dik's household (tent 11), contributing to it. In tent 12 lived their sister Miryam, who had once been married to

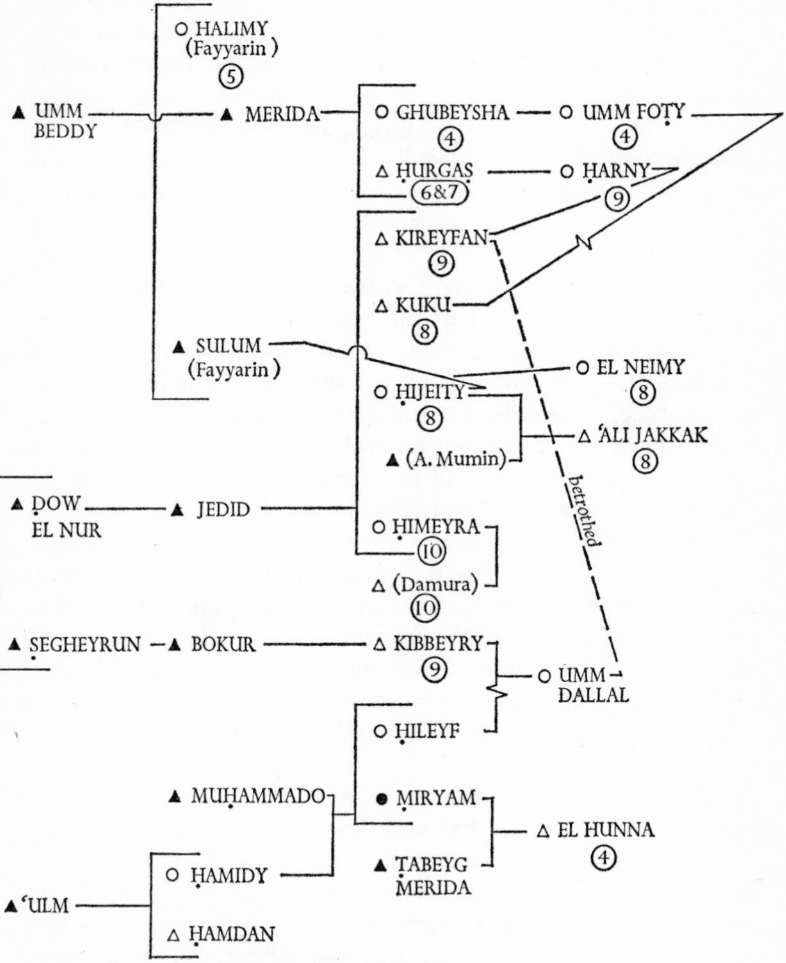

FIG. 6. Extended family of I. Jedid, with I. Bokur.

Ḥurgaṣ, and who had recently married a member of the local police from a different omodiya whose work had taken him temporarily to this camp. Tents 13–15 were associated with *'Iyal Adim* (Fig. 5). The only surviving son, Merida, had two wives, one of them from

'Iyal Ganiṣ in tent 14 and the other from another omodiya in tent 15.[13] Tent 13 belonged to his sister, who had married into the Faḍliya omodiya; she was on a short visit with her husband. Merida's other sister was Simeyḥa, Ḥurgaṣ's wife in tent 7.

Abu Dik and Adim were two brothers who combined their tenuous resources to try to start a family. *'Iyal Jedid* (Fig. 6), on the other hand, were interested in a different kind of manipulation. Tent 9 belonged to a man called Kireyfan, Jedid's eldest son, and he resided there with his wife Ḥarny, a daughter of Ḥurgaṣ, and their two small children. Tent 8 belonged to Ḥijeyty, Jedid's elder daughter.[14] She had had four husbands and lived here with the issue of two of them. Her daughter El Neimy came from her marriage with Sulum of the Fayyarin omodiya, who had been a brother of Ḥurgaṣ's mother (tent 5). Her son 'Ali Jakkak came from her marriage with a man of another lineage of the Mezaghna who had died. That 'Ali, a grown son (he was about sixteen), lived here and not with his father's brothers arose out of an accident which had happened to his mother: a throw from a bull had left her slightly lame, though she was still active. Because of this the mother preferred to live with her own paternal kin, to ensure as much help as possible around her tent; 'Ali had grown up in this camp, and his guardians had agreed that he should stay rather than go to them at the age of seven. Ḥijeyty herself had few cattle; 'Ali had about a dozen head, and these provided milk also for the occupants of tent 9, his mother's brother Kireyfan and family, for Kireyfan had only one bull. Living on tent 8 was Kuku, Kireyfan's younger brother, who had once been married to a daughter of Ghubeysha (tent 4). He had no cattle. Ḥarny cultivated a garden for tent 9, and Ḥijeyty and El Neimy together cultivated for tent 8, while 'Ali spent all his days with the herds.

As the only father of a family, and the eldest brother, Kireyfan was leader of this group. He had some additional prestige from his job as a local authority policeman.[15] In spite of his salary, his domestic responsibilities had prevented him from getting a herd, but he still considered himself quite fortunate in having 'Ali's cattle at his beck and call. His position at the time was more difficult than usual because he was trying to take a second wife in an expensive marriage, and in

[13] Merida's wife and Miryam's husband both belonged to the Kelabna lineage of A. Kamil, with whom I. Ganiṣ had close relations.

[14] Tent 10 was that of another sister, who was paying a short visit with her husband from another surra.

[15] The nazir had kindly released him from his police duties so that he could help me in my work.

fact he married her within a year: most of his money went in gifts to this girl's mother. This girl was the daughter of a paternal second cousin of Kireyfan, called Kibbeyry.[16] The girl's mother was also a woman of 'Iyal Ganiṣ, but she was now married to a man of Dar Bakheyt major lineage, and mother and daughter lived in his camp. Kibbeyry was a bachelor, and on his many visits to the camp his kinship and prospective affinity led him to live on Kireyfan's household.[17]

Kireyfan, with his job, his relative seniority, and his established family, was undoubtedly head of this group, and had authority even though he had no cattle of his own. Yet it was quite clear that, through his sister, he was successfully attaching 'Ali's animals. In order to consolidate his position, he would have liked later to marry his ten-year-old daughter to 'Ali Jakkak. If this succeeded, it would mean that 'Ali would certainly remain in the camp, under Kireyfan's authority, in view of his mother and his other connexions there. Kireyfan would have performed a substantial coup: for if 'Ali's guardians made the first move to persuade 'Ali to marry a girl of his own lineage or surra, then he would go off to their camp, taking with him his mother, his sister, and his cattle. Kireyfan would be left high and dry, with two wives, a growing family, and no milk.[18]

Kireyfan was in a still stronger position, as his sister's daughter El Neimy had been handed over (again because of her mother's lameness) by her Fayyarin kin to himself and Ḥurgaṣ, her father's sister's son, as her effective guardians. Kireyfan and Ḥurgaṣ were thus in a position to retain El Neimy and any cattle she might have; and before I left the field she had duly become engaged to a man of 'Iyal Ganiṣ, instead of having been married off by her father's kin to a man of the Fayyarin; El Neimy's and her husband's animals remained with 'Iyal Ganiṣ, and Kireyfan could still influence their disposal. So Kireyfan managed to retain about him more people than a cattleless position would normally enable a man to do, and he remained the master of this group, with a respected name.

I have discussed the arrangements of domestic families out of which some men emerge to political position. The significance of the residential group, with the extended family as its basis, is clear: however mixed the origin of a residental group may be, it takes its name from

[16] Kibbeyry was the only surviving representative of another extended family, *I. Bokur* (Fig. 6).

[17] In addition, Kibbeyry had earlier been engaged to two of Kireyfan's sisters, but had not actually married either of them.

[18] I am now (1964) told that 'Ali married a girl of I. Adim, and still lives in the same camp.

the extended family with which it is associated. A man's reputation for wealth is to some extent confused with the reputation of his extended family, and this reputation in turn depends to some extent on the number of its dependants and of their cattle. The cattle of a residential group are a unit; they are all associated with the extended family that (at least for the time being) controls them. It so happened that Kireyfan had under his control cattle which belonged almost exclusively to other lineages; but the cattle are used for the benefit of all the members of the residential group. This is not done by appropriating cattle for the use of specific members, but rather by so organizing the residential arrangements within the group that a reasonable sharing of resources is assured. And, since the inheritance rules of Islam are not adhered to strictly, there is the opportunity of evening out to some extent, after a death, the variations of cattle ownership among the male members of the extended family. In this respect the cattle of these members can be regarded as stock held in common by and for the extended family.

Ḥurgaṣ, Kireyfan, and Merida were leaders of their extended families and the people dependent on them. The extended family and the residential group, however, give a man only limited scope to show his ability to attract kinsmen as economic dependants and as adherents in a more general sense. Discussion of surra and camp will bring out wider possibilities.

5

CAMP AND SURRA

As a group of neighbouring tents is associated with an extended family, so a camp (*ferig*) is associated with a lineage of the kind known as 'surra'. One or more camps constitute a mobile physical framework for accommodating surra members. Humr regard the surra as the ideal camping, migrating, and cattle-herding unit, as well as the limit of intimate and undifferentiated brotherhood. A camp should, in ideal circumstances, consist of the males of a surra and those dependent on them; they should camp together, move together, look after their herds together, and share together the burdens of hospitality; they should make up a named unit exhibiting complete solidarity. In practice, however, this ideal is continually thwarted by economic necessity and the changing relations of surra members.

COMPOSITION AND RESIDENCE OF 'IYAL GANIṢ

The surra of 'Iyal Ganiṣ takes its name from Muḥammad[1] Ganiṣ, 'Muḥammad the Hunter', who is said to have been alive when the Humr moved east from Wadai. Seven generations are counted; the supposed date of the migration, 1775, makes it possible that no telescoping has taken place.

Fig. 7 shows how the founders of the extended families of 'Iyal Ganiṣ are related to one another. The diagram is not a complete representation of the higher generations of the lineage: I have omitted from it those men who produced only daughters, or who were childless; the question of the extended families of ex-slaves is deferred to a later section. The most recent men shown are those from whom the present extended families take their names. Ganiṣ is said to have had five sons, all of whom can be linked by patrilineal descent with living people. But the order of the sons is not remembered; accordingly 'Iyal Ganiṣ have no notion of senior and junior lines, and all extended families

[1] I write 'Muḥammad' in the recognizable form, but Humr say 'Meḥimmed'. Many other names have unusual pronunciations, as, for example, 'Abd el Raḥman, which becomes 'Adderḥaman.

are of equal status if their founders were of the same generation.[2]

With the exception of Ḥamdan, all the founders of extended families were dead. Their sons were alive, and, with 'Iyal Merida, some granddaughters and a grandson already had children. But mostly one extended family consisted of the adult sons (with their young offspring)

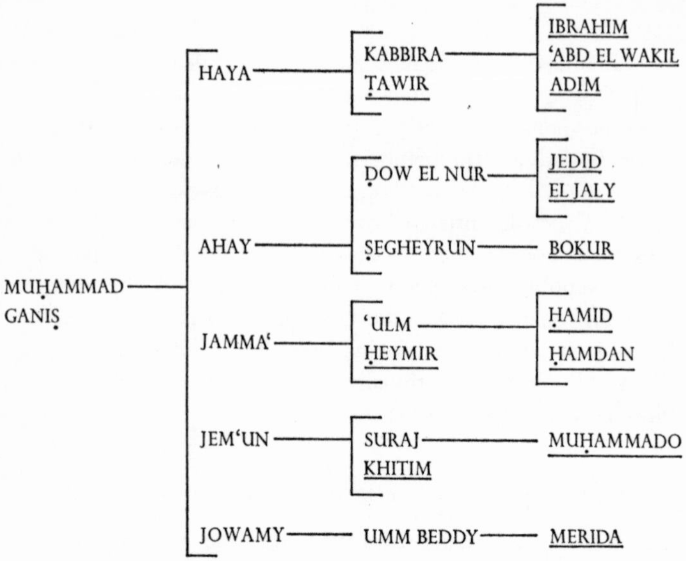

FIG. 7. Extended families of I. Ganiṣ, 1954. The figure shows their relationships to one another and their descent from Muḥammad Ganiṣ through males. Names underlined are founders of extended families now recognized as such. In each case the founder was dead and his sons were alive, except for I. Ḥamdan, whose founder was still alive. Note: the order of the five sons of Muḥammad Ganiṣ is not remembered.

of a dead man after whom it was named. Ḥamdan was an old man, so weakened with age that he had practically stopped migrating and lived at the granaries for most of the year.

Although the surra itself had clear agnatic segments, those intermediate between the surra and the extended family were not named.

[2] The extended families deriving from Ṭawir, Ḥeymir, and Khitim are a generation older than the others. The eldest man in these extended families, El Khatim Ḥeymir, had the honorific title of *judul*, 'tree-stump', which is given to the living man of the surra who is closest to its source. He was accorded no special respect, and I did not notice that the possession of this title made any difference to the way people behaved towards him.

Thus the descendants of Ibrahim, 'Abd el Wakil, and Adim, were never mentioned together as forming a group called 'Iyal Kabbira; similarly, the descendants of Kabbira and Ṭawir together were never mentioned as forming a group called 'Iyal Haya.

It is consistent with this that the members of one extended family cohere more than the members of closely related extended families. During most of my fieldwork the members of 'Iyal Ganiṣ resided mainly in two camps. The main camp, which was under its leader Ḥurgaṣ, contained most members of 'Iyal Merida, 'Iyal Jedid, 'Iyal Bokur, 'Iyal Adim, and 'Iyal Ḥamid, as well as some ex-slaves and their descendants. The splinter camp consisted of 'Iyal Ḥamdan, 'Iyal Ṭawir, and 'Iyal Ḥeymir. Thus the descendants of 'Ulm were split: 'Iyal Ḥamid were in the main camp, while 'Iyal Ḥamdan were in the splinter camp. The descendants of Kabbira were also split: 'Iyal Adim lived in the main camp, while 'Iyal Ibrahim and 'Iyal 'Abd el Wakil lived in various other places. As among the larger segments of the tribe, alliances are formed within the surra which cut across those lines of cleavage which agnatic descent provides.[3] This is a feature of segmentation at all levels.

The last chapter gave some details of households and extended families in the main camp. I show now where the other members of 'Iyal Ganiṣ were residing. The splinter camp existed under the name and the leading spirit of the old man Ḥamdan, although he himself lived in it only when it was near Muglad. The focal person around whom the other members of the splinter camp gathered was Ḥamdan's old widowed sister, Ḥamidy (Fig. 8). She had six daughters, who had been married; these were by her marriage to Muḥammado, the founder of one of the extended families; and through these marriages, she held cattle in trust for her daughter's children. The fact that she had these cattle in hand allowed her to move with 'Iyal Ganiṣ independently. Her only son, Kabbashy, now lived with his wife from 'Iyal Ganiṣ in another surra; if Ḥamidy had been poor, she would have lived with him. Although she was the daughter of 'Ulm, she was considered as belonging to the extended family of *'Iyal Ḥamdan*, named after her brother. Amongst 'Iyal Ḥamdan, the elder son had married a daughter of Ḥamidy and Muḥammado, and the other was a bachelor, who was later to become engaged to El Neimy (tent 8, main camp). Another

[3] In some respects, the intermediate groups between surra and extended family have statuses relating to their varying depths in a system of agnatic lineages. Examples: a claim to marry a girl of the surra can be upheld only if no closer agnatic cousin wishes to marry her; residual rights in property accrue to the closest surviving agnatic group; guardianship rights revert in the same way.

daughter of Ḥamidy was the mother of El Hunna (tent 4) by Ḥurgaṣ's brother.

'Iyal Ḥeymir also lived here. El Khatim, the only son, was an oldish man with some dozen head of cattle. He had previously married a daughter of Ṭawir, but this had ended in divorce, with no children. He then married a woman from another surra, and their children were not yet married. Finally, *'Iyal Ṭawir* were present; the group consisted of Mas'ud, who had a wife from another surra; his brother Mulah, who was married to a woman of 'Iyal Ibrahim; and the bachelors El Hireyky and Bashir, who contributed in various ways to the upkeep of Mas'ud's household, and lived with him.

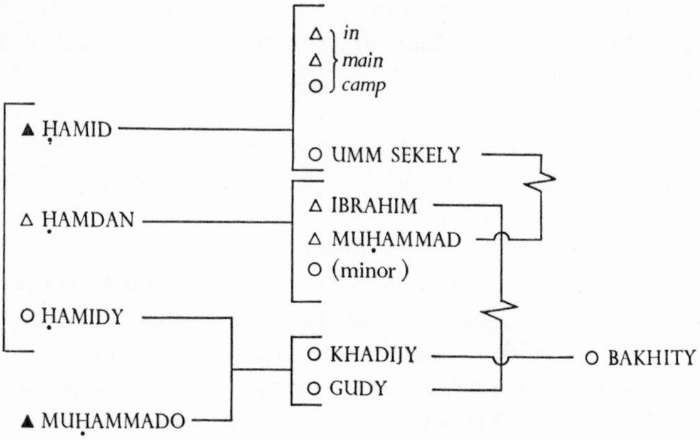

FIG. 8. The nucleus of the splinter camp of I. Ganiṣ.

Some of the extended families were not represented in either of these two camps. Among *'Iyal Ibrahim*, one man worked as a policeman in Muglad and lived there with his wife from the Jubarat omodiya; another married a woman of the Kelabna lineage of Awlad Kamil and lived with his affines. Two of the daughters of Ibrahim had married out; a third was working in Muglad cooking at the girls' school, and the youngest was the wife of Bakora (of *'Iyal Khitim*), a cotton grower, who spent his spare time bringing hides from Dinka. From *'Iyal 'Abd el Wakil*, Ḥasan had married a woman of 'Iyal Ḥamdan; a hunter, he spent most of his time on the Bahr. His brother Adim, and his wife from another lineage, lived with him. El Medir was a bachelor who went from place to place engaging in trade in a small way. Of the daughters, one was married to Kabbashy Muḥammado and never lived with 'Iyal Ganiṣ, and another was married out. The only son of *'Iyal el Jaly* had married into 'Iyal Belebbo surra, with whom he lived; his sister had married into another surra. There were two senile half-brothers of Jedid and El Jaly, whose mothers had been Dinka. One was a frequent visitor at the main camp, where he lived on tent 8; the other lived with a married daughter. *'Iyal Khitim* seldom visited either of the camps. The eldest of the sons had died, leaving a daughter married in 'Iyal Belebbo surra. The other three were alive: Rashid herded sheep in the camp of his Awlad Mumin affines; his brother Timan, who had previously been married to a daughter of Ḥurgaṣ, was often with him. The other was Bakora, mentioned above.

At this time 'Iyal Ganiṣ had thirty-four males of what I took to be marriageable age (about twenty years) and over. Of these, eighteen were married, eleven divorced, and five had never been married. Thirteen were in the main camp, seven in the splinter camp, and fourteen elsewhere (four of these were at their wives' camps; three, all of them old men, were living with daughters or sisters who had married out; three were wandering merchants; two spent their whole year on the Bahr cultivating cotton and hunting; one was a policeman in Muglad; one lived with his wife, also from 'Iyal Ganiṣ, in another surra; and one bachelor lived with his brother and his wife in another surra). Thus twenty men resided in the two camps of 'Iyal Ganiṣ; and three others lived in different surras of Awlad Salamy; this meant that two-thirds of the men of 'Iyal Ganiṣ were usually within easy reach of their own leader in an emergency. Those staying with female relatives were old men; those away as merchants and cotton cultivators had no cattle and were trying to get capital. The temporary shortage of cattle in the surra had, I think, led to a greater dispersal of males than was normal. But there was still a strong nucleus of 'Iyal Ganiṣ men available, and when, a few months later, an attack was made on Ḥurgaṣ in his capacity as omda, all the males of 'Iyal Ganiṣ gathered in Muglad, where the conflict was staged, except the merchants who were out of the country.

At this same period there were forty-seven women of marriageable age (which I took to be about sixteen) and over. Of these, thirty-one were married, seven were widowed, six were divorcees, and three had never been married. Twelve were in the main camp and four in the splinter camp. Twenty-three lived with their husbands in other camps. Four widows were living away with their grown-up sons in their late husbands' camps; three middle-aged women were working for wages in Muglad and Abyei; and one girl had run off to Nahud. The dispersal of women is thus marked in comparison with that of men. Humr say their women are like water-melons,[4] because they spread far from their roots. Nevertheless, the extended family of birth always remains the focus for divorced or widowed women, unless it happens that they have grown-up sons to look after them in the camps of their affines. The surra is where the family of origin is, and where they make appeal in times of difficulty.

THE CAMP: PHYSICAL

Quite obviously 'Iyal Ganiṣ did not achieve the ideal association of camp and surra. I doubt if any surra does so permanently. The last section showed the residence of members of this surra at one point of time. Different seasons would show different residence patterns; different material conditions within the surra would also lead to different residence patterns over a longer period. Yet we are not left with a situation completely without form, because a camp, although its membership changes, yet retains an identity through its association with a surra. No camp consists of males of more than one surra in regular co-residence. A camp's identity, and such stability as it has, derives from this association. The problem now turns on the relation between surra and camp. I discuss this in general terms before considering 'Iyal Ganiṣ in more detail.

A camp has four named parts: the ring of tents, the inner area where the livestock are kraaled, the tree under which the men sit in the daytime, and the hearth where men sit in the mornings and evenings and where bachelors sleep.[5]

Tents of a camp are pitched as evenly as possible in a ring which varies in diameter with the number of tents to be accommodated and the number of cattle to be kraaled.[6] The various sites differ in the roughness of ground, the disposition of shady trees, and the position of anthills, and these account for any difference there may be in the distances

[4] *El 'ayyin biṭṭeykh.*

[5] The camp is *ferig* (the word implies a unit of residence; it refers also to the tents of one extended family, i.e. to an arc of the camp's circle). The livestock enclosure is *dor*; the tree is *shejera*, or more fully *shejerat el juma'a*, 'tree of the group'; and the hearth is *ḍarra*.

[6] While the camp is usually circular in shape, when it is pitched beside a watercourse or meadow in the Bahr region it is semicircular (as in the sketch of the main 'Iyal Ganiṣ camp on a watercourse, Fig. 2). The open side faces the water or grazing, to which the cattle have free access at night. A semicircular camp does not have its circumference cut at any particular place, but the tents associated with one extended family always remain adjacent. Bad ground sometimes leads to camps on the Bahr being pitched in a straight line, or a gentle curve.

Men's tree at a hot dry season camp on the Bahr

(*Facing p.* 64)

between the tents. When the man directing a caravan has chosen the camp site, he indicates to the first woman who arrives where she should unload her bull and the direction in which her tent should face. The women following behind know what position to occupy with reference to the first. No member of camp, not even the leader, has any prerogative in regard to the position or the orientation of his tent.

The point in the camp circle at which a woman should pitch depends on two things: first, the recognized position in camp of the extended family to which she is attached, and second, her own place within the extended family. Although tents belong to women, the pattern of residence is based on the kinship relations of men. A father's tent is pitched with those of his sons in descending order on its right, and the position of the father's tent is determined in turn by the position which he occupied, in relation to his extended family, at the time he first established a household, and so on. Thus not only are the positions of fathers and sons established but also the relative positions of extended families, all deriving from the application of the same rules over past generations.

As the camp consists ideally of all the extended families of the surra, so each surra has a plan according to which all of its extended families can be accommodated in the same camp. But as all of the extended families, and all of the associated tents of each extended family, are seldom at the same camp at the same time, the circle is adjusted accordingly. Those members and their dependants who happen to be camping together form an even ring of tents; if some other members and their dependants form a second camp, they also form an even ring. In each case the relative order of pitching is determined by the ideal plan, but the gaps in the circle left by those who are absent are filled up to give the impression of a complete and undifferentiated unit. At any time other surra members or their dependants may be living away with relatives, or absent for some reason of economic need; such may be cultivators, merchants, or hunters, or those seeking wage labour. The camp is thus divided into arcs, each composed of some or all of the tents associated with one extended family. Those tents which do not belong to wives of camp members are those of divorced or widowed members of the surra, of widows whose sons are members, or of temporary visitors. These women pitch their tents in the arc associated with the extended family to which they are related, and beside the tent of the closest married male.

Inside the ring of tents the livestock sleep at night and are milked morning and evening. Tethering ropes or small thorn enclosures are placed there for calves and small stock. If lions are about, the whole area inside the tents is enclosed with a thorn fence (*zariba*); a similar fence is built when a camp is near standing grain. Inside the circle, log fires are set at night among the cattle to provide smoke to keep off insects. Here, too, the camp's drum is slung over the limb of a convenient tree.

The general situation of a camp is chosen so as to be within convenient reach of water and grazing. Its actual site is selected so as to be within about a hundred yards of a tree which provides good shade. At this tree the men of the camp and their guests spend the hours from nine to five, roughly, if they are in camp at all. The angereybs are brought out; the men sit, pray, feed, rest, and work during the daytime and guests are received at the tree. It is the centre of the men's social life.

When the cattle are brought back from grazing in the late afternoon the men move from the tree to the hearth, which is normally situated on the camp's circumference close to the tree. This hearth is the equivalent of the tree for the mornings and evenings. At it the men have their evening meal and bachelors sleep. The less important guests also sleep here, but those accorded special respect are not brought in among the cattle; they sleep at the tree. Men congregate at the hearth at dawn for prayers and early morning milk and tea, and move out to the tree only when the cattle have gone to graze, or the sun becomes too hot to sit without shade.

There used to be another integral part of the camp. Domestic slaves built their shelters in an outer circle immediately behind the tents of their owners. Today those Humr (few by comparison with former slave-owners) who have Dinka servants or herders place them in the positions which slaves formerly occupied.

CO-OPERATION IN CATTLE MANAGEMENT

Of the two main economic activities, millet cultivation involves co-operation on the basis of the household and cattle husbandry involves co-operation on the basis of the camp. Cattle husbandry has to go on all the time, and thus seasonally the household is faced with the problem of simultaneously herding and cultivating, while those households which grow cotton have work in yet a third place. Cattle herding invites large-scale co-operation, and in some circumstances a few members of a camp have a joint responsibility for all the cattle. At all times the members of one camp recognize general responsibility for all their cattle.

When cultivation is not in progress the daily grazing is organized by means of a camp roster of herders. Each cattle owner, or two or three together, in turn provides a youth (or sometimes a girl or an adult) to go out with a grazing herd.[7] In the camp in which I stayed, each cattle owner provided a youth who herded five successive days and then rested. The owner of no, or very few, cattle is not normally asked to provide a herder; if the owner of a large herd is temporarily without herders this is no matter: the duties are still carried out. Adults herd the cattle if the terrain is difficult or if the grazing itself is scarce or distant. Sometimes the cattle of a father and those of a son are counted, for the purposes of the roster, as one unit. Arrangements vary widely from camp to camp. A rich man may employ a Dinka to herd his cattle for a year in exchange for food and clothing and a nominal wage. Ex-slaves of a family, or their descendants, or other dependants of a rich man, may act as herders and receive in return gifts or loans of cattle. A gift or loan in the past compels a poor man to serve in any capacity: even if he does not go herding, he assists in milking, in fetching logs, and in general supervision of the cattle at night.

Thus it often happens that the grazing duties are undertaken by youths of one household on behalf of the cattle of all camp members. A different herding system is used in the special circumstances of the planting and harvesting seasons. It is used also at other times when, for various reasons, it is advisable to remove the cattle from the main camp: for the sake of mobility if the grazing is scarce and sporadic, or to ensure that women will not take milk that calves should be drinking, an important precaution in hot seasons when there is little greenery. This arrangement involves the division of the camp into two parts, the one being the cattle camp, and the other consisting of those people who stay behind with the heavy baggage.[8] On these occasions the cattle go off under the charge of youths and girls, with occasionally one or two adults for general supervision and a woman to do a little cooking. Those who stay behind in the main camp retain a few cows to provide some milk. Here again, each owner does not need to supply a youth for the cattle camp; if he can spare no one, he still knows that his cows will be properly tended.

[7] By a 'grazing herd' I mean not the cattle of one man but a group of cattle that normally go out to graze together. It may consist of the cattle of more than one owner; or it may consist of part of one man's herd. The cattle of one camp are sometimes formed into one grazing herd, but two or three can exist in one camp. The criterion is usually numerical: see next section.

[8] Respectively, *'azzaba*, from *'azab* and *'azaba*, bachelor and spinster, for those who go with the cattle are usually youngsters; and *tegeliya*, from *tagil*, meaning heavy.

During the short periods before planting and after harvest when cattle are set to manure the gardens, the camps themselves break up into single tents or into small groups. Those of the same surra who happen in any year to be gardening near one another herd their cattle together, and have them spend the nights in successive gardens.

With these various arrangements a man can have his cattle tended at all times, be he rich or poor, with or without family, with or without interests elsewhere. In particular, they allow of prolonged absence on the part of individual members of the camp for the sake of activities such as marketing, trading ventures, fetching grain from distant granaries, giraffe-hunting, wage labour, and so forth. Any member can go away and be sure that his cattle will be herded and that his camp mates will keep a watchful eye on his beasts.

A grazing herd is much more stable than a camp of men and women. Cattle get to know their herds, and stay with them. Beasts which are moved to another grazing herd always cause trouble for a few days: when grazing, they wander off after the herd they have left. Changes are avoided as much as possible. Men and women, on the other hand, are continually on the move for a variety of reasons: a man may visit his in-laws for a brief spell, or go to another camp until a grudge wears off, or go away to contract business or take a job. When he does so he leaves his cattle in their original camp and grazing herd. To take his cattle away would be a sign of acute difference with his camp mates. If he leaves his cattle he implies that he intends to return soon, and also that he has not lost faith with his kinsmen to the extent that he fears they will neglect his animals during his absence.

THE INFLUENCE OF CATTLE NUMBERS ON SURRA ORGANIZATION

The way a surra is organized depends to some extent on the number of cattle the members own and the distribution of this ownership. A surra with few cattle may have all its beasts as a single grazing herd. A surra with many cattle may divide them into two, three, or more grazing herds, and if they are so divided the divisions tend to be permanent while the cattle numbers remain constant. Brothers, or a father and his sons, usually have their cattle in the same grazing herd, but within the surra close cousins are no more likely than distant cousins to have their cattle together.

Humr recognize an optimum size for a grazing herd. A very large one becomes unwieldy: the tail end straggles out of sight through the trees; towards the end of the dry season, when grazing may be scarce, a large grazing herd is bad because the fast cattle trample over the small patches of good grazing before the slower cattle arrive. Humr do not enumerate their cattle, but it appeared to me that about 150 head was the largest convenient size for a grazing herd that would suit all seasons. If grass is ample, young herders may join their grazing herds together as they go out so that they can chat and play as the cattle graze; but the division into herds of this size ensures easy handling in the more difficult seasons. Watering from wells also limits the useful size of a grazing herd. But herds vary widely in the number of their cattle: the owner of a thousand head, unable to find the hands to deal with six or seven herds, may have to divide his beasts up as conveniently as he can in relation to the labour available; and conversely, many people break away from their main camps and herd their cattle on a very small scale.

If the cattle owned by members of one surra are split into more than one grazing herd, as they usually are, various arrangements are possible. Under one of these, all the cattle are kraaled inside the same camp. Each herd has its own sector of the enclosure; each herd is provided separately with its roster of herders; each herd is provided separately with its own smoke fires; and the small stock and the calves of each herd—or sometimes of each owner—are tied up or enclosed in separate thorn fences. The cattle know the herds to which they belong, and if they leave camp at night of their own accord to go to nearby grazing, they go out and return by herds. This arrangement does not lead to any other differences in the organization of a camp. The men still sit together under the same tree; they entertain guests in common; the tents form an unbroken circle; although the cattle are taken out in different groups, they leave at the same time; the camp has a unified grazing policy, and moves from site to site as a unit.

Under an alternative arrangement, the tents of the owners of different grazing herds are pitched in adjacent circles, and each herd is kraaled in a separate enclosure. Here, the two or more camps still usually have a unified grazing policy, decide together on times of moves and on new sites, and move in a single caravan; and while there may be much intervisiting, each camp has its own tree and its own hearth, and the men do not entertain guests in common.

A third possibility is for the owners of different herds to camp quite separately, perhaps many miles apart. If there is a tendency in this matter, it is that on the Bahr in the dry season the camps are small and scattered and that in the Babanusa in the rains the camps are large. These arrangements are consistent with the situation of water and

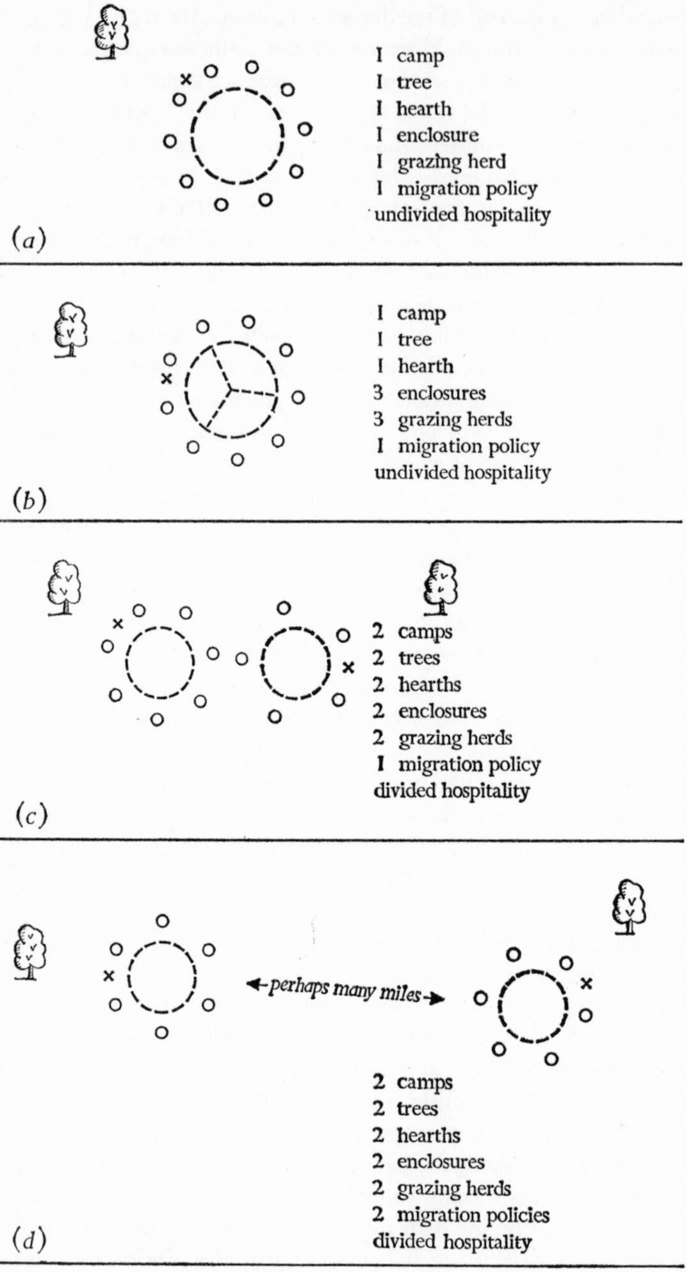

FIG. 9. Some possible types of camp formation.

grazing; and moreover, Humr say that during the rains, if mosquitoes have penetrated the Babanusa, it is better to have big camps, for they create more smoke.[9]

These alternatives cover the possible cattle-herding arrangements at times when there are no separate cattle camps. Extended families of more than one surra hardly ever join together in a single camp. But when there are separate cattle camps, the cattle of more than one surra may join together in one large enclosure. In the early part of the southward migration, and during the harvest period when cattle are taken to eat the regrowth in the Goz, cattle camps of two or three surras may join together, with many hundreds of head inside the ring of the few rough shelters that the women present may build. Large concentrations are possible and even suitable at these times because the herding can be left to children, and one or two adults are enough to deal with any emergency that may arise. Likewise in the first few weeks in the Babanusa this arrangement is useful; safety in numbers is then sought by the young people, who do most of the herding while elders work in the gardens. The cattle which combine on these occasions usually belong to surras which are closely related, or which at least belong to the same omodiya. There is a strong element of chance in the combinations: cattle camps which happen to find themselves close together may temporarily amalgamate to form a single enclosure. The cattle continue to be taken out in their individual grazing herds.

Whether a surra moves and camps as a single unit or in separate groups, and the lines along which it divides, are thus matters which are to some extent determined by the number of cattle the surra owns and the way in which the ownership is distributed among the surra members. The limiting factor is the convenient size of a grazing herd, but the availability of water and grazing leads to seasonal variations. The arrangements in operation at any time may take account also of the relations of surra members with one another.

LEADERSHIP AND SOCIAL CO-OPERATION WITHIN THE SURRA

The convenience of herding may be itself be an adequate cause for the splitting of a surra into different units for the purpose of cattle husbandry, and the fact that the males of one surra camp in different places does not by itself indicate strained relations. Cattle may be so

[9] When insects are about, camps of many different surras are often pitched close to one another, forming a big encampment called *dukuk*. Smoke from one camp covers others instead of drifting uselessly into the forest.

numerous as to cause a united group to form more than one cattle-herding unit. On the other hand members split up for other reasons, and the few head of cattle of a small surra may be divided into a number of grazing herds in widely separated camps even though it would be quite practicable to graze them all together.

Each surra has a generally accepted leader, who, in this capacity, has no administrative recognition; but he may happen to be an administrative officer such as an omda, or a tribute sheikh, or be known to the administration as a 'notable' of the tribe. The surra has no administrative function as far as the Government is concerned, although its importance to the Humr is great. The man recognized as its leader is called the *reis* (head); he has his position from the fact, usually, that he is the wealthiest of its members in cattle; but a man who is already an omda or sheikh, or is brother or son to a past one, may have the position. Spokesmanship and general diplomatic ability are also good qualifications, but they have to be backed by wealth. In his capacity as leader of a camp rather then leader of a surra he is known as *reis el ferig*. A splinter camp also has its own leader.

The name of a surra usually includes a form of the name of its founder. But Humr may mention instead the name of its leader; thus 'Iyal Ganiṣ could be called *nas Ḥurgaṣ*, Ḥurgaṣ's people. The splinter camp was never referred to as 'the camp of 'Iyal Ganiṣ'; it was usually 'the camp of 'Iyal Ḥamdan', or 'the camp of Ḥamdan', or, very occasionally, 'the camp from among Ḥurgaṣ's people' or 'the camp from among 'Iyal Ganiṣ'.[10] It seems to be general that the splinter camp takes the name of its own leader and not the name of the surra leader or the surra founder; this is an implied insult to the surra leader and the founding ancestor.

The ideal behaviour is for members of one surra to show a united front.[11] They should be seen to camp together, and be mentioned

[10] The phrases used are in the form *ferig 'Iyal Fulan*, *ferig Fulan*, *ferig nas Fulan*, and *min nas Fulan*. The use of the word *ferig* followed by the name of the splinter-camp leader is in line with the use of the word *ferig* applied to the section of a camp associated with one extended family.

[11] Although it may be split by temporary quarrels, the surra retains a formal unity much clearer than that of lineages of other kinds. Some of the characteristics of this unit are are as follows. Its male members should form a single camp with their dependants. Members should give the outside world the impression that they are all brothers of an equal degree of kinship. They should play down to the outside world any cause of shame in their behaviour to one another. Marriage within the surra is preferred. A man does not boast, as he boasts of other exploits, that he has made love to women of the surra or to wives or ex-wives of its members. If he wants to marry the ex-wife of a fellow-member he first seeks the permission of her ex-husband, even though the divorce has been final and

together in a phrase linking them to their common ancestor, in the "Iyal Ganiṣ' form. A large camp is a matter for admiration, and one which has more than about fifteen tents gives rise to approving comment: the leader has many followers, and their relations are harmonious.

But when a surra has divided and a part of it has camped at a distance for reasons not connected with the needs of the cattle, those in the main camp, who still follow their surra leader, speak ill of their kinsmen. There has been a quarrel, but the comment goes beyond the immediate reasons for it, to state the the splinter camp is showing disrespect to the ancestor who founded the surra. To move away is to exhibit undue pride: the name of the leader of the splinter group is mentioned at the expense of that of the surra ancestor or the man upon whom his mantle has fallen, the surra leader. Moreover, people who move away impair the notion that their surra is united and undifferentiated.

What Humr find most offensive about a split is connected with the value of generosity. Often those who break away give as an excuse the meanness of the surra leader, who, after all, is usually the wealthiest man in it. But those in the main camp reciprocate with an accusation which is much more devastating: that they are avoiding their obligations of hospitality. For as a general rule Humr treat their guests with a generosity and formality which varies in relation to their social distance. If a man from a closely related surra drops in to see a friend or a relative, he goes straight to the tent concerned and has the freedom of the camp. People from distant surras are received at the tree. Those who are not very close kinsmen come as guests not of a single person but of the whole camp. A traveller looking for a place to spend the night inquires in the locality and goes to the camp of the man in the neighbourhood with the best reputation for hospitality. I lived in the camp of an omda whose generosity was a tribal byword, and hardly a night passed without the obligation to feed and accommodate guests. The arrival

---

irrevocable. If a man leaves his surra and joins another, the surra of his birth still bears important responsibilities if he should inflict death or injury: the surra is a man's blood, which is indivisible. Until recently blood-money could not be claimed against a fellow-member. No claims for damages by cattle to crops are made against fellow-members.

These established rules apart, there are other indications: some surras have a drum beat which is exclusively theirs; some have an exclusive cattle brand; some have an exclusive ear-clip for their stock. Many instances have recently arisen in which those people who are on the books of one sheikh for the purposes of taxpaying are exclusively the members of one surra.

I set these points together here for convenience. Some of them have been discussed; others will be amplified in due course.

of a guest is an immediate excuse for a party. It is the duty of each extended family to produce tea, milk, sour milk, and a grain dish. A ram can be seized from anyone's flock for the entertainment of the visitor. The men of the camp serve the guest in addition by feeding, watering, and tying his horse, supplying water for ritual ablutions, and providing an angereyb and comfortable bedding for his sole use to sit on by day and to sleep on by night. A traveller seeks out a renowned leader of a surra, and his visit affects all those in the same camp. Those who camp separately from the leader of the surra attract fewer guests. Accordingly those who leave, and pitch camp apart, are accused of conserving their resources at the expense of their kinsmen. The visitor sees less food prepared in his honour, and sees a smaller camp, than he would do if the surra camped in one circle.

CO-OPERATIVE ASPECTS OF CULTIVATION

Although the household is the main unit of co-operation in agriculture, some activities connected with it involve a wider group. We have seen how, for sociability and if convenient, owners of nearby gardens may camp together at sowing and harvest, and how they use their cattle together for manuring. In the use of garden land, the protection of stored grain, and to some extent its transport, groups larger than the household share common interests.

Humr have communal grazing rights over the whole of their country but they own garden land as individuals: whereas in a broad sense grazing land is abundant, land suitable for cultivation was in the past comparatively scarce.[12] Individual ownership gives garden land a special meaning: more than any other place, the Humrawi nomad looks upon his garden land as his 'home'. Members of an extended family often cultivate close to one another, and together they regard the site as their home. The same is to some extent true of the surra. For 'Iyal Ganiṣ the rain-pool called El Bieyṭy was the main cultivation area of the leading extended family, 'Iyal Merida, and had much the same relation to the surra as the Muglad had to the whole tribe: it was, so to speak, their *dar*. But each person has various places which he goes to and cultivates. A single garden may retain its fertility for five

[12] The recent deep bores in the Babanusa supply dry-season water for those wishing to open gardens there. When Humr first settled their present country the question of defence encouraged the concentration of gardens and granaries in the single area of the Muglad. The cultivable area in the Muglad is much smaller than the Muglad itself, since the staple bulrush millet is grown only on the sand ridges.

years or so; a move is then made to another garden which may be some miles away, and this may be cultivated for another five years and in turn may be regarded as 'home'. Most surras have two or three blocks of land where most members have gardens, but these blocks are not exploited in a unified fashion: some gardens are depleted sooner than others; families sometimes move away out of dudgeon with their fellows, and so on. Yet the association of individual, extended family, and surra with particular pieces of land persists, and indeed the only even semi-permanent structures of Humr nomads are the granaries which serve groups of neighbouring gardens and which persist so long as anyone is cultivating them.

The gardens lie for the most part near the migration trails of their owners. The millet gardens of the Mezaghna omodiya are nearly all inside a strip, about twenty-five miles long and about three miles across, running north and south through the Muglad. Within this area, there are gardens belonging to other omodiyas as well and to Muglad townsmen; gardens of Awlad Kamil, Faḍliya, and Jubarat are intermingled with pockets of Mezaghna.

Most of the garden land in the cultivable areas of the Muglad and along the Wadi el Ghalla has long been exploited and blocks of it are associated with particular surras. This association derives from the method of opening up garden land, which follows the sequence of events I witnessed when a member of 'Iyal Ganiṣ found an excellent tract for cotton cultivation on the Bahr. He discovered this land, about half a square mile, when he was out herding. He mentioned it on his return to camp, and next day all the available men of the camp went to see it. The took axes and cut a sign like the cattle brand of 'Iyal Ganiṣ on the tree trunks. In this way they reserved it against all comers: anyone might graze there during times when it was not planted, but as far as cultivation was concerned it was Ganiṣ land. The discoverer divided it unasked among the other members of the surra who had gone with him and who wanted to add to their cultivations. When men from closely related surras begged him for shares, he refused.[13]

Thus tracts of garden land came to be associated with surras; within the blocks the ownership of sites is personal, and is handed down from father to son. Individual ownership is strictly recognized, but there is very free give-and-take among members of one surra, who

[13] I. Ganiṣ have an exclusive cattle brand, but even if they share a brand the discovering surra owns the cultivation rights. I. Ganiṣ had not used it by the time I left the field, but the rights in it are theirs so long as the signs remain visible on the trees.

use one another's land with permission. In any year all or most of the surra's land which is in a cultivable state is put to the most convenient use. Once land has lain fallow for some time it is readily loaned to members of other surras, who do not, however, gain title to it.

Thus, despite this association, in any year the worked gardens of one surra are dispersed; no one block is used in its entirety at one time. And the blocks of one surra are interspersed with gardens belonging to members of other surras and even other omodiyas.

Small groups of tents form at sowing and again at harvest. The farmers co-operate in manuring the gardens, and in making thorn enclosures to contain millet heads as they are cut and to keep off livestock; when the cutting is over each household takes its turn to have its grain stamped: children ride bulls round and round over the heads of grain. The crop then has to be stored for the period when the camps are away from the gardens. Those of the same surra who cultivate near one another have a number of granaries, built on stilts, in one place, often enclosed by a thorn fence. Details of the arrangements for storage and protection of grain differ. Each granary site has a guardian, and arrangements vary in relation to the distance between the gardens of one surra, and the number of people who are willing to remain in the Muglad to guard the grain. Thus the crops may be stored in one, two, or more clusters of granaries and guarded by different numbers of people. Those who are willing to remain behind include senile people and those with obligations to care for them; men with no cattle; and ex-slaves, also with no or few cattle, who live in a semi-dependent position upon their former masters. The grain guardians may build a semi-permanent 'village'[14] of grass huts beside the granaries; they usually cultivate intensively themselves; and they have a reward for guarding the grain.[15]

A household takes with it on the southward migration only as much grain as a bull—or perhaps two—will carry. In order to be supplied during the course of the dry season grain caravans called *jangala* leave Bahr camps to go to the granaries, and return laden. The transport is organized sometimes by a single household but more often by a camp, available bulls being sent with available men to bring grain for those households that need it. In some camps there is an arrangement whereby all the grain brought south in one transport is divided equally among the households, even although the household itself may not

[14] The Humr call it *hilla*, the usual term for a village of a non-nomadic tribe.

[15] Often a *midd* (about seven pounds) for every bull load (about 210 pounds) removed from the granaries they are guarding.

have grain stored. This has the effect of conserving for the calves the milk which the household would otherwise have to drink.

Cotton demands different patterns of residence and co-operation. Most people cultivate millet, but the recently introduced cotton is a matter of choice. A few people have given up the cultivation of millet entirely, and depend on the proceeds of their cotton crop to buy grain. Where cotton has been longest cultivated, notably among the Salamat near Lake Keylak in the east of the country, most people work at it during the rains after sending cattle camps off northwards. These who remain follow after the weeding, but stay in the north for only a month. The Salamat have what amounts to almost permanent camps, with tents more elaborate than the usual Humr tent. Some cultivate grain in the region of Keylak. But further west only a few members of some surras grow cotton. During the season (May to August for planting and weeding, and November onwards for harvesting and selling) they live in villages, also called *hilla*, of grass huts, or tents if available. At one cotton centre, Seidana, the village consisted of members of half a dozen surras, each group forming their own small circle of tents or huts within the village. Nearly all were Mezaghna in whose summer area the village was situated, but it included a few Faḍliya and Awlad 'Umran. Cotton has thus led to a new form of residential arrangement, to which we may relate the scarcity of suitable high ground in the Bahr region and the fact that very few Humr cultivate cotton and those who do seek the company of their fellows.

MODES OF CO-OPERATION AMONG 'IYAL GANIṢ

The organization of 'Iyal Ganiṣ is to be understood in the light of these general comments on the organization of camp and surra and how they are related. 'Iyal Ganiṣ formed two camps following a dispute over the marriage of one of the women. Ḥurgaṣ, the leader, decided to give his half-sister Umm Una in marriage[16] to an influential middle-aged man of the 'Ariya major lineage of the Mezaghna. In this decision his main antagonist was the old man Ḥamdan 'Ulm, who wanted the girl to go to a youth of 'Iyal Ganiṣ: either to his own son Muḥammad, or else to El Hireyky, son of Ṭawir. The custom is to give preference to someone of the girl's surra, but Ḥurgaṣ, as the wealthiest man and an

[16] In fact Sheybun, his young half-brother and full brother to Umm Una, would normally have had control of her destiny. But Sheybun was much younger and had received financial and other assistance from Ḥurgaṣ, and it was difficult for him to go against him.

omda, felt in a position to force the issue. He wanted a marriage into the 'Ariya for political reasons and he arranged it, although he must have guessed the consequences. Nevertheless, the breach was not wide enough to endanger seriously the permanent unity of the surra; the splinter group, without exception, gave him moral support during the later attack upon him.

In 1954 the groups comprising these two camps co-operated in varying degrees. At the end of 1953 all the cattle had made the southern migration together as a single cattle camp, but when the first full camp sites were formed on the Bahr, 'Iyal Ḥamdan and their followers camped separately. Each group went to four sites independently before they reunited at the end of the dry season: then in March they camped in adjacent semi-circles at the side of the Regeba Angol. The splinter camp began its northward move a day earlier than the main camp; and it was not until their second rains site in the Babanusa that they came together again in adjacent circles. At the return to the Muglad in September they moved separately. Then gardeners went to their gardens and the people of each camp organized their own cattle camp. For the Goz grazing before harvest the cattle of the whole surra reunited, and shared a big kraal with the cattle of a closely related surra and those of a surra of the 'Ariya lineage. Once more they returned to the gardens and split up until the southward migration, when they slowly reunited as chance dictated throughout its course.

It was useful to have arrangements of this kind. The splitting and reuniting of herds answered the practical problems of cattle management and agriculture. In this case the splitting and coming together of cattle tallied with the accepted procedure: concentration of cattle in the Babanusa and in the Goz at harvest time, dispersal on the Bahr. The detailed arrangements were made in the context of a quarrel which had divided the surra. In the course of my fieldwork 'Iyal Ganiṣ never camped in a single exclusive circle of tents: 'Iyal Ḥamdan and those with them never agreed to share a single tree with the leader of their surra, and so did not help him to entertain his guests. They often visited one another, sometimes for argument, but sometimes out of friendship. The brotherhood of surra fellows is taken for granted, and has the strength to contain a dispute of this nature. While still bitter towards one another the members continued to take responsibility when occasion arose for one another's cattle.

In these camps marital connexions within the surra appeared to add to the value of those ties which already existed through close agnatic kinship. Those who resided in the splinter camp did not have the same kinds of connexions by marriage with Ḥurgaṣ and his extended family as did 'Iyal Adim, 'Iyal Jedid, and 'Iyal Ḥamid.[17] Those who had such connexions through extant marriages all remained in the main camp. No doubt the wealth and prestige of Ḥurgaṣ as omda added force to the obligation of his surra in-laws to live with him, although sometimes it was a struggle for them to do so. The case of Abu Dik is one in point. As brother's son to Ḥamdan he was in a delicate position. Although Abu Dik was living in the main camp with his wife, Ḥurgaṣ's daughter, he struck up a close friendship with his cousin El Hireyky, with whom his sympathies lay in the dispute, and he seldom sat at the omda's tree. A member of the camp commented: 'He cannot be angry, he has eaten the sweets of Ḥurgaṣ and married his daughter; yet he has to show some anger if his uncle Ḥamdan is not to tax him with neglect simply because Ḥurgaṣ has given him a wife.'

Another factor affecting the groupings was no doubt the shortage of cattle in the surra at the time. It was because of this shortage that some men were away from both camps earning enough money to start herds. In order to survive, 'Iyal Ganiṣ were forced to cluster round those with cattle. This clustering arose from economic dependence, but in turn it led to dependence of a more general kind. The biggest owner by far was Ḥurgaṣ himself, although in the main camp El Hunna and 'Ali Jakkak both had about ten head. Likewise the splinter camp clustered around the nucleus of the widow Ḥamidy's cattle and those, rather fewer, of El Khatim Ḥeymir. Ḥamdan could lead this break-away on the practical basis of his sister Ḥamidy's cattle. Most of the other members of these camps had no more than a riding bull for the household and perhaps a cow or two.

These two factors affecting alliances—differential riches and marital links—are themselves closely connected; a poor man, like Abu Dik, has a better chance of marriage within the surra, for a surra wife costs less, and additional allowances for poverty are more likely to be made within the surra than outside it. The marriage itself accordingly creates a sense of indebtedness. There are two consequences: first, the felt indebtedness is repaid by loyalty; and second, the husband knows that in great hardship he can rely—if not on his account, then on account of his wife and her children—on his richer affines.

The distribution of cattle ownership thus affects not only the composition of households, but that of camps also: men with few cattle cluster round those with many; poor people live beside their richer

[17] See diagrams in previous chapter.

affines; a man who has given or loaned a cow attaches the recipient to him in perpetuity.

NON-ARAB DESCENT

So far I have mentioned only those members of 'Iyal Ganiṣ who are said to be of Arab descent. These include some people whose mothers were Dinka, Nuba, Fur, or other non-Arabs. Humr used to take slave women as concubines; descendants of these unions are as completely 'Arab' as other Humr, and through their fathers they have a firm place in an extended family.

'Iyal Ganiṣ and most other surras also have attached to them people whose paternal ancestors were not Arabs. They claim to belong to surras, and are accorded membership in various degrees and with some misgivings. They fall into a number of different categories. We have to distinguish between those with a male ancestor who was a Dinka (or less commonly a member of another tribe) who was not a slave; those with a male ancestor who was a freed slave, or who themselves were ceremonially freed; and those of a slave line, of whom none were ceremonially freed.

The Humr dialect does not distinguish between a person who was a slave to a Humrawi and a person who was or is a pagan. The word '*abid* refers alike to domestic slaves and to people who, because they were pagans, could have been appropriately captured and turned into slaves. Nowadays the word applies to any Dinka (and the few Nuba who are in this position) hired by Humr to herd their cattle and to cultivate, and, more widely, to the southern Sudanese in general. But a 'good' Dinka, one who has adopted Islam, or who follows some Humr customs, or who lives (as a few do) in independence among Humr, may be mentioned more respectfully as Jengayi, or Dinka.

Domestic slavery came under administrative control with the Condominium and was supposed to be abolished finally by 1924. Many of the domestic slaves of 'Iyal Ganiṣ remained with them voluntarily. At any time a slave could be freed by being declared free by his owner. A slave was his owner's 'son'; a freed slave ('*atig*) became a 'brother'. The liberation ceremony, which continued to take place after the official abolition of the system, consisted in a declaration of the owner; the freed man was then ridden on horseback round neighbouring camps and greeted with applause; he would receive presents of money or small stock, some of which he used for a sacrifice. Once liberated, a male slave and his offspring were Arabs and full members of surra and tribe.

An unliberated male slave's child was himself a slave and was inherited like his father; a female slave was never liberated, but could be taken as a concubine (*serraya*) by her owner, and her children would then be freeborn; alternatively her owner might marry her off to another slave.

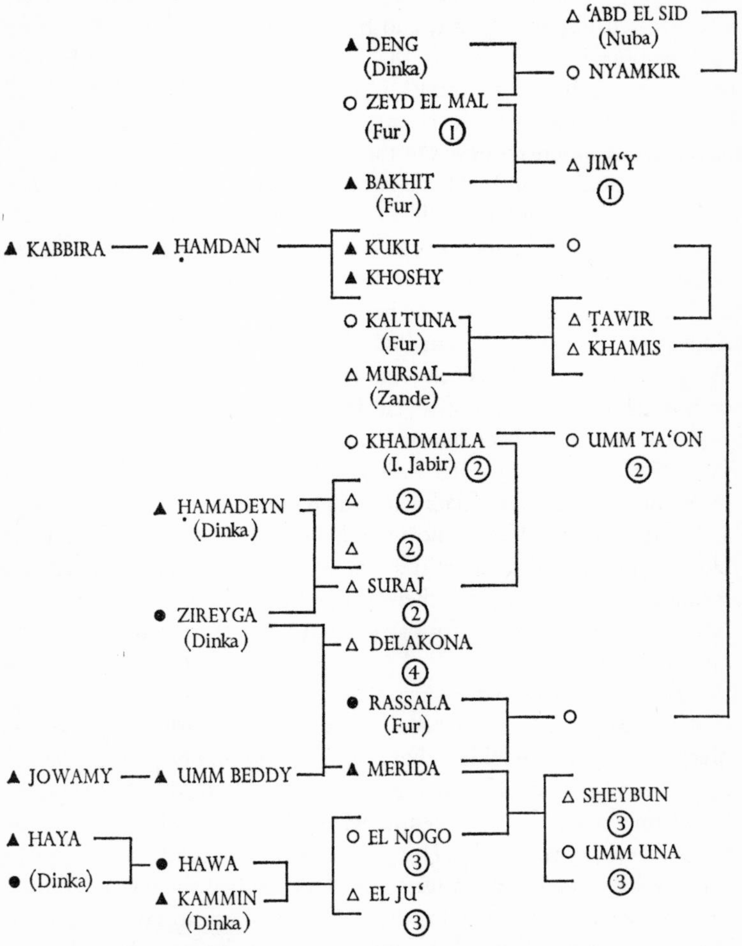

FIG. 10. Non-Arab descent in I. Ganiṣ, showing residence in main camp (cf. Fig. 2) and links with I. Merida, etc.

'Iyal Ganiṣ had people belonging to all these categories. In the main camp, tents 1, 2, and 3 consisted largely of people with non-Arab descent in one line or another. To take first tent 3, whose household has already been described in terms of its relationship with Merida:

the woman who owned it, El Nogo, and her brother El Ju‘, were children of a Dinka called Kammin. He was not a slave but a ‘good’ Dinka who spent much time in the ‘Iyal Ganiṣ camps. He married Hawa, who was the daughter of Haya, one of the five sons of Muḥammad Ganiṣ; Hawa’s mother was also a Dinka. El Nogo and El Ju‘ were treated like real Humr, and both were Muslims. El Ju‘ was no more subservient to Ḥurgaṣ than were others without cattle who depended largely on him. But El Ju‘ suffered one disability: he belonged to no extended family of the Humr, and he took no part in the payment or receipt of blood-money. On the other hand if he had been injured there is no doubt that ‘Iyal Ganiṣ would have put forward a strong case for blood-money on his behalf.

The household of tent 2 was connected through Merida’s father, Umm Beddy, to the people of tent 3. Umm Beddy had, amongst others, two Dinka slaves, a woman called Zireyga and a man called Ḥamadeyn. Zireyga as Umm Beddy’s concubine bore Delakona, the old man who was still an occasional visitor at tent 4. Then Umm Beddy married Ḥamadeyn off to Zireyga. Ḥamadeyn was ceremonially freed, and their son Suraj later married Khadmalla, a freewoman from ‘Iyal Jabir surra, and brought her to live in the camp. The other members of the household were Khadmalla’s daughter by a previous marriage, and two young children who were half-brothers of Suraj. Suraj and his child brothers thus constituted an extended family of Humr, ‘*Iyal Ḥamadeyn*, and they had their part in blood-money transactions. A freed slave receives a formal status higher than that of a ‘good’ Dinka.

Tent 1 belonged to a woman called Zeyd el Mal; she and her late husband Bakhit had both been slaves of Umm Beddy, and later of Merida. Although Bakhit’s character was still highly praised, he had never been freed. Zeyd el Mal and her son Jim‘y made up this household. Jim‘y was in his late twenties when I knew him. He and his mother had been inherited by Ḥurgaṣ on Merida’s death; Ḥurgaṣ then ceremonially freed him. In terms of blood-money the effect, although he was now by courtesy a ‘brother’ of Ḥurgaṣ, was to give him a position in a separate ‘extended family’ of which he was the only male member: he would pay and receive a share equal to that of each other extended family of the surra. But outside this formality he had disabilities. Although he was courting, and spending much money on, the step-daughter of Suraj (tent 2), his antecedents made it likely that she would not be allowed to marry him. He was without cattle, and was on Ḥurgaṣ’s own roster of cattle herders. His ceremonial freedom created a sense of indebtedness in him, which had been strengthened by loans of animals from time to time.

On Bakhit's death Zeyd el Mal married Deng, another 'good' Dinka. The daughter of this union, Nyamkir, married a slave of Merida called 'Abd el Sid, who was destitute and who now frequently helped Ḥurgaṣ in herding; some years he would stay behind in the Muglad to guard the granaries of 'Iyal Merida. In the same position also was El Siteyb, with his sons; he was the son of a Nuba woman who had been a slave of Umm Beddy, and had married another slave from 'Iyal Belebbo surra. El Siteyb himself married a slave of 'Iyal Jabir surra. None of these were given ceremonial recognition of their freedom; none had cattle, and all had depended upon the omda for their upkeep in one way or another.

Lastly there was a group which did not move with the camps at all, but lived in a permanent village near one of the cultivation areas of the surra. A man called Mursal, who had been a Zande slave of a Ganiṣ man, married a Fur slave woman and had a number of children. On the official ending of slavery the family set up the village. There were two sons, of whom one married a daughter of Merida and a Fur slave woman; the other married the daughter of Kuku Ḥamdan, the brother of Mursal's 'owner', and a free woman. These were close kin to 'Iyal Merida because Kuku was also the father of Ghubeysha's daughters in tent 4.

Umm Beddy and his fellows had other slaves as well, but they had emigrated and I could only get the vaguest information about them. Some lived in Kadugli. But for those ex-slaves still present, it is noticeable that they have become connected by blood ties with the families that owned them. The marriages and concubinages of these people were in the hands of their owners who seem to have made a point of creating these ties. In the event, when the slaves were freed by Government order or were given ceremonial recognition of their freedom, many already had their economic dependence reinforced by kinship with their former owners. The family of Mursal apart, all those mentioned were still dependent on Ḥurgaṣ economically, and served and supported him.

Descendants of slaves, even though ceremonially freed, do not fully enjoy the privileges that Humr do. Personality enters in to some extent, but usually the knowledge of non-Arab descent is enough to make Humr attribute a lower status to slave descendants. There is a contradiction apparent in the difference between descendants of 'good' Dinka, who do not achieve recognition in terms of blood-money, and freed slaves who do, for the offspring of good Dinka seem, in general, to have better standing than the offspring of freed slaves. Thus El Juʿ and El Nogo were hardly distinguishable from Arabs as most freed slaves were. This distinction is further emphasized by the word applied to slave descendants of one surra as a group: *melekiya*, which is connected with the word *melek*, to own. Slave descendants are still ʿ*abid* or *melekiya* behind their backs. In general they find difficulty in marrying or courting free-born women.

Within the *melekiya* a distinction exists between those who go with the cattle and those who, like Mursal, are independent, relying on agriculture for their livelihood. Many villages like Mursal's exist in the Muglad and round about, each being called the *melekiya* of the surra, or of the man who would have inherited them had slavery continued. Their way of life is now more akin to that of Berti, Ma'alia, and other settled tribesmen in the area. But they sustain special relations with the surra from which they derive; Mursal said he was a member of 'Iyal Ganiṣ, and most of his family married people with connexions there. Between Ḥurgaṣ and Mursal there was a relationship of a kind in which they emphatically and jokingly emphasized their humility towards one another: at Mursal's for lunch one day, Ḥurgaṣ said he was as nothing and poor, and living on Mursal's generosity; Mursal was the big chief there and Ḥurgaṣ was at his command. Mursal retaliated by bringing the lunch himself, instead of having a woman do so; and brought it, moreover, running. The economic independence of Mursal and his people distinguished them from those who served in the camps, for the latter were in a clear position of subordination to the cattle owners for whom they worked.

THE EXTENSION OF PERSONAL FOLLOWINGS

The way in which I have described the organization of the Humr units, from household to camp and surra, has involved much alternation between social and economic facts. These groups are those which co-operate actively in exploiting the economic resources of a difficult country. There has to be co-operation, and different purposes need co-operation at different levels. Humr who co-operate are kinsmen in the same household or camp or surra. But while everyone is involved in co-operative activity of different kinds, the composition of co-operating groups is very variable. Flexibility arises from the freedom of movement of the individual, who can still rely on his kinsmen to see that his cattle do not suffer. No group of people has to remain in a state of permanent co-operation. The surra is the ideal herding unit, but it can and does split up for various reasons. At any time the camp is the actual herding and residential unit, but the composition of the camp changes with the seasons and its members' personal relations. The freedom to graze one's cattle anywhere in the country and the existence of alternative lands for cultivation allow social strains between kinsmen to be translated into physical distance. Humr suit their residence to their friendships. This is true for political relations at higher levels as well; lack of group rights in specific stretches of land, and the differing weather conditions and the variety of ways in which the land can be exploited from year to year, together make unlikely the exploitation of available resources by permanent large-scale groups.

The existence of cattle as the main form of property gives room for manipulation of alliances, and allows scope for the rich man, through loans, gifts, and marital links, to gather dependants as followers. His primary responsibility is for his nuclear family; responsibility for his extended family runs a close second. Variations in wealth force upon him further responsibilities which can extend readily to embrace people throughout the surra and their dependants. This is his real basis for further political advance; his wealth and generosity are by now proven. Ability to advance beyond this stage does not depend so heavily on economic factors.

6

SOME FEATURES OF HUMR MARRIAGE

HUMR women are often present in the camps of their own surras, dependent for their maintenance upon their agnatic kinsmen. The agnate may be the husband, or may be a male who is looking after a divorced or widowed woman. Two features of marriage, the amount of mating within the surra, and the amount of divorce, thus have an important bearing on the residence of women. Seen from the point of view of men, the effect is a concentration of maintenance and effective guardianship of female members of the surra and their offspring. Thus both marriage and divorce contribute in different ways to the interdependence of surra members. Yet significant though intra-surra marriages may be, outside marriages exist as well and have their own significance. In Humr society this does not arise from a common interest brought about by bridewealth negotiations, payments, and receipts, and by lasting interest in bridewealth cattle: for bridewealth is a relatively small cash payment, and its negotiation is mostly the concern of the bridegroom and the bride's mother alone. Rather, the significance stems from the links contracted between individuals, and it varies with the political importance of their immediate kinsmen.

DISTRIBUTION OF MARRIAGE PARTNERS

The Humr constitute an agnatic lineage, and so everybody, in one way or another, marries his patrilineal parallel cousin.[1] They state that the closer the cousin, the better the marriage; that the tribal ideal is marriage with father's brother's daughter; but that if a relative of this category is not available, it is much better to marry at least within the surra. In fact marriages within the surra are common—marriages in which the partners have known one another personally all their lives, and have lived, perhaps in the same camp, in the company of their connecting relatives.

Some tables will provide a basis for discussion of the problems.

[1] An insignificant number of marriages is contracted with members of other tribes.

Although the figures are inadequate for generalization, I am satisfied that they represent the situation for three different surras, and from casual inquiries elsewhere I believe that the ratios for different types of marriage which they suggest furnish a reasonable guide for the situation of the Humr as a whole.

TABLE 4. *Distribution of marriage partners in two Mezaghna surras*

		Per cent.
Marriages within surra	56	36
Marriages within minor lineage but excluding own surra	48	30
Marriages within major lineage but excluding own minor lineage	21	13
Marriages within own omodiya but excluding own major lineage	12	7
Marriages within 'Ajaira section of tribe but excluding own omodiya	19	12
Marriages into Felaita section	2	1
Marriages outside tribe	1	1
	159	100

Totals were reached by including all marriages of males and those of females who had married out: i.e. whose marriages were not included in the males' total.

TABLE 5. *Distribution of marriage partners in a surra of A. Kamil*

		Per cent.
Marriages within I. Habily	9	17
Other marriages within I. Dakir	19	36
Other marriages within Dar Umm Sheyba Zerga	6	11
Other marriages within Dar Umm Sheyba	6	11
Other marriages within A. Kamil	4	8
Other marriages within 'Ajaira	5*	9
Marriages into Felaita	Nil	
Marriages outside tribe	4†	8

* Includes one mother's brother's daughter.

† Includes one marriage into Berti and one into Birgid tribes. These are families of settled farmers in the A. Kamil cultivation areas.

Working off the genealogies of the two surras I knew best, 'Iyal Ganiṣ and 'Iyal Rigeyby (two closely related surras of the Mezaghna omodiya), I asked about all marriages. The information of 159 of these seemed reliable, and provided the basis for Table 4.

Figures from 'Iyal Habily surra of Awlad Kamil omodiya (Table 5) are not strictly comparable, since that surra is the product of an extra step of segmentation. Here there is not the same marked gradual diminution from the surra outwards. I account for the comparatively few marriages within the surra by two facts: the surra is small; and the minor lineage of which it forms a part has many cultivations close together, and the members cultivate intensively and remain a long time as a local community.[2]

These tables show especially the preference for close agnates as marriage partners: in 'Iyal Ganiṣ and 'Iyal Rigeyby together, sixty-six per cent. of the marriage were within the minor lineage, and in 'Iyal Habily, fifty-three per cent. These are impressive percentages, and I think we are on safe ground in supposing that close agnatic marriage is a marked feature of Humr society; equally clearly, they show that it is by no means an invariable custom. They show that the stated Humr ideal is at least to some extent carried into practice: for, generally speaking, far more marriages are contracted with the few marriageable close relatives than with the many marriageable distant relatives.[3]

The figures of marriages within the surra show how far the ideal of marriage to father's brother's daughter is practised. In Table 6, I class together first cousins and their lineal descendants, second cousins and their lineal descendants, and so on. For the three surras the distribution is rather uneven, particularly with regard to the preponderance of first-cousin marriages in 'Iyal Rigeyby. The figures do, however, suggest that the concentration on father's brother's daughter is not particularly marked. But we are dealing with a small number of people, and there is less chance of finding an unmarried first cousin of suitable age than there is of finding a suitable partner within the surra as a whole or the minor lineage.

From one point of view the table is misleading; for the greater number of intra-surra marriages are first marriages, that is to say marriages in which there is considerable constraint on a girl (and a smaller measure of overt constraint on a boy) to marry the person whom

[2] A rough combined total of these two tables may be found by amalgamating the third and fourth categories of I. Habily, i.e. by counting medium and major lineages together as equivalent to major lineage. The result is: marriages within surra, 30 per cent.; within minor lineage excluding surra, 32 per cent.; within major lineage excluding minor lineage, 16 per cent.; within omodiya excluding major lineage, 8 per cent.; within 'Ajaira excluding omodiya, 11 per cent.; within Humr excluding 'Ajaira, 1 per cent.; outside tribe, 1 per cent.

[3] As there is, in spite of the ever-changing patterns of residence, a rough correspondence between kinship and geographical separation, it would also be true to say that far more marriages are contracted with the few marriageable close neighbours than with the many marriageable people who live far away.

guardians think appropriate. For Table 7, which deals with this point, I counted those male surra members only for whom I have the relevant information.

TABLE 6.

Distribution of marriage partners in intra-surra marriages for three surras

	I. Ganiṣ	*I. Rigeyby*	*I. Habily*	*Total*	*Per cent.*	*Percentage of all marriages*
Marriages with:						
FBD	6	13	3	22	33	10
FBSD	2	1	—	3	5	1
FBSSD	2	—	—	2	3	1
				27	41	12
FFBSD	9	1	4	14	22	6
FFBSSD	7	—	1	8	12	4
FFBSSSD	1	—	1	2	3	1
				24	37	11
FFFBSSD	10	1	—	11	17	6
FFFBSSSD	3	—	—	3	5	1
				14	22	7
				65	100	30

TABLE 7. *Intra-surra marriages as first and subsequent marriages*

	I. Ganiṣ	*I. Rigeyby*	*I. Habily*	*Total*	*Per cent.*
Marriages considered	88	61	44	193	100
Marriages within surra	35	16	9	60	30
Total of first, including only, marriages	48	35	26	109	100
First or only marriages within surra	23	12	8	43	39
Number of second, third, etc., marriages	40	26	18	84	100
Number of second, third, etc., marriages within surra	12*	3	1	16	17

* This includes six wives of one man.

While thirty-nine per cent. of all first marriages took place within the surra, only seventeen per cent. of all subsequent marriages took place within the surra. This can be expressed in another way. Of all the marriages within the surra which took place, some seventy-two per cent. (forty-three out of sixty) were first marriages.

TABLE 8. *Proportion of surra marriages ending in divorce compared with proportion of outside marriages ending in divorce*

	I. Ganiṣ	*I. Habily*	*Total*	*Per cent.*
Surra marriages completed	23	3	26	100
Surra marriages ending in divorce	18	2	20	77
Outside marriages completed	29	17	46	100
Outside marriages ending in divorce	14	8	22	48

For this table I had information on the marriages of some males in only two of the surras.

TABLE 9. *Proportion of divorces to total completed marriages in two surras*

	I. Ganiṣ	*I. Habily*	*Total*	*Per cent.*
Completed marriages considered	112	27	139	100
Completed marriages ending in divorce	62	14	76	55

Since most first marriages are surra marriages, and since there is much divorce, it is to be expected that surra marriages will show a high rate of break-up through divorce. Table 8 gives figures concerning this. In order to obtain as large a figure as possible for an estimate of the amount of divorce, I took the completed marriages of Ganiṣ and Habily males and added to them those of females in these surras who had married out. On the basis of this small number of marriages considered, we can consider that around fifty-five per cent of marriages contracted end in divorce.[4]

THE IDEAL AND THE PRACTICE

Whatever the quantitative material may show, Humr leave one in no doubt about the preferred marriage. The father's brother's daughter is best of all; failing this, a girl from the surra. Two customs support

[4] The Humr have the Arab custom whereby a man may divorce his wife and then call her back within a specified period. The divorces considered in these tables are, however, only those which were not followed by resumption of the unions.

this ideal. First, a man may lay claim to (*jelkak*) a girl in his own surra. If he does so, claims of more distant suitors ought not to be considered. Before proposing marriage a suitor should make sure that no closer relative desires the girl.[5] Although he is sometimes under pressure, a young man can marry where he likes. For the girl the final decision comes from her male relatives, although the girl's mother, or the girl through her mother, occasionally manages to force through a marriage the men do not want. There is pressure on young men and young women, but that on a girl is much heavier, and the completion of the contract depends upon the goodwill of her kinsmen. If her guardians see a close suitor they are liable to give him preference over a more distant one, regardless of wealth and character. The closest is father's brother's son; after this mother's brother's son and father's sister's son are equal so long as they belong to the girl's own surra; no special preference is given to mother's sister's son. Next follow other males of the surra, the closer the better. If a man of the preferred degrees wants to marry, he simply lets the fact be known, and this virtually seals his claim to her. He can do this if he is the closest relative or has ascertained that closer relatives than he will not claim her. The split in 'Iyal Ganiṣ shows what can happen if the girl's relatives should disregard a claim to her hand from a close kinsman.

I have mentioned that Muḥammad Ḥamdan of the splinter camp, who had wanted Umm Una, became engaged to another girl in the main camp. This girl, El Neimy, was under the guardianship of Ḥurgaṣ and Kireyfan, her close cognates. The engagement ran roughly: Muḥammad offended his prospective in-laws in a number of ways, and Kireyfan spoke his mind to him and said: 'Remember I did not give you the girl because you were a man of good character; I gave her to you because you are our brother.' The character of Muḥammad may or may not have been good, but by refusing the match, however unsuitable in terms of personality it might be, Kireyfan would have fallen in the esteem of his kinsmen. It was a bad match, but a good marriage. Where marriage within the surra is concerned, character is irrelevant. The right to lay claim to a girl in the same surra is strongly upheld, even across divisions of this kind.

The second custom which acts as an incentive to close marriage consists in a modification of the usual marriage ceremonies; a smaller cash outlay is therefore required. One of the ceremonies, a betrothal

[5] A suitor from a different surra can enter negotiations for marriage after ascertaining that no members of the girl's own surra wants her: he need not inquire about a suitor closer than himself but outside her surra.

party which usually costs about five pounds, is dispensed with altogether; and a husband from the surra pays about a third less bridewealth than an outside husband pays. The total saving may represent the value of five young bulls or two cows.[6] The recipient of bridewealth is the girl's mother; to her father its amount is irrelevant.

Humr use many arguments to justify this preference for close marriage. I take these from the point of view first of the woman and her guardians then from the point of view of the marrying men; they are also the justifications which are given when the matter is discussed, outside the context of a particular marriage, in support of the ideal as one which is universally held.

Guardians have their sisters' children as their concern. They say that the child whose parents belong to the same surra is better off. If you give your sister to a stranger, they argue, the stranger takes her to his camp; then the child will be living in a camp where its mother is a stranger. She is not among her sisters, and so she is less likely to receive help when she needs it. In that camp her child is only 'brother's child' and not 'sister's child' to other residents: the point of this observation is that to a child the mother's brother is a special friend, who cossets it and has its interests constantly at heart.[7] Further, the lack of mother's sisters in camp means that the child, left alone playing among the tents with the other children, is at the mercy of father's sisters, who tend to share in the father's more authoritarian attitude. It is the maternal relatives who can provide the child with that extra amount of love and care: the males provide protection; the females provide intimate help.

Moreover, men do not readily give their sisters to outsiders because their sisters' children would be as strangers to them, living far away, and potential enemies.[8] The surra is the only unit within which there is some kind of obligation to settle disputes without force, and even to

[6] Sometimes this rebate applies not only to marriages within the surra but also to marriages within the minor lineage. Thus the bridewealth paid by husbands of I. Dakir for wives from the same minor lineage was usually about £14, as against £20 for wives from outside. Note (Table 5) that there were fewer marriages within I. Habily than there were between I. Habily and other surras of I. Dakir.

[7] The mother's brother's position is shown especially in the male circumcision ceremonies. It is he who holds the boy protectively during the operation, helping him to sustain the pain and the girls' challenges to bravery. The father, if present at all, is a silent onlooker.

[8] Informants discussed this potential enmity in detail; and it is a live issue, and a worrying hazard of marriage. I was present when mention was made in camp that a girl had just been betrothed to a man of the Felaita. The men at the tree reacted with exclamations of disapproval: 'too distant', and 'enemies'.

keep the fact of disputes secret. But if words arise between a surra and another into which a sister has married, not only the sister but her children also are endangered, for force may come to be used, and their position, although they would not be harmed physically, would be most uncomfortable. One consequence might be the cessation of communications between the two surras. This is very likely, as social separation is often followed by wide physical separation.

Marrying men share some of these sentiments and have an eye to the position of their future children, although not to the extent that the girl's relatives do. They too have an economic advantage in close marriage. A man who marries in the same camp retains for the use of his household the produce of his wife's cattle as well as his own. If he marries a woman from another surra his wife's cattle are not with him, for her brothers retain them in their own camp. Humr give two reasons for this custom. Firstly, it is a kind of insurance against the day when the girl may be obliged to part with wealth as compensation. When she marries, she remains squarely in her natal lineage, who continue to be responsible for her morally, economically in a broad sense, and legally. The only responsibility of which they are relieved on her marriage is that of day-to-day maintenance. They remain responsible for her debts. By keeping her cattle with them her brothers are making sure that they will not have to part with their own to pay their sister's debts, for if she took her cattle with her, they would lose effective control of her wealth.

Secondly, they retain the cattle as an insurance, more generally, against the girl's old age, and the minority of her children. They fear that if she took the cattle with her, then her husband might talk her into selling them, perhaps even to enable him to take a second wife. This is the stupid sort of thing that women would do, say men. In acting thus, her kinsmen are realizing the proverb with runs 'A woman's best is for her husband, her worst is for her family'.[9]

Otherwise marrying men have mixed feelings on the matter. They recognize the greater security of close marriage, in the sense that kinsmen of both parties are present in camp, or at least joined in the unity of surra brotherhood; disputes have a better chance of settlement, and children are better tended. At the same time a close cousin, as a wife, is cheap, disrespectful, and a poor servant, while a stranger wife who comes to live in another camp is on her best behaviour because she brings with her pride in her own lineage. Such is the myth. Moreover, towards foreigners like myself Humr seemed a little bit ashamed

[9] *El mara' kheyrha le rajilha wa shirrha le ahalha.*

of their customs of cousin marriage, thinking it was a special, somewhat risqué indulgence of their own. For they are brought up to treat their surra cousins as sisters; sexual familiarity with them out of marriage is ill thought of; when they marry a close cousin they speak of 'marrying a sister'. One informant who had had a succession of 'stranger' wives explained that he did not see why he should spend a lot of money on his close cousins, and anyway distant women were much more interesting as women. On the other hand a man who was happily married to two surra wives said: 'Distant women are easy to love, close women are difficult to love, but if you do love them, there really is fire in your belly.'

In the face of the ideal of close marriage, the actual state of affairs is indicated by the figures. Humr society has only a preferred marriage with close kin: there is no endogamous group, although pressures may be brought against those wishing to marry distantly without some strong justification. It is clear that in their first marriages youths tend to follow the ideal and to yield to the expectations of their elders and betters. But many first marriages end in divorce, and in subsequent marriages men, and more significantly women, are free to marry where they will; later marriages are more often made on a basis of romantic attachment.

MARRIAGE AND POLITICAL RELATIONS

Some marriages are arranged for political convenience. Ḥurgaṣ gave his half-sister to a distant suitor against the will of his kinsmen for this purpose; he had arranged a previous marriage into the family of the Nazir Umum. I have also given an example of the kind of marriage which could lead to the maintenance or extension of a man's wealth and influence. Marriage may be used as a political weapon; while admittedly placing children of the marriage in some danger, a distant marriage for political ends is a gamble on the part of a politically significant or aspirant person to create a bond of common interest with a lineage which might be a rival, or with a source of power already established.

Given that marriage creates a link of common interest, we have yet to define the nature of this interest. We have seen the grounds for the diffidence with which distant marriages are viewed. The objections recognize that the Humr are a feuding society, and that open hostility is liable to arise between surras. Humr regularly carry spears, after all, for personal defence against sudden attacks of vengeance. Now it is possible to classify marriages into those entered for various reasons: because primarily they are of the preferred kind, or they bring some economic advantage, or they bring some political advantage, or they are romantic. But the distribution of marriage partners can be considered independently of the motives behind particular marriages. A surra has marriages at any time binding members with others, with closely related surras, with other minor lineages, major lineages, and omodiyas, and our figures suggest that there is a diminution of incidence the more distant the relationships are. In the last chapter it was shown how marriage ties within the surra strengthen existing links of close agnation and influence alliances. We have now to consider whether marriage links between more distant lineages have a similar effect.

I think not. In many societies which have a superficial resemblance to this one the process of marriage mobilizes wide groups of kinsmen on both sides in the negotiations about, and payment and receipt of, bridewealth. Here, this is not the case. The payment itself is not expressed in terms of cattle, nor does the value of the payment amount to the value of large numbers of cattle. This is not the place to analyse the marriage payments, but only to note that the total cost for a first marriage may run to about forty pounds, of which a large part goes to buy household furniture, a trousseau, and silver ornaments. The remainder of the payment goes entirely to the bride's mother to do with as she likes. She can spend it on tea, sugar, scents, and cloth; but if she buys animals with it, these do not become hers; she keeps them in trust for her daughter and daughter's children. Although there is often argument about the amount of bridewealth to be paid, the debate is not between the two families concerned; instead, the men of both families unite in argument to try and beat down the price which the bride's mother, backed by the women of her family, is demanding. Women agree to this more readily when the bridegroom is a close kinsman.

A youth gets financial help only from his very near relatives (father, brothers, mother's brother); although he might try and raise loans from other people, he is expected to find most of the money by himself. The men of the girl's family show little interest in trying to fix the bridewealth until at the end they attempt to persuade the mother to be reasonable in her demands.[10]

[10] The final word is that of the bride's mother absolutely. One way she can try to stop a marriage that she or her daughter do not want is to refuse to lower the price. They say *neṭarḍa bil mal*: let us chase him off with our demands (lit. with wealth).

Thus the process of marriage itself does not entail the participation of a wide body of kinsmen on both sides. In intra-surra marriages it is a matter between the guardians of the two parties, involving at the most the members of two extended families. It is the same with other marriages, however distant they may be. Ḥurgaṣ did not marry off his half-sister to Ḥammoda in the expectancy of creating an indissoluble alliance between his own lineage and the politically awkward ʻAriya; he did so to gain the wise and powerful voice of Ḥammoda himself on his side. Ḥammoda in his situation, and other in-laws in other situations, acted as intermediaries in times of tenseness. Distant marriages are not always, or even largely, politically actuated. The effect is not to link lineages in alliance, but to link families belonging to potentially hostile groups in common interest. Such marriages exist simultaneously with others which have as their effect the concentration of social interest within the surra. The ideal of close marriage, and the frequent breach of the ideal, mean that the marriage links created in any surra have a variety of side effects which, taken together, both enhance the bonds of dogmatic brothers and make inroads into the autonomy of different lineages.

7
A SEGMENTARY LINEAGE

SYMBOLS OF SEGMENTATION

As the Humr all belong to a single agnatic lineage, we might be led to suppose that this lineage and its segments were the groups and sub-groups which, in different situations, entered political relations with one another, and had leaders, spokesmen, or groups of elders who represented them to outsiders and exerted some kind of authority, however weak, internally. In some respects, political and otherwise, Humr are organized on the lines of lineage segmentation. This chapter indicates some ways in which they are so organized, but I will later show that much Humr activity, including political activity, involves groups which are not congruent with the lineage or its segments, and further that the agnatic framework changes through time and at any moment exists in various versions. I deal now with that version which is the one strangers first learn from Humr. This 'dogmatic' mode differs from others, which are products of greater genealogical detail.

Writing of the Sanusi of Cyrenaica, Evans-Pritchard said that 'authority is distributed at every point [of segmentation] in the tribal structure, and political leadership is limited to situations in which a tribe or a segment of a tribe acts corporately.'[1] This statement is, in some measure, applicable to the Humr. The segments of the all-embracing lineage, the extended families, the surras, the minor lineages, the major lineages, the omodiyas, and the two main divisions of the tribe, have or potentially have recognized leaders. But they are leaders in some respects only because, while these men may be recognized as leaders by other Humr, their leadership is not necessarily accepted by all the members of their respective groups. At any time a lineage may be allied for political action with other groups of remote agnatic relationship. A leader of a group may or may not also be a leader with Government recognition.

Owing to the segmentary nature of the lineage, some men are leaders of groups of more than one order. Thus an omda, as well as

[1] *The Sanusi of Cyrenaica*, p. 59.

being the Government-recognized leader of his omodiya, is also the unofficial leader of his extended family, his surra, and his minor and major lineages. One important consequence of this is that, while an omda is supreme in his capacity as administrative head of an omodiya, yet he has counterparts in his capacity as unofficial leader of subordinate groups. As the leader of an omodiya he has the leaders of the major lineages other than his own to contend with. Within his own major lineage he has the leaders of the minor lineages other than his own to contend with concerning the policies of his major lineage; within the minor lineage he has the leaders of other surras to contend with concerning the policies of his minor lineage; within his surra he has the leaders of other extended families to contend with in formulating policy for the surra. It is only in his capacity as omda that he holds an office and an authority unique in the omodiya, but it is in this capacity that rivalry, hostility, and aggression are most often directed against him. Yet his omdahood is only a part of him. He has assumed a large number of different social personalities. The situation is true, *mutatis mutandis*, for nazirs, and for lesser leaders like those of major and minor lineages and surras.[2]

To some extent all positions of leadership, whether or not they are recognized by the Government, have the same attribute as they had in pre-administration days: they exist by consent, and people can withdraw their support. The fact that the Government backs certain leaders has modified the readiness of individuals to change their allegiance and follow others. This Government recognition extends to nazirs and omdas; the official recognition of tribute sheikhs is more limited. Yet, recognized or not, leaders are attacked and their following changes. A lineage need not at all times have a leader who is recognized by all its members.

Although there are many reservations to be made about using the agnatic lineage as a model, it is clear that Humr see their own social organization in terms of it. The all-embracing agnatic lineage furnishes for Humr a statement of the way in which the tribe ought, according to the ideals of the brotherhood of the closest, to be arranged. It pro-

[2] I have simplified matters here a bit as far as the nazirs are concerned. The Nazir Umum is official head of all the Messiriya, but not of the ʻAjaira, whose official head is his brother, Nazir ʻAli. Nazir ʻAli is official head of the ʻAjaira, but not the official head (omda) of A. Kamil, to which he belongs: the omda comes from a different major lineage. For the Felaita, Nazir Sereyr is the official head, but he is not the official head of his omodiya, the Jubarat, which is in the hands of his brother Subeyr. Nevertheless the Nazir Umum retains great influence over the ʻAjaira, the Nazir Umum and his brother ʻAli retain great influence over A. Kamil, and Nazir Sereyr retains great influence over the Jubarat.

vides them with a key to the behaviour which is appropriate when strangers meet. Identification is not made by comparing ancestors, but after greeting another a stranger asks: 'Where are you from?'[3] The other will answer that he is from 'Ajaira or Felaita, or perhaps by the name of his omodiya. If the omodiya is Mezaghna, the questioner goes on 'And within the Mezaghna? . . . And within Dar Abu Timani? . . . And within Awlad Salamy?', eventually narrowing identification down to the surra. The knowledge thus gained gives a clue to other things; it suggests the part of the country the other comes from, as well as defining the social distance between them.

In many respects the significant groups of Humr, in action, in symbol, and in sentiment, appear to be the segmentary lineages. Yet the agnatic segmentary principle is seldom alone operative.

The distribution of the various cattle brands within the tribe furnishes a good example. Quite clearly the basis of the distribution is the lineage, but there is no great regularity in the order of segmentation of those groups which share brands in common. The tribe is divided agnatically into the two sections 'Ajaira and Felaita; associated with each of these sections is a cattle brand, the *shelga* being that of the 'Ajaira and the *guna'* being that of Felaita. The phrase 'The Humr, *shelga* and *guna'*' is used, in precisely the same way as the phrase 'The Humr, 'Ajaira and Felaita' is used, to mean the tribe in its totality. Yet within the 'Ajaira the following groups do not use the *shelga*: the Fayyarin omodiya, Dar Nala minor lineage (that of the nazir, in the Kelabna major lineage of Awlad Kamil), and the Beni Helba minor lineage (Dar Abu Timani major lineage of the Mezaghna). Among the Felaita the Ziyud, Salamat, and Jubarat omodiyas do not use the *guna'*. These have only lineage brands. They all, with the exception of Dar Nala, are among the sections which appear not to be derived from the tribal ancestor. Accordingly these two brands seem to be badges not of the 'Ajaira and Felaita but of those lineages which are their members by genealogical descent.[4] Thus the actual use of the brands, as distinct from the symbolic use of the terms, relates to a different mode of grouping the sections of the tribe.

In addition to these brands referring to the two major sections of the tribe, it is quite common for major or minor lineages to have exclusive brands. Thus among Awlad Serur, apart from the *guna'*, which they all

[3] *Mineynak?*—literally 'your whence?'.

[4] For Dar Nala, see later. I did not confirm whether the converse is true, that *no* stranger lineages among the Humr use *shelga* and *guna'*. I was told that the stranger Barokela use the *shelga* as other A. Kamil do, but did not personally confirm it.

use, there is a brand for each of the six major lineages. Other omodiyas have more elaborations. Among the Mezaghna, Dar Abu Timani major lineage has no single and exclusive cattle brand, but the minor lineages have brands as follows: the Terakana use the *taffer* across the back legs and the *rukab* on the front leg of the cattle; Dar Ḥantor use the *rukab* on the front leg; Awlad Mumin use the *matarig* on the front leg; Beni Helba do not, like the other, use the *shelga*, but instead have the *ashbur* in the same position, on the back leg; Awlad Salamy use the *rukab* in varying positions according to surra, except for 'Iyal Ganiṣ surra, which has the *jerrai* and the *taffer*, and for one extended family of 'Iyal Damura surra, affinally related to 'Iyal Ganiṣ, who adopted the *jerrai* (but not the *taffer*) from them.

These brands are a help in the search for stray animals.[5] As a sign of ownership, men cut the same signs on trees over stretches of agricultural land they have reserved. But Humr see them also as a means of protection, in a mystical sense, for their cattle, and they change them when they appear to be no longer effective. Dar Nala, the 'Ajaira nazir's lineage, has not used the *shelga* since 'Ali Julla, the first nazir, held it responsible for the heavy loss of stock. As a protective measure Humr cut the brands on the trunks of trees with very thick foliage when they use them for shade, for these are supposed to harbour harmful spirits.

The drum call is another important badge. Each surra has at least one drum, which is carried on a bull in caravan, and is slung from the limb of a convenient tree in camp. Sometimes it is taken down to be used at singing and dancing sessions, but its more serious purpose is that of indicating the position of the camp to men and cattle. The drum call attracts those who have straggled from the caravan when a new camp is formed, and is used also to indicate the position to herders should they be lost, as they are quite likely to be in the thickly wooded Babanusa.[6] It is also beaten out on the evening before a move, once the decision to shift camp has been finally taken, thus announcing the intention to the whole neighbourhood.

The drum calls are short phrases, beaten out in different rhythms, each rhythm corresponding to a verbal phrase by which the drum call is known. The distribution of the different drum calls does not correspond with the distribution of the different cattle brands. The biggest

[5] Earclips also are used on animals for identification. I think that most surras have an earclip of their own, but I made no comprehensive collection of them.

[6] There is a popular belief, without foundation, that cattle can recognize the particular rhythm of their own camp's call.

unit which shares a drum call is the major lineage. Among Awlad Kamil there is one drum call for each major lineage except Dar Umm Sheyba, where the three medium lineages have one each; Awlad Tuba and the Kelabna major lineages have the same drum call, but they make a distinction by giving them different names: Tayi Gum and Kayi Durr. Only Awlad Serur have a correspondence between drum-call and cattle-brand distribution, each major lineage sharing a call and a brand exclusively. Among the Salamat each surra has its own drum call, except for two surras which share one; and one extended family has a call of its own. Although many brands and calls are repeated among sections of different omodiyas, I do not think this has any significance: it is not an indication that the groups sharing them were once closer than they are now.[7]

Drum calls used to be jealously guarded, and a group using one to which it was not entitled would incur the revenge of the group claiming it. Such behaviour led to force. Humr now realize that the Government would hardly regard such misappropriation as an excuse for the use of force, and have left off applying it. However, they do use drum calls for political comment. When the omda of the Mezaghna was under attack from the 'Ariya major lineage, the youths of 'Iyal Ganiṣ, the omda's surra, beat out the 'Ariya call, '*Kuku, sidd el derb*', in such a way that it was recognizable, but with variation to create a comic effect. This gave great delight, although some of the more responsible men present were anxious about the consequences.[8]

Humr associate the two main sections of the tribe, and different omodiyas, with idiosyncracies of one kind or another. Some are true, and some are false. As between the 'Ajaira and the Felaita, there is much backbiting based on popular conceptions of their natures. When I was leaving 'Ajaira country on a tour among the Felaita I was told to 'watch out; and take plenty of food'. The Felaita, as seen by the 'Ajaira as a whole, are untrustworthy and inhospitable. My experience did not confirm this judgement. Felaita counter by referring to the darker complexion of 'Ajaira ('Ajaira are in closer contact with Dinka and have presumably mixed more with them). Humr remember well how an early nazir of the Felaita used to refer to 'Ali Julla, the first nazir of the 'Ajaira, as 'Zunji', the Arabic word which comes closest, among the

[7] For example, in A. Kamil, the major lineages of Dar Mota and A. Tuba both have the *soṭ* brand, the former on the neck and the latter of the foreleg. Genealogical statements do not indicate any specially close connexion between them.

[8] Lists of brands and drum calls are given, with their distributions, in Appendixes 3 and 4.

Baggara, to the tone of the opprobrious English 'nigger'; Felaita likewise often call the 'Ajaira '*abid*.[9] Awlad 'Umran are characterized as tolerating *seligy*, tea without sugar: this is a reference to their distance during the hot dry season from any market. The Ziyud are known as particularly negligent cultivators who go in March and April for long periods on milk alone.[10] The Salamat build tents of a different (oval) kind and let their spears go rusty, and are generally more settled than the other omodiyas. The Fayyarin have some vocabulary which members of other omodiyas do not use: they say '*amajan* instead of *desheran* to refer to cattle grazing in the morning before milking, and they have some other words of their own. The Mezaghna say *nina* instead of *naḥna* for 'we'. It is lineages of the size of the two main sections and of omodiyas which are given characteristics of these kinds.

Lineage autonomy appears also in one form of blood-money transaction. This applies in the special case where a Humrawi has killed, or has been killed by, a man of another tribe. The blood-money then has the name of *diat el soff*. Before the Condominium I do not think that blood-money was paid between tribes at all; raiding and counter-raiding marked inter-tribal relations at the time. It seems, however, that a kind of *diat el soff* existed between 'Ajaira and Felaita in the past: the component *bedanas* of each major division took part in contributions and receipts. Nowadays this kind of blood-money payment is made only in respect of non-Humr.[11] Howell recorded an example in his manuscript. In 1947 the son of the omda of Awlad Serur was killed in an affray with a man of the Messiriya. As an act of vengeance a man of Awlad Serur killed a Messiri. He was sent for trial and received a life sentence; the payment of blood-money involved the Humr as a whole. A meeting was first held to assess the market value of sixty head of the specified grades. One-third of the total value was contributed by the close family of the killer, assisted by those with whom they had pre-

[9] Above, p. 80.

[10] Under the influence of their omda, Adim Yusuf, many Ziyud young men went to wage-labour in Omdurman for two years, living so austerely there that they were able to buy good herds when they returned. I have no figures, but it was generally thought that the Ziyud made far better use than others of the herd-raising possibilities of wage-labour.

[11] Arrangements made in the presence of officers of the administration between Humr and Messiriya and between Humr and other tribes have resulted in the following scales of reciprocal blood agreements: Humr with Messiriya, 60 head of cattle; Humr and Messiriya with Rizeygat, 71 head; with Hamar, £60; with western Kordofan Nuba, 15 head of cattle; with Kadugli Nuba, 33 head; with Hawazma, 33 head; with Rweng and Ngok Dinka, 45 head; with Malwal Dinka, 30 head. There is, I believe, no agreement with Nuer, and the agreement with Rweng Dinka is an informal one.

vious agreements. Responsibility for the remaining two-thirds was then divided among the other omodiyas of the Humr as follows: one share from all omodiyas except Awlad 'Umran who paid two shares (Menama and 'Addal paying one each), and Jubarat, Salamat, and Faḍliya which, being small omodiyas, paid a half each. The whole tribe thus co-operates, through its omodiyas, in restoring relations when one of its members has been involved in a homicide leading to breach with another tribe.

These various signs of lineage autonomy do not, however, tell us very much. Anyone can wear a badge. What they do tell us is that in some respects the lineage and its segmentary nature are significant to Humr. But this is only an extension of the fact that the Humr groups which have names are agnatic lineages: each named group takes its name from the man who is said to have founded it, and any named group implies an assumed common ancestry. We have yet to see how far and in what other spheres these groups have meaning in social action.

ADMINISTRATION THROUGH AGNATIC GROUPS

An important part of the answer concerns the position that this arrangement of people has in the administrative organization of the tribe. When it imposed a system of formal administration, the Condominium Government used existing agnatic groups as administrative units. The first appointments to be made were those of two nazirs: one for each of the main sections, 'Ajaira and Felaita.[12] Up to 1911, these two nazirs operated through 'senior sheikhs' and 'sheikhs', who had Government recognition: in the early days of the administration there were no omdas. According to the Intelligence Reports of December 1905, at that time the 'Ajaira section under Nazir 'Ali Julla was in two parts, named Awlad Kamil (under 'Ali Julla himself) and Awlad 'Umran (under Sheikh Abu Shama Ṭaha). The following table of the divisions of the 'Ajaira is taken from the *Sudan Intelligence Reports* of the time. The third column gives the names of the sheikhs, and the fourth the amount of tribute at which the divisions were assessed.[13]

In Fig. 11 I have put together the divisions of the 'Ajaira as they were

[12] The nazir of the 'Ajaira, 'Ali Julla, was 'nominally Nazir of all the Humr, but [had] no influence whatever with the Humr Felaita and very little with his own tribe' (*Sudan Intelligence Report* (hereafter *S.I.R.*) 90, Jan. 1902). Early administrators often called the two main sections different tribes.

[13] *S.I.R.* 137. I have changed the spellings of the sections to make them conform to my own. Some were rather remote: e.g. Abu Ghadeya was spelt Ghighideir, but there is no doubt that it refers to the same section. I have standardized the names of the sheikhs which are recognizable.

in about 1905, and as they were in 1955. There are noticeable differences. Then, the 'Ajaira were divided primarily into two main groups, Awlad Kamil and Awlad 'Umran, each of which was a *bedana*,[14] and these were divided into major lineages, each of which was a *khashm beyt*; now the 'Ajaira are divided into five main groups, each of which is an omodiya. Then, the Mezaghna and the Fayyarin were major lineages of Awlad Kamil. The tribute figures show that they had

TABLE 10. *Tribute divisions of the 'Ajaira in 1905*

Bedana	*Khashm beyt*	*Sheikh*	*Tribute*
A. Kamil (Sh. 'Ali Julla)	Kelabna	'Ali Julla	£15
	Dar Mota	Ḥamdan 'Abdalla 'Azoza	16.5
	Dar Umm Sheyba Ḥamra	Mas 'ud Idris	8.5
	Dar Umm Sheyba Zerga	Digani 'Azoza	8.5
	Dar Salim	El Dai Manje	16.5
	A. Kimeyl	(not named)	5
	El Mezaghna	'Ali Ḥamda	40
	El Fayyarin	Adim Abu Khalil	40
A. 'Umran (Sh. Abu Shama Ṭaha)	Abu Ghadeya	Abu Shama Ṭaha	44 (Abu Ghadeya to Abu Isma 'in, bracketed)
	Nige 'y	Raḥma Ḥamid	
	Abu Ḥammad	Ḍow el Beyt Ḥassab	
	El Nowashy	El Milḥ el Nebi 'Abdalla	
	Abu Ḥimmeyd	Jodat Gheyib	
	Abu Isma 'in	Muḥammad Junkola	
	Umm Jod	Aḥmed 'Arig	30.5
	Dar Zebaly	Ḥassola Ḥamid	15
	Dar Heyballa	'Ali Wagga el Dagga	15.5
	Dar Banat	Muḥammad Eygal	15
	Raḥma	Ṣugheyir Fiḍeyla	5
	Faḍliya	Naṣr Wenesa	25

more cattle than the other sections (though there is no indication of their human populations); and on the establishment of omdas, they both became omodiyas. The other sections of Awlad Kamil were the present-day major lineages, although Awlad Tuba and Barokela were not in the list. Of the divisions of Awlad 'Umran given for 1905, the first six are the major lineages of the 'Addal, one of the two omodiyas which now compose the Awlad 'Umran omodiya; and a note states that these six paid their tribute through Sheikh Abu Shama. The remainder, who represent the Menama omodiya of today, paid their tribute as a group directly to 'Ali Julla. In the earlier table the Faḍliya are shown as a major lineage of Awlad 'Umran; in the later table they are shown twice, as a major lineage of the Menama, and as a separate

[14] See p. 8, n. 25.

omodiya. They applied for, and were granted, an omodiya in the 1930s but a few of them remained with the Menama.

The Intelligence Reports do not detail the Felaita sheikhs of the early period, but Captain Lloyd, who compiled the 'Ajaira list for the Intelligence Reports, published an article in 1907 in which he stated: 'The Felaita, who are only half as numerous as the Ajaira, are divided into the Metanin . . . the Walad Serur . . . the Salamat and Gubarat',[15] a statement which omits only the Ziyud from a complete list of present-day Felaita omodiyas. The Ziyud, who had been part of the Metanin, emerged as a unit of equal status after the establishment of omdas.

While the administration initially used agnatic groups as corporate units in fiscal, disciplinary, and other matters, agnatic groups in turn used the administration for their own purposes. Provided they could satisfy the administration that they had some claim to autonomy in terms of their numbers and their place in tribal history, they could use the new system to forward their interests in two ways: by becoming a named omodiya the lineage would gain wide recognition as a component unit of the tribe, and by having an omda the lineage might manage to gain advantage by the presence of their own official in high places. Apart from the honour of having one's own body of kin elevated, a few material advantages could be expected. An omda may, for instance, attain such a position with his nazir that he can influence appointments to minor posts in local government: nearly all the local authority police[16] at Muglad are Humr, and the work is highly valued as a source of locally obtainable income. Many advantages are perhaps only alleged ones: the widely held belief that the presence of a close kinsman as omda will sway lawsuits and offer general protection against various administrative actions may or may not be true. Yet this belief concurs with the Humr view of power, and the closer the kinsman in office, the more likely are his power-attributes to be of positive service, at least with men of similar personalities.

Of the major lineages to rise to the status of omodiya, the Faḍliya are the latest example. The story of their emergence is recorded in the Kordofan provincial files for 1938 as follows.

The Fadliya are the only parent branch of the Humr[17] without an omodiya.

[15] Lloyd, 'Some notes on Dar Homr', p. 651. *S.I.R.* 171, Oct. 1908, also names these sections as those entitled to have sheikhs.

[16] These act in various capacities: as messengers on local government business, as detectives, etc.; and, being armed, they often accompany sheikhs or omdas in tax-collecting troubles to make a show of force.

[17] The founder of the Faḍliya is often said to have been a son of 'Ajar, the founder of the 'Ajaira.

1905

- ʻAjaira — NAZIR
  - A. Kamil — Sen. Sheikh
    - Kelabna — Sheikh
    - Dar Mota — ״
    - Dar Umm Sheyba
      - Ḥamra — Sheikh
      - Żerga — ״
    - Dar Salim — Sheikh
    - A. Kimeyl — ״
    - Mezaghna — ״
    - Fayyarin — ״
  - A. ʻUmran — Sen. Sheikh
    - A. Ghadeya — Sheikh
    - Nigeʻy — ״
    - Abu Ḥammád — ״
    - El Nowaṣhy — ״
    - Abu Ḥimmeyd — ״
    - Abu Ismaʻin — ״
    - Umm Jod — ״
    - Dar Zebely — ״
    - Dar Ḥeyballa — ״
    - Dar Banat — ״
    - Raḥma — ״
    - Faḍliya — ״

  (Umm Jod, Dar Zebely, Dar Ḥeyballa, Dar Banat, Raḥma, Faḍliya:) although officially under the senior sheikh of A. ʻUmran, these sections paid their tribute to the senior sheikh of A. Kamil, who was also Nazir of the tribe.

1955

- ʻAjaira — NAZIR
  - A. Kamil — OMDA
    - Kalabna
    - Dar Mota
    - Dar Umm Sheyba
      - Ḥamra
      - Zerga
      - Barokela
    - Dar Salim
    - A. Kimeyl
    - A. Tuba
  - Mezaghna — OMDA
  - Fayyarin — OMDA
  - A. ʻUmran
    - ʻAddal — OMDA
      - Ghadeya
      - Nigeʻy
      - Abu Ḥammad
      - Nowaṣhy
      - Abu Ḥimmeyd
      - Ismaʻin
    - Menama — OMDA
      - Umm Jod
      - Dar Zebely
      - Dar Ḥeyballa
      - Dar Banat
      - Raḥma
      - Faḍliya
  - Faḍliya — OMDA

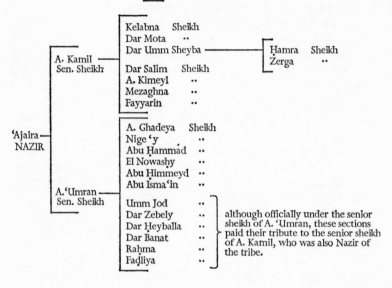

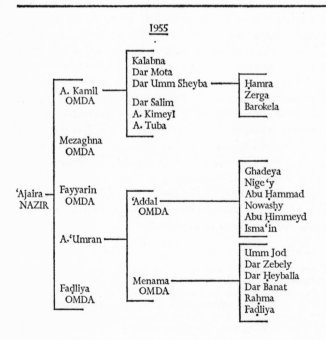

Until about the middle of the nineteenth century the Fadliya were under their own sheikh and a main section of the tribe but as a result of a feud between the clans they lost their status and became merged with the Awlad Umran. The story is given in a note by Mr. Dee [when Assistant District Commissioner of the Baggara], who wrote: 'At one time the Fadliya had a separate sheikhship but a Fadli killed a Jubari. The Jubarat [Felaita] came for dia [blood-money] and the Mezaghna, A. Kamil and Fayyarin ['Ajaira] being a long way off, Sh. Sheyhat of the Menama Umm Jod got the A. Umran to assist in paying dia. When Shaib Mwati abu Hurriya, the leader of A. Kamil, heard of this he was furious. He was apparently a strong imperious man who would not have dreamt of paying dia straight away.[18] He went to Sh. Sheyhat and caught him by the beard and vest and hit him a blow. The A. Umran wanted to fight but Sh. Sheyhat stopped them saying this was talk for elder men and that he knew why Shaib Mwati had hit him. Shaib Mwati then asked why the A. Umran had paid dia as if they only were the brothers of the Fadliya, and left out A. Kamil, Mezaghna and Fayyarin. Eventually, it was agreed that these should pay back part of the dia to A. Umran. This dia was not paid back for some time and in the mean time one of the A. Kamil and one of the A. Umran had a quarrel at a dance. A. Fadli took up the side of the Umrani and so a quarrel sprang up between the A. Kamil and the Fadlia and the former never paid their share of the dia. The Fadlia were a weak section numerically and in those days there were always raids and counter raids and the Fadlia joined up with the A. Umran for protection.' During the Mahdiya the Fadliya flag was born by the Emir Kebir el Nuwar, the A. Umran following their own Emir, Abu Shama Tahir,[19] but after the occupation the section again placed themselves under the A. Umran leaders. Numeric weakness and lack of any outstanding character may have been the principal causes of their self defacement [*sic*] but times change and the old spirit has ever been present. . . . It is alleged that years ago Mukhtar Effendi wished to give the Fadliya their own omodiya but the then omda of A. Umran bribed the sheikh to say they did not want to break off. . . . The nazir himself is most anxious to award the Fadliya a separate banner. . . . Over two thirds of the section favour El Naim Omr.[20]

[18] His anger arose also because the other 'Ajaira groups, apart from A. 'Umran, had the right to participate in blood-money payments to Felaita creditors.

[19] i.e. Abu Shama Ṭaha, the first sheikh of A. 'Umran.

[20] El Na'im 'Omar was thereupon appointed and is still omda. The account is in Kn. P. CR/66/E.13, p. 317.

FIG. 11. Comparison of certain units of the 'Ajaira in about 1905 and 1955. All the 1905 groups with sheikhs over them are shown, and are repeated in the 1955 diagram to indicate their positions in the present system of segmentation. The Mezaghna and Fayyarin became omodiyas in about 1911, and the Faḍliya in 1938. The latter left a small group behind among the Menama. Awlad Tuba and the Barokela did not appear on the 1905 list.

Thus the Faḍliya became one of the 'Ajaira five. On their achievement of omodiya status, they showed a little bit of independence from Awlad 'Umran by starting to move slightly west of their previous routes, and they now tend rather to accompany the Mezaghna although their axis lies between the two. Nowadays as a group the Faḍliya have a status which is equal to that of the other omodiyas of the tribe, except for that surra which remained among the Menama and still belongs to that omodiya.

When the administration first took over, they used agnatic groups as units of administration. While the system of administration underwent changes, the units of administration were still agnatic groups. The principle of administration through lineages has remained, but in the process the relative status of the lineages has altered. To the administration this is simply a change of administrative status; to the Humr, it marks also a rearrangement of the relations of agnatic groups to one another—although it is important to bear in mind that this change refers to one only of the recognized methods of segmentation. Humr readily admit putative links as being equivalent to genuine ones in the establishment of any lineage. Equally readily, they admit the possibility of change in the relative status of lineages to one another within the total system.

It is tempting to suggest that with regard to the particular mode of segmentation we are discussing at this point, Humr do not think in lineage terms but in terms of administrative units. This would be an error. The groups are lineages in a system of segmentary lineages, and they are administrative units at the same time. I have been tempted to speak of them as 'administrative lineages'; what has prevented me from doing this is the separation, at lower levels of segmentation, of agnatic segments from administrative units, a point which will emerge later. The equal voice which all omodiyas have constitutionally, and the equality of status in the eyes of the administration that all omdas have, may have influenced Humr to give equal status to omodiyas considered as lineages.

It was in 1911 that the 'omodiya' and the office of omda were established, and with them the opportunity for lineages to seek to enhance their status. No record appears to have been kept of the omdas before that given in the provincial files in 1921[21] by which time the Ziyud and the Fayyarin had achieved omdaships; the Faḍliya emerged finally in 1938. District notebooks make it clear that omdas were established in order to remove from 'Ali Julla, the first nazir, some of

[21] Ibid, p. 3.

the excessive power he had managed to amass. Originally the nazirs kept a tenth of the tribute collected from their people, and they could impose fines on litigants and keep the fines themselves. After the appointment of omdas and the establishment of a local treasury manned by civil servants, the omdas collected the taxes from their sheikhs and delivered them to the treasury, the omdas keeping a third of ten per cent., and the sheikhs keeping two-thirds. Omdas had the power to fine, and kept the fines. The post of omda was lucrative, and men made out a case for the establishment of more omdas. Later the omdas were salaried, they were denied shares of the tax, and they no longer had power to fine. Today it is only the sheikhs who keep ten per cent. of the tax money.

The various administrative officers have well-defined functions. The nazirs of the 'Ajaira and the Felaita both have courts at which suits are heard from within their own sections and to which appeal is made from a number of localized courts under specially appointed court presidents. Appeal from there is to the court of the Nazir Umum. The nazirs are ultimately responsible for the good behaviour of their sections, for passing on to them instructions from the administration, and for seeing that the appropriate taxes are paid by members of their units. They are the chief spokesmen to people higher in the administrative hierarchy. They have considerable influence in the appointment of omdas and court presidents. The duties remaining to omdas are the general ones of keeping their omodiyas in order. They are responsible for good behaviour, for producing men wanted by the administration, for the production of the tax money through their sheikhs, for acting as spokesmen to higher authority, and for passing on to omodiya members the instructions of higher authorities. They are also recognized as arbitrators in quarrels within their omodiyas; this task and their exhortations to produce tax money together take up a large part of their time. Most suits from an omodiya are first heard informally by the omda, but he has no power of coercion, and if he fails to arbitrate to the satisfaction of both parties then the suit goes to one of the courts. Sheikhs are primarily responsible for extracting tax money from their followers, but they occasionally have other administrative tasks to perform.

The other important political posts are those of court presidents and of members of the Rural Council. Both these appointments are made through the agnatic system. The court presidents are those of the local courts: the courts they administer answer the needs of the shifting population of particular localities, according to season, rather than the needs of lineages, but the offices are awarded to men who happen to be suitable within an omodiya which is chosen, on account of its close associations with a particular place, as appropriate for the work. Members of Dar Messiriya Rural Council are elected, one for each omodiya, by the members of each omodiya.[22]

Because the administration recognizes nazirs and omdas as heads of agnatic groups, and because council members and court presidents are appointed as representatives of agnatic groups, it follows that the man with political aspirations has to work through the agnatic system to gain the popularity required before he can enter these positions.

The administration also finds the lineages a useful means of organizing certain activities. We have noted that tax-gathering in the early days was done through them. Then, too, 'administrative fines' were imposed on agnatic groups under the sheikhs for failure to produce tribute and other misdemeanours. Most years, about November, there is a mass cattle inoculation and census, and the camps of the whole tribe are called to within reach of Muglad. Days are appointed for the cattle of each omodiya to be inoculated. During the Parliamentary elections of 1954 voting booths were erected in various parts of the country, in some cases one for each omodiya, in other cases one for two omodiyas which used it on successive days. The first census of the Sudan which reached the Humr in 1955 used the omodiyas as units of enumeration.

THE BROTHERHOOD OF THE CLOSEST

In all these ways the administration makes use of the agnatic groups within the tribe. I have indicated also some of the ways in which these groups are significant to the Humr themselves. Although this arrangement of lineages is not an accurate reflection of political, as distinct from administrative, relations, it is accurate enough for certain purposes; moreover, it has a certain prestige in that it represents an ideal arrangement which Humr extol, and from which they are concerned to correct deviations.

As many societies which are based on a lineage organization express political relationships in kinship terms, so do the Humr. The notion of living together in peace and friendship is expressed in the word *khua*, brotherhood, derived from *akhu*, a brother: in Arabic generally, and not only among the Humr, the word for brother is commonly used to mean friend. The Humr apply it to the real brother, to close cousins,

[22] While the method of appointment changed after 1958, the representation—by omodiyas—remained the same.

and to distant cousins. Since Humr are all agnates it is an appropriate mode of address between them. Other kinship terms such as those meaning father's brother, son, and brother's son are used also to express kinship with people of obviously different generations. Because all Humr are agnates a link through a woman takes precedence in address over distant agnation, for this is adding a quality, an additional bond of kinship, to agnation (which all Humr already share). Thus *wald ummi*, my mother's son (implying also common fatherhood), is the term of address used by men to their closest friends. But Humr likewise extend the word brother to non-Humr: many have made friends with settled farmers of Berti or Ma'alia or other tribes near whose farms they camp in the rains, and these are brothers. They have made useful contacts on a purely business basis with one or two merchants in the markets; they address as 'brother' also Dinka from whom they ask help or seek favours.

Humr would agree to the proposition that they are all brothers and ought to behave as such. They would further agree that a man of the 'Ajaira was less of a brother to a man of the Felaita than another of the 'Ajaira, and so on, down to the closest of brotherhoods, which applies to men of one surra. *Khua* is a relative concept with a different force according to context. All disputes involve a breach in the ideal of brotherhood, and the closer people are the graver are the implications of the breach. To behave in a way that might be expected of a brother is one of the elements of manliness, and is an important part in the continuing good relations between men and between groups.

There is much in common between the higher administrative divisions of the Humr in the early days of the administration and the present divisions. Most of the former units still remain as units now, although, as in the case of groups that attained omdaships later than the others, there has been a rise in status. But always the groups concerned were, to the Humr, *bedanas* or *khashm beyts*, lineages of one or another order of segmentation. To the Humr they are groups of kinsmen, deriving from similarly named groups of kinsmen who existed before the Condominium. Some kinship units then became administrative units, and they are still talked about in kinship terms; indeed, the only way that Humr refer to political groups is in terms of brotherhood, which implies common lineage. Although we do not know the exact meaning of the 1905 list (which was given in administrative reports and simply represented those groups which paid annual tribute as units), the groups mentioned must nevertheless have been meaningful to Humr, because they declared themselves as units in the face of a demanding administration. But the 1955 list has now, we have found, a meaning to the Humr beyond its administrative function, for it is through the arrangement provided at the top by the administrative units that people define their relations to one another, and it is with reference to this arrangement that people explain to strangers the composition of their tribe.

Humr are well aware that other segmentary arrangements exist. In the way that things gave been arranged by the administration, at least in the upper levels, the Humr are 'two'—'Ajaira and Felaita;

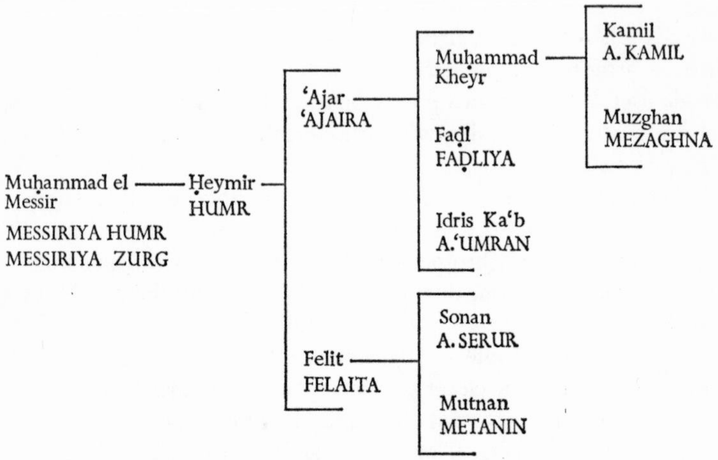

FIG. 12. Usual version of relationships between groups held to be descended from Muḥammad el Messir. The most common variant is to give Muḥammad Kheyr two sons: Muzghan, and 'Awaḍalla whose three sons, Kimeyl, Kalbon, and Kamil, founded A. Kamil lineages.

the 'Ajaira are 'five'—the constituent omodiyas—and the Felaita are also 'five', as shown on Fig. 1, p. 10. Now according to Humr idiom, this implies to them that 'Ajar, whom they know as the ancestor of the 'Ajaira, had five sons, each of whom founded one of the present omodiyas; and the same for Felait, the ancestor of the Felaita. But this is only one mode of segmentation, and it is the only one in which the 'Ajaira are five. With this dogmatic mode, Humr speak first of their groups and then derive them from ancestors from which the groups are named. Other versions give primacy to genealogy, and derive groups and their relative statuses from names mentioned in the genealogy and their genealogical relationships to one another. On one genealogical version, the commonest, the 'Ajaira are three and the Felaita are two. Fig. 12 shows the upper reaches of the genealogy which accounts for this arrangement. Since they are strangers and not really descended from the tribe's ancestor, the Fayyarin, the Ziyud, the Jubarat, and the Salamat are excluded from it. But this is only one of many versions of the genealogy. Macmichael recorded another, already quoted, in which Felaita and ʻAjaira were related much more distantly. Short of recording hundreds of *nisbas*,[23] which I did not do, it would be difficult to compose a genealogy which would represent a consensus. Even then one would be likely to end in confused failure.

Without comparing and cross-checking their nisbas, Humr think that the ʻAjaira are five and the Felaita are five. They also think that the ʻAjaira are three and the Felaita are two. Sometimes they think that the ʻAjaira are two, because Faḍl is often forgotten. Yet again, they think that the ancestor of the Fayyarin is included amongst the sons of Muḥammad Kheyr, thus denying the strangerhood of the Fayyarin and including them in close relationship with Awlad Kamil, with whom they are said first to have made brotherhood on joining the tribe. The assertion of one mode of segmentation does not preclude the assertion of a different mode of segmentation by the same person.

Later chapters show that political action may be related to more than one mode of segmentation, and that the principle of lineage segmentation itself may be of little use in trying to account for some political episodes.

[23] A *nisba* is an ascending list of direct male ancestors. Few people can recite more than three or four of these with confidence; a handful of old men can recite some fifteen or twenty, but the versions all differ markedly. Howell came to the same conclusion; his efforts to get agreement in small meetings were mostly unsuccessful.

8

SOME HUMR IDEAS ABOUT POWER

I ENDED Chapter 5 by suggesting that the basis for access to power within the surra differed from that for access to power over people beyond its confines. Within, what counts is economic ascendancy: members are obliged to cluster round those with good herds of cattle. The ability to be of direct economic assistance to other people and thus to have authority over them stops with the extended family and those dependent upon it. The effect of differences in cattle distribution becomes more even the wider the group considered, and I heard of no surra becoming economically dependent on another one. Nevertheless, the process which allows a man to attain ascendancy within can lead him further to gain political sway outside. Direct economic interests unite, or can unite, surra members, but not members of larger lineages; thus direct economic interests are not a factor in the alignment of one lineage against another. But it has to be borne in mind that a man's ability to extend his influence depends in the first instance on a dominant position, based on economic ascendancy, over family and surra. If I have spoken here of 'direct' economic interests, this is purposely done in order not to exclude economic interests which may arise indirectly as a result of the close association of a group with a man in a position of power.

The Arab nomad is popularly supposed to hold no man his master. For the Humr this supposition is manifestly false. Their history is filled with accounts of men leading the tribe or parts of it. Yet there is a clear distinction between the kinds of power and authority that exist here, and those that exist in societies with constituted and hereditary chieftainships: a man is not bound to a particular leader, and leaders do not have control over all those who reside in a particular territory.[1] In the past there were leaders, certainly, but they led only those men who wanted to follow them. They had no formal powers of

[1] The one exception is that the Nazir Umum controls the Humr who share Dar Humr; subordinate leaders are leaders of sections of the population and not chiefs over sections of the land.

coercion; they had no courts, and there was no body of executives. The positions were not hereditary. The establishment of the Condominium Government changed matters in many ways, but still for the most part a leader leads only volunteers. This chapter deals with some of the ideas which Humr have about the nature of power and authority, and the positions to which they give rise. It deals with them in terms of the expectations which Humr have about the practices, the rights, and the duties of those who lead, and of their acceptance of these ideas of power and authority. It will thus furnish an introduction, in terms of values, to the subsequent chapters, which deal with the various kinds of political groups and leaders in existence.

Certain qualities are expected of men who are chosen as leaders; and these qualities are similar, Humr say, to those which a man with ambitions in the directions of wealth and women must hold if he is to be successful. These various objectives—wealth, women, and power—form a complex of closely related aims, and the man who succeeds in their pursuit comes close to the Humr ideal of manliness. Manliness, the compound of many qualities, eludes exact definition, for it is impossible to construct an ethos which would be acceptable in all its parts to all Humr at all times. Many ideals of behaviour are situational, and some are downright contradictory. Brotherliness and the spirit of vengeance, generosity and thrift, stubbornness and reasonableness, are admitted values which are inconsistent. Although the Humr term 'manliness' includes them all, it has different connotations in different circumstances, and a man who is a loyal and stubborn avenger to his friends can appear, through the same behaviour, as a pig-headed trouble-maker to others.

The value of manliness connects success in the fields of women, wealth, and power. This connexion has been mentioned in Chapter 3. The list of qualities can be extended to include, apart from piety, asceticism, industry, physical hardiness, and pastoral skill, also loyalty, common sense, responsibility, brotherly love, and the spirit of vengeance. The logic of the connexion of these virtues with success is somewhat circular: in order to attain success in these fields a man must have these qualities, and God's favour in addition. Failure to achieve success indicates to Humr the lack of one or other of these qualities, while achievement is proof of their possession.

I have discussed wealth as a springboard to power. It is also a springboard to women; and women in turn play a significant informal part in the power careers of men.

WOMEN'S ROLE IN THE STRUGGLE FOR POWER

A young married man said: 'What is the point of anything without women? Why do you work hard for wealth if it is not to spend it on women? Without women no one would bother to amass wealth. Why does a man want to be a nazir or an omda? Only because of the fame it brings him, and fame is good because women will get to know about him and remember his name, and when they stir their meal they will talk about him and say "So-and-so has said this and has said that".' This informant mentioned as the prime motive for effort the regard of women; others mentioned ownership of many cattle, and others preferred the esteem of fellow men through the achievement of office. But whatever the avowed objective may be, the amassing of wealth, the favours of women, or accession to office, success in any one sphere is closely bound up with success in the others.

Women play no formal part in Humr political life.[2] As in many Islamic societies, they have in relation to men a somewhat separate existence and a socially and legally inferior position. In day-to-day life the women's place is at the tents, and the men's place is at the tree. This division of the camp, where people spend most of their lives, into a female sector and a male sector is representative of the division of functions of the two sexes. Women's life is private life. Men have their private hours, but their life is by and large public. Women sit, work, and talk in small groups. Women of a tent or of two or three neighbouring tents carry out their domestic activities together. Men sit in large groups; the males of a camp spend the daylight hours together at one place, the tree, usually with a succession of guests from other camps. While women's labour is confined to domestic chores, that of men is public and open. Their responsibility for the camp as a whole, humans and animals, is a public responsibility, which effects many households of one camp. They deal with movements, and their policies in this respect are of interest to other camps. The men of a camp, in their capacity as a surra or as a part of a surra, decide the kind of relations they will sustain with other groups. The tree is a forum for all kinds of political discussion, in which women have no direct voice. The tent is the place for talking about the minutiae of domestic affairs, and whatever is discussed there has no direct impact upon the decisions reached at the tree. The separateness of women is well symbolized in the feeding arrangements common throughout the tribe. Men and women eat separately, the men at their tree, the women in their tents.

[2] For extended discussion, see my article on 'The position of women among the Humr'.

Although men may be seen eating by women, it is not allowed that women should be seen eating by men, and elaborate precautions are taken to avoid this.

While women occupy no formal position in political life, they do have a profound influence on politics in two respects. Firstly, they are arbiters of men's conduct, and they can make or break a man's political career. They do this by singing songs of praise or alternatively of mockery. The brave man and the cowardly man have their fame spread. The man who is undistinguished in either direction goes unsung. The songs sweep the country, and reputations are made and broken by them. Secondly, a policy decision that the men of a camp or a surra make is influenced by the kind of reaction that the women of the group are likely to have towards it.

A few years before I went to Dar Humr there occurred an episode which was still talked about when I arrived; and it was still being talked about even when I left the country over two years later. In it, women forced a policy decision and later spread the reputations of men who had comported themselves well or ill in carrying it out. A party of Humr had gone into the Sahaly, in Upper Nile Province, and had been apprehended for poaching giraffe by a posse of Nilotic policemen. At the time the men were away from the hunting camp. After some discussion, the police agreed to return to the hunting camp with them in order to pursue the matter there. They sat down, had tea, and a meal. The men eventually agreed to go and be interviewed by the District Commissioner of this portion of Nuerland, many miles away. From the camp the women heard the turn of the conversation, and as the men were preparing to saddle their horses they shouted 'So you're letting yourselves be taken away by '*abid*!' and so on. As a result of these provocations the men turned on the police and in the ensuing fight killed four of them. Police reinforcements eventually arrived and took the Arabs into custody. On this occasion, having killed their men, they gave themselves up, except for one who ran away when the reinforcements appeared. The women were thus very successful in challenging the men's honour. They forced action in terms of the values they held, of the superiority of Arabs over pagans, of physical bravery, of the spirit of revenge, and of hardness in the pursuit of wealth.

After the episode became known women began to compose songs, which were still being sung years later. These songs paid special attention to two men. They sang in praise of the one who was the acknowledged leader of the group and who, having taken his revenge by killing one of the police, did not try to escape the consequences.[3] They sang in mockery of the only man who ran away; his reputation was ruined, and he had to live in the knowledge of women's scorn for years afterwards.[4]

From the time of boys' circumcision, when girls cluster round at the operation singing 'If you cry I won't sing for you',[5] through their teens when girls give boys presents of finely burnished spears with the challenge to kill an elephant or a giraffe, through courting and early marriage when girls and their mothers demand expensive presents and wedding gifts, to seniority when at weddings old women sing of the physical powers of men of their own generations, the Humrawi male is under a constant impetus to prove himself in terms of the values that Humr women hold good. These are so close to the values that men hold good that the songs are listened to as avidly by the men as they are by the women who make them up.

POWER AND THE GOVERNMENT

The Humr have on the whole respect for the Government,[6] which, they agree, has done great things for them. The Government 'increased the Arabs'.[7] The Humr have increased because the Government has prevented the warfare and raids that once led to loss of life, introduced

[3] For example:

El Dubeyb Ḥimeydan
Riding 'Bortugan' [his horse]
They took him to Malakal [the provincial headquarters]
They brought the Koran
He took the oath and denied nothing.

(El Dubeyb Ḥimeydan
Sid el Bortugan
Waḍḍo Malakan
Jabo el kitab
Ḥalaf ma nakar.)

[4] For example:

They shouted for ——	(——korako lo
His little heart failed him.	Gileyba aba lo.)
—— is no good	(—— ma amina
A woman is better than he.	El mara' akheyr mina.)

[5] *Kin tebki ma baghanni leyk.*

[6] The Government, for most of the time I observed affairs, consisted of senior British and junior Sudanese; towards the end of my stay a Sudanese Provincial Governor and District Commissioner were in office.

[7] *Raggat el 'Arab*; the phrase seems strictly to mean 'increased the status of the Arabs', but Humr told me they meant increase in number.

health measures to help them and their livestock, and ensured overall peace, and so widened the areas in which their cattle can graze in safety.

They respect the Government also because it is commendably fair, and the officials are not held to be open to bribery; they contrast it with previous kinds of government in which, under the various sultans, the Jellaba of Zubeyr Pasha, the Turco-Egyptian rule, and the Mahdiya, they had neither general peace nor security for their cattle. Certainly there is still tax to be paid, but this is predictable and no longer sporadic and arbitrary.

The Humr seemed to have a genuine liking for many of their District Officers, and this was probably in some measure their response to the genuine liking that their officers had for them: Humr wit, ingenuity, strong individualism, and physical hardiness were much admired by the British staff. Humr were apprehensive about the first Sudanese District Commissioner before he took office, but he was soon met with an affection which he reciprocated. There is no doubt that the personalities of two nazirs during the formative years helped to create much of the mutual respect between Humr and the officers over them: Nazir Babo, with his wit, geniality, and ability, and Nazir El Ḥaj, with his judicious and aristocratic bearing.[8]

Another part of the respect they have for the Government concerns its manifest power. To the Humr, the Government wields a kind of power vastly superior to that of any of their own people. It gets things done; it usually catches up with offenders; 'it rides on a donkey but can catch a gazelle'.[9] It has boundless wealth at its command, has regimented armed soldiers, and vehicles that can move quickly about Dar Humr, at least in the dry season. It is also the source of stable justice, of hospitals, schools,[10] and jobs; good cloth and tea came with it.

[8] This mutual respect did not extend to relations between Humr and junior Government officials, whom Humr tended to bracket in their general way of life with the Jellaba. However, the few Humr who have junior Government posts are more liked that the others.

[9] *Terkub fi ḥumar o teshibb ghaẓal.* Humr may see the results in particular cases as unfortunate, but the possession of the power to effect these results is admirable. Cf. for instance the boasting lines of the song sung at all weddings:

> We are mighty Turks
> Tough to the poor man. . . .
> (Nina Turuk shaddin
> Ghaṣi lel meskin).

The word *Turuk*, Turks, is a generic term for foreign rulers.

[10] The inclusion of 'schools' in this list of benefits may seem strange in view of what I have argued elsewhere, that Humr have largely rejected educational opportunities. The herdsman is faced with a decision: schooling for his child or neglect of his herd. This does not mean that he denies the power-and-wealth-bringing

It gains an odd additional prestige through the chance that government as they now know it started about the turn of the century; so that the calendar (the year is expressed as 54 rather than 1954) represents to them the number of years since the Reoccupation.

Humr were accustomed to the idea of power. They themselves try to wield power and in so doing to get wealth from their fellows. They wielded it to great advantage in Dinka-raiding days; raiding was the source of wealth and all its derivatives. They have a great respect for power. The Humr man of power could summon horsemen to raid slaves and hunt elephants. The adherents needed for such raiding or hunting are still required today for other purposes: for you may have wealth, but without the personality to attract a following beyond your surra political position will be difficult to obtain. In the early years of the century district officers constantly referred to a man's power by the number of spear- and gun-bearing horsemen he was seen to muster.

Power, moreover, Humr see, enables men to get still more wealth. This is clearly shown by the gifts of money which nazirs receive on their personal travels around the camps. These gifts are brought and received openly. In the course of half an hour I counted £17 taken to one nazir while he was actually hearing cases. Known as *ḍeyafa*, these are gifts to honour a guest where it is impossible or inappropriate to bring a beast for slaughter.[11] Humr resisted with great heat my suggestion that these gifts could be construed as bribery for favours generally or as some kind of insurance in respect of risks in future court cases. They replied that so many contributed that the nazirs could not possibly remember who had done so and who had not.

Apart from this custom, it is widely held that those in offices of importance get a good income in bribes. For they say that to achieve office a man has to be wealthy, not only to be able to sustain a steady flow of guests, but also to take to the nazir in secret enough to mark himself out in the nazir's eyes from other candidates trying to do the same. Whether or not this bribery occurs, the important point is that

[11] It is a common practice in N. Sudan generally to take gifts of money in public to certain categories of people; to minstrels, good dancers, and so on, as well as at weddings and funerals. In Dar Humr singers and beautiful women dancing get presents: the former of coin, the latter often of paper money, which they tie in their hair. Among political personages I have seen this money taken only to nazirs. District officials would not accept it; people of lower position are not influential enough to make it worth while. Presumably much of it, like tribute, is redistributed to the tribe in the form of meals and cash presents. The higher the position, the more hospitality it is required to give.

potentialities of education which are open to the more fortunate sons of nazirs and omdas, who have both herds and salaries.

Humr myth says it does. The myth here helps to underline two aspects of Humr belief about power: you need wealth to get office, and once you have office you cannot help accumulating more of it.

More than that, to the Humr power gives you some right to wealth. It is not a bad thing to be *ḥaramy*[12] and use what power you have to try to effect transfers of wealth to your own person. I was discussing Western societies with a respected elder, and the conversation turned to gangsterism and armed hold-ups. He said that a society in which it was possible to gain wealth by these means could not be all bad, and it was the best example he had heard of the potential fruitfulness of power. But in Dar Humr, he said, gangsterism would, alas, be impossible. Everyone knew everyone else, their guns were too clumsy, and anyway there was not the loose cash and jewellery there to make the trade pay.

To use your power to gain wealth is not a bad thing. What is the point of power if you cannot so use it? You are justified in using it in this way because you have the power and have presumably worked hard to obtain it; and, moreover, you suffer greatly, being involved in endless harangue, argument, and persuasion. A nazir is *ḥaramy* because, by free-will offerings to him, he gets money gifts from his subjects. This is power in its most beautiful expression: here the mere aura of power brings wealth to you unasked. But the government is also *ḥaramy*: by enacting laws backed by force it gets tax money from the Humr. It used to extract fines in cattle or cash from whole sections of the tribe, as well as from individuals, for non-payment of tribute or other signs of rebelliousness.[13] Humr aver that much of the money thus collected does not return to them in services. The nazirs are *ḥaramy*, the Government is too; but they have the power and they deserve to be. As a result Government action in this sphere is not resented. You try to hide your cattle, but if the Government catches up with you, you pay.

There is a general assumption also that people in a position to do so embezzle or 'eat' wealth, and this is an accusation commonly used in intrigues to depose political office-holders or to down rival aspirants.

[12] The word in Sudan Arabic means simply thieving, or a thief. In Dar Humr, in addition to its general meaning it rather implies the use of cunning or force, both of which are almost positive virtues, to obtain wealth. An impoverished Dinka, breaking and entering, would simply be '*sarrag*', a thief.

[13] For instance in 1903, on non-payment of tribute, the Government seized cattle to three times its value. But this was returned on payment of the full tribute plus a fine of £40 (*S.I.R.* 104, p. 4). In 1920 a number of people were fined for refusing to go to El Obeid for a ceremonial gathering in honour of General Allenby, who was then High Commissioner for Egypt (Kordofan provincial files).

I do not think Humr make a moral distinction between transfer of wealth of this kind and transfer of wealth with legal sanction; between, for instance, what we would regard as embezzlement or fraudulent conversion, open gifts to nazirs, and taxation or legally imposed fines. They distinguish between the consequences of the actions, of course, and see that some are open and others are secret; but ethically they make little distinction, and so in this respect there is to them a similarity in the behaviour of all power-holders, from the Humr political authorities themselves up to and including the Government.

When a tax-gathering sheikh 'ate' £100 of his own lineage's money, and his trading venture with it brought disaster, there was great sympathy for him and his brothers when, at the end of the year, the Government demanded the missing cash. No one wanted him jailed for fraudulent conversion. Members of his minor lineage not only combined to produce enough money to pay the tax but went so far as to provide him and his brothers (who had sold their cattle in an attempt to put things right) with capital to start a herd again. In dealing with the Government in such a way, Humr are not ashamed: by hiding their cattle Humr 'eat' the Government in withholding tax; if the Government discovers the cattle and imposes fines, then it is the Government which is 'eating' the Humr. The game is one in which the Government is every bit as *ḥaramy* as the Humr, and just as manly.

POWER AND THE BARAMKA ASSOCIATION

While Humr dislike some of the measures and activities of the Government, they respect it for the power it wields. Power is not a new idea for the Humr; they recognize it as a fact of social life and comprehend it, having exercised it in a limited way among themselves and in their dealings with others. But the Government introduced, along with a much greater power than they had known, a bureaucratic hierarchy and a different way of life for officials.

These elements are the theme of the ceremonial of an association called the 'Baramka'. This association, which exists ostensibly in honour of tea-drinking, brings out the confused relations that Humr have to power-holders generally. The fact that tea is used as a symbol of these confused relations is particularly appropriate.

The association was described by Arber in 1940.[14] He said, 'In its

[14] Arber, 'The Baramka', which is the source of information in this paragraph. Lampen mentioned the movement in his paper, 'The Baggara tribes of Darfur', in 1933. Arber refers to a report by C. Nicholls concerning the association among the Felaita section of the Humr, but I have not seen this.

simplest form a Baramka club is a collection of members, mainly youthful, for the ceremonial drinking of tea, usually with songs in praise of tea and sugar.' Some tribes, but not the Humr, organized agricultural co-operation through the Baramka clubs. The movement appears to have spread some time after 1914 from the Nile Valley to the Habbaniya Baggara of Kordofan, and thence to other Baggara tribes and later to the Nuba. Among the Humr it was first reported in 1926. It came to the notice of the Government, who banned it among troops and police as being possibly subversive of discipline, and many tribal nazirs put it down, including the nazirs of the Humr. The subversion was supposed to consist in the way the young men, at their parties, aped superiors, and 'in this way the elders saw a challenge to their constituted authority: and this was the reason for the numerous complaints to District Commissioners by Nazirs and the subsequent breaking-up of the club in different areas'.[15] The Baramka have now been reinstated, and flourish in Dar Humr.

Among the Humr the clubs were organized by lineages. The Mezaghna, for instance, had four clubs, one in Dar Bakheyt, one in the 'Ariya, and two in Dar Abu Timani, where Awlad Mumin and Beni Helba shared one, and Awlad Salamy, the Terakana, and Dar Ḥantor shared the other.[16] Women have counterpart clubs and hold parties inside tents. Active members, as Arber suggests, are mostly young men.

Humr are never so neatly and cleanly dressed as when they attend a Baramka party. They seat themselves in a circle on the best available mats, with the Baramka office-bearers on angereybs.[17] The office-bearers are the Sir,[18] Nazir, Omda, Sheikh, Kadi,[19] Effendi,[20] and Askari;[21] the young men adopting these offices have a temporary

[15] According to a note from Darfur quoted by Arber, a group of Baramka on trial there 'averred that they were only continuing a local custom, by which in the days of the Sultans young men at dances would assume the title of Sultan, Shartai [Sultan's local representative], etc., even in the presence of the real holders of these offices'.

[16] It was, no doubt, because of the feud existing between the Terakana and A. Salamy that the latter club had only one small meeting during my stay.

[17] If a genuine office-holder (unlikely to be a member) is present as a guest, he also is allowed to sit on an angereyb.

[18] Sir, the English word; here it derives, I think from the honour given to the late Sayed 'Abd el Raḥman el Mahdi, the then leader of the religious sect and political party with which the Humr are all associated.

[19] Judge in Islamic law.

[20] Clerk or white-collar worker mainly employed by the Government. The word dropped out of normal usage in the Sudan after independence.

[21] Soldier or policeman; 'chucker out' as Arber says. Note that the positions are all those held by Sudanese; the British staff (perhaps now also the Sudanese district officials) were not mimicked.

authority over others present of the kind that their namesakes have in real life. Offences against the code of proper behaviour are heard by the Kadi, who imposes fines, the 'pounds' of the fines being paid in piastres, which go to purchase tea and sugar for future parties. The Askari can eject any member guilty of a grave breach of etiquette.

Baramka distinguish themselves clearly on Baramka occasions from people who are blatant non-Baramka, whom they call Kamkara.[22] The Kamkary does not appreciate the etiquette of tea-drinking, and he goes ill-dressed. Baramka vilify the Kamkary, saying that he sits with his smock above his knees, or wears no drawers; a 'grey-mouthed donkey', he keeps a dirty tea-pot, and so on. Most Baramka songs bring in some pejorative reference to him:

> The Kamkary's neck is thick and grey
> The buttocks of his wife are big and fat
> The Kamkary found the Baramky's tea-leaves on the ground
> And took and filled his dish with them.[23]

Baramka songs, although inspired at the outset by tea, lead also to the subjects of politics and women. Here are extracts from a song sung by an old Baramky while addressing a cup of tea in his hand:

> The Maramky drinks you
> The holy man drinks you
> Sultan Babo drinks you
> Nazir Babo who from the beginning never cursed anyone
> Never hit anyone with a stick.
> Our Nazir's mouth is bright as electric light

[22] The word is based on a pun: Kamkary is something like the reverse of 'Maramky' (= Baramky, sing. of Baramka) in name and in behaviour.

There is no association of Kamkara as there is of Baramka. Although the word is often bandied about, and applied specially by Baramka to those who normally flout the conventions of tea-drinking, or hunt the monitor lizard, few actually call themselves Kamkara. (The monitor lizard is unclean to Muslims, but the meat is edible and the skin has a good commercial value. Hunters, to avoid spoiling the skin, go after it with their bare hands. The art is skilful, but because of the victim it is derided as being quite unmanly. What makes it worse, monitor hunters are supposed to get their skill by the use of charms and talismans—'*urug*, sold by Westerners. To the Baramky, the lizard has almost the status of a totem. He does not eat it, and there are many stories which relate to the protection which he gives it.)

[23] Regebat el Kamkary ghabsha o takhina
Wa ja'bat marata kebir o semina
El Kamkary haffa ligi tifl el Maramky
Khamma mela bea moa'ina.

These songs are not sung at the Baramka gatherings, but by members, or others, on any suitable occasion.

His beard is like thunderclouds
His beard is thick and black.
If the young men of his family come
He pulls up an angereyb and spreads a sheepskin on it
And talks with them, the kettle black
Forever boiling on the fire....

He goes on to praise the nazirs and omdas of the Humr, then describes the route the tea has taken to reach the tribe:

Your steam train they brought from Halfa
They brought it to Omdurman
To Aba Island
The great one took off his hat[24]
The small one prayed
It came by Kosti....[25]

There follows a line about railway signals and tickets which, though in itself meaningless, duly introduces these two elements of 'Government' culture in the context of tea. Then the tea came by El Obeid, 'where the merchants walk about in fours', and finally to Muglad. The singer goes on to praise the nazirs of the Humr and the Rizeygat at great length.

The aping of certain aspects of the Government and Government *mores* is very evident in Baramka parties, as the praising of them is evident in the songs. Nowadays it is only by some connexion with the government that a Humrawi can habitually wear clean white clothes.

[24] i.e. the European on board removed his hat as he passed Aba Island, in respect to the home of Mahdism.

[25] Beshribak el Maramky
Beshribak el faghara
Beshribak Sulṭan Babo
Beshribak el Naẓir Babo min tabba ma 'ayyer zol be khashma
Ma ḍarab zol be 'asa
Khashm naẓirna abyaḍ ily kin kahraba
Dign naẓirna majurat maṭara
Dign naẓirna ghulad o zerga
Naẓirna jo leo johala ahla
Zeggel el 'angereyb ferresh el furwa.
'Amal ma'hum wenesa kafateyrta zerga
Min el nar ma mtedilla....
Baburak jabo min Ḥalfa
Jabo Umm Durman
Jezira Aba
Kebirhum ṣill el barneṭṭy
O ṣaghirhum ṣalla
Kharrama be Kosti....

There is the emphasis on Government-inspired rank, on proper etiquette, on cleanliness and, especially, correctness of clothing, and on 'manly' behaviour in general. Scorn is directed against the Kamkara, who have no interest in these things. Some of the values expressed oppose values held by Humr in general outside the Baramka situation: the emphasis on dress opposes the dictum that clothes do not matter and that expenditure on personal accoutrements is money wasted; the solemn assumption of a hierarchy of authoritative officials hardly tallies with the opportunist nature of Humr politics. Indeed, Baramka adhere to Baramka values at times only: the Government and its *mores* are not really useful models for pastoral nomads. The point became very clear when I casually asked a close friend why, when teapots and even cooking pans were kept clean, kettles were always kept covered in soot. He snapped back: 'Who do you think you are, the Government or something, that you want us to have everything clean?' My friend was 'Nazir' of the local Baramka club.

Movements with similar mimicry of prestige-bearing offices have often been reported elsewhere, but many of these originated in towns or in situations where groups of vastly different culture and status were in close contact.[26] The interpretations of these are not directly applicable to the Baramka, because, in the first place, the Humr are aping fellow-tribesmen and fellow-Sudanese, although the positions they occupy are largely European innovations; and secondly, because Humr are not in constant and intensive contact with Government officials, and indeed spend most of the year in camps remote from Government centres. There is nothing like a class struggle within Dar Humr itself, although Humr are of course well aware that high Government officers lead lives which are easier and wealthier than their own. But for the most part they delight in their nazirs and their nazirs' hospitality, and I have never heard objection in principle to their institution. But the nazirs and other office-holders, with steady salaries, some

[26] In the Mbeni dance Mitchell (*The Kalela Dance*, p. 12) saw a 'vicarious participation' of Nyasalanders in the European social structure, but he denied that it expressed any hostility towards the ruling group through the satire of mimicry. The Kalela dancers of the Rhodesian Copperbelt (op. cit., p. 14) wear 'the smart clothes of the European business or professional men: Africans have come generally to accept the standards of these men as those to which they aspire'. Thus his interpretation differs from that of Banton for the 'Dancing Compins' of Sierra Leone (*West African City*, p. 182), which, he claims, 'develop partly in reponse to the need for role differentiation—for developing in a confused situation a new structure of roles and status. The most successful course is to take over an already known and attractive pattern. Titles of European derivation suit this purpose admirably . . . they have a connotation of power.'

of them leading sedentary lives, and all of them having power and frequent contact with Government officers, are themselves partly identified with the Government.

For these reasons I see the Baramka association in a different light, and regard it as a response to a confusion in the value system of the Humr. This confusion concerns the relations between manly behaviour, power, and the Government.

The harsh necessities of life for most of the Humr are a contrast to the comparative physical ease which is enjoyed by their nazirs and higher Government officials; Humr respect power and what it can bring them, but they respect also the hard work and asceticism that can lead to it, realizing at the same time that few of them can attain it. At the same time they respect the kind of life led by the cattleman with many followers, who is content with his cattle before him but who, should he lapse from his austerity, will see his herds dwindle.

The part which tea plays in daily life makes it a suitable symbol to express this confusion of values. It is of great importance to all Humr. It is drunk by everybody at dawn, and he who does not drink suffers a day-long headache.[27] It is drunk on two or three other occasions during the day. It is the immediate and indispensable offering to the fleetest and most casual guest. The luxury of meat is spoilt if it is not followed by tea as a chaser. Often it is used medicinally, like brandy to others. Its making, serving, and drinking are marked by care for etiquette, and there is some suggestion of ceremonial behaviour about the whole performance.[28] Yet at the same time Humr say that tea is a softener of men, that the Arabs have become slaves to it, that they sit around camp drinking it when they should be out on horseback looking for better pastures, that it takes money which should be spent on stock. It is new: Humr did not drink it before the Reoccupation, and the fact that it arrived at the same time as the new form of government made the association between the two close. In the songs all references to the Government and its officers are friendly: they lift their caps to Aba Island; God bless the Government, it brought us

[27] Called *giryef*. The complaint is justified, as I discovered when, on the Humr dietary régime, I sometimes had to forego my glass at daybreak.

[28] To make tea Humr boil a kettle; they take a drinking glass of tea and pour it into a teapot, followed by one or two glasses of sugar. They pour the water into the teapot and infuse it on embers. The tea maker pours out a glass to taste it for strength and sweetness, then puts it back to mix the brew. Glasses are poured, on a tray, to the number present, and handed round from right to left. A guest drinks two or three glasses, not one or four.

matches, torches, soap, *shibb*,[29] and tea; the District Officer's path goes through the tents of the most beautiful Humr women. A kind of tea-glass is named after the calf of an officer's leg; another after the waist of an expatriate wife.[30]

On their ceremonial occasions the Baramka appear to reflect values, as Humr see them, which are associated with the power of the new kind which the Condominium Government introduced, with its trappings of bureaucracy and authoritarianism and its association with dress and cleanliness. Humr can admire the Government for the power which it has; but at the same time they resent some of its aspects, and among themselves they scorn behaviour of the kind which officers of the Government practise, for this is no way to achieve wealth. It seems that for Humr tea is a symbol: it has become an integral part of their lives, but at the same time they experience a feeling of guilt because their use of it has made them lapse from the austerity which they claim as a necessary part of manly behaviour. At the same time tea is associated, for them, with the admired power-holders, the nazirs and others who dispense it most, and this in a sense justifies its use.

[29] *Shibb*, alum, a mineral collected on the Red Sea coast by pilgrims and used to purify water. Because the stuff came first during the Condominium, the Government is somehow responsible for its introduction.

[30] *Sag Safil*, the calf of Saville's leg, presumably in riding kit (Saville Bey was Governor of Darfur); *sulb el sitt*, the lady's waist.

9

TRIBAL POLITICS

THE relation between agnatic groups, political leadership, and administrative action, broached in Chapter 7, can be seen in more detail from certain events concerning the higher politics of the tribe. For evidence about their nature it is necessary to use historical and semi-historical material which is scarce and variable in reliability. My own inquiries yielded little historical information, and I have used the important article by Henderson[1] and notes placed at my disposal by Sayed Abu Jabr el Ḥaj[2] dealing with last century. Information on more recent episodes was elicited from various people in conversation.[3]

FIGHTS AND ALLIANCES IN THE NINETEENTH CENTURY

Before they came to Kordofan leadership of the tribe had lain with the Metanin group of Felaita,[4] who have since continued to lay claim to it on grounds of tradition. But the first hero of the Humr in their present territory was 'Ali bu Gurun, a holy man of Awlad Serur, whose leadership secured the Muglad for them. He is said also to have been responsible for adding considerably to the Humr population by attracting to the tribe the Salamat, the Jubarat, the Ziyud, and the Fayyarin.[5]

[1] 'A note on the migration of the Messiria tribe into South West Kordofan'.

[2] A brother of the present nazir of the Felaita. Hill's *Biographical Dictionary of the Anglo–Egyptian Sudan* acted as a check on some material and provided additional information on some personalities.

[3] Obviously this account has no claim to historical accuracy, yet the material collected in this way is all that can be used in discussing the problems this chapter raises. But although it includes inaccuracies, and perhaps even fabrications, nevertheless it is, in my opinion, justifiable to use it. This is because the material consists of statements of a kind which are current in the society, and which are local interpretations of, or beliefs about, historical events. The actual events may not have occurred as stated, but at least members of the society assert that they did. We can thus say that the events related are of a kind that Humr, with knowledge of the ways of their own society, reasonably believe could have happened, that the events are not inconsistent with what Humr know of their own social processes.

[4] Henderson, op. cit., p. 52. [5] Ibid., p. 65.

The ascendancy of Awlad Serur under ʿAli bu Gurun aroused the jealousy of the Metanin, the traditional leaders. ʿAli was followed as leader by another Seruri, Ismaʿin abu Jefna, and the latter's son, Jibril. No doubt much of the fighting hinged upon this jealousy. There were some straight quarrels between the Metanin and Awlad Serur. A dispute between them over garden land was settled when mediators found the Metanin were in the right. A Mutnani (i.e. one of the Metanin) agreed on another occasion to buy a female slave from a Seruri for goats, took the woman, but did not pay. The lineage of Awlad Serur concerned raided the camp and seized four cows, which led to a fight

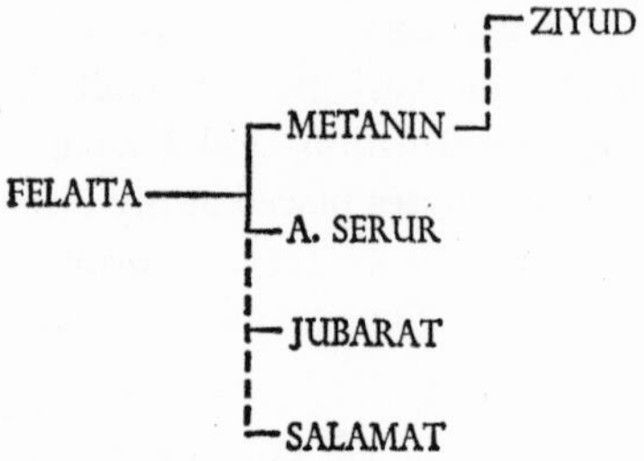

FIG. 13. Felaita bedanas during the Turkiya. The broken line indicates the incorporated strangers.

between the two sections. Again, some traders from the Hawazma, another Baggara tribe, were staying as guests among Jubarat and Salamat and during their stay bought cows, a slave, and a horse. On their way home some Metanin fell upon the merchants, took their booty, and released them. The merchants then sought help from their former hosts, who, with Awlad Serur as mediators, attempted to make the Metanin restore the goods. The Metanin refused, the others fought and defeated them.

Yet the alliances and hostilities shifted from time to time. On one occasion Awlad Serur allied themselves with the Metanin, raided Salamat and Jubarat at Lake Keylak, and inflicted a defeat. Jubarat and Salamat then banded together and beat Awlad Serur in revenge. This episode closed when Metanin and Awlad Serur allied themselves with some Hawazma and some Nuba and together defeated the Jubarat and Salamat. At one time the Metanin attempted to win the Jubarat and the Salamat over to their side in the leadership dispute, and during friendly negotiations a Mutnani killed two men, one each from the Jubarat and the Salamat. These thereupon rose and killed many of the Metanin in battle.

These events, whose chronological order is not known, were followed by an episode which led to the intervention of the Turkish Government. A Mutnani looted a slave and cattle from a Seruri. The Seruri pursued him, but was killed in the ensuing fight. A pious old Mutnani out looking for a stray beast came to a camp of Awlad Serur and was killed in vengeance, and his dead body was violated. In return for this the Metanin killed a Seruri and took his horse. Now the Metanin, Jubarat, and Salamat collected followers, beat Awlad Serur, and looted grain. Awlad Serur then ambushed and defeated them. Subsequently Awlad Serur went to the country of the Zurg to seek an alliance. This episode, noted by Sayed Abu Jabr, is a link with events related by Henderson, according to whom the move of Awlad Serur to Zurg country was made necessary by the inability of their leader Gebrin (i.e. Jibril) to keep the Metanin in hand. Under previous leaders, Awlad Serur had been strong enough to do so. Now, when a Seruri had killed a Mutnani, Jibril had refused to pay blood-money, and alienated the rest of the tribe from his leadership. The Messiriya Zurg, it appears, declined to receive him, so he attacked them and suffered a severe defeat.[6] From this period onwards the question of tribal leadership was affected by the contact established with the Government of the Sudan, the 'Turkiya'. According to one version of the history, after Jibril had been defeated he went to El Obeid to meet the governor of the province[7] and returned saying he had been recognized as nazir; for a short time after this he was the only man around whom the tribe would gather.

But at about this stage leadership reverted at long last to the Metanin in the person of Faris Ṣaluḥa. Henderson states that eventually Jibril, who had been in hiding, returned and made his submission to Faris. But external force was now coming from two directions: the Government of Kordofan was centred in El Obeid, and Zubeyr Pasha was operating from Bahr el Ghazal province, trying to win over the Rizeygat in order to effect a defeat upon the Sultan of Darfur. In the absence of Faris in the north, Zubeyr Pasha made contact with some Humr on the Bahr el Arab, persuaded one 'Ali Mesar of Awlad Kamil (Kelabna section) to collect a thousand head of cattle in tribute, and recognized him as head of the 'River Humr'. Later he also managed to appoint a merchant friend as *sanjak*, or military ruler, over the tribe, based on El Odaya. Presumably this strengthened the trading alliance

[6] Ibid., pp. 66–7. Henderson dates Jibril's defeat at about 1865.

[7] It will be remembered that Dar Humr was not an integral part of the administrative province of Kordofan.

which had existed between the Jellaba slave-merchants and the Humr. But Zubeyr Pasha went to Egypt and was forced to remain there in exile; and Gordon, the new Governor-General, in an effort to eradicate slavery, encouraged the Humr to hunt down and plunder their former Jellaba allies. 'Ali Mesar thus went out of favour, and his place was taken, according to popular choice, by 'Azzaz Idris, who was also of Awlad Kamil but of Dar Umm Sheyba section; and he is said to have been recognized as nazir by the Government at El Obeid. He lasted until he was shot in a camp of Awlad 'Umran six months later, and was succeeded by his brother Dud, who, with another brother

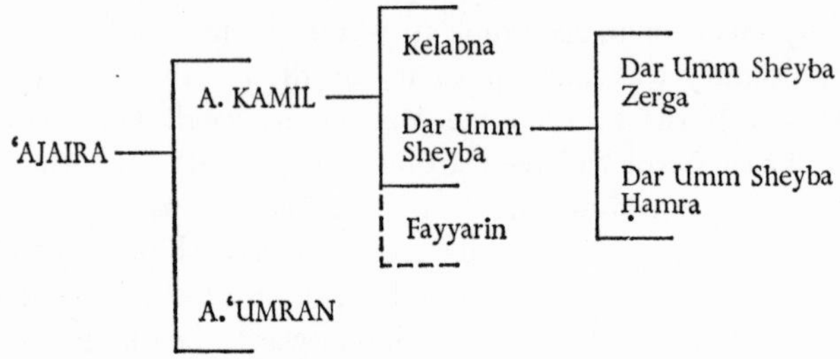

FIG. 14. 'Ajaira bedanas (in capitals) and sections mentioned in the Turkiya and Mahdiya episodes.

Mas'ud, accused 'Ali Mesar of complicity in the killing. The brothers allied themselves with the Rizeygat and even got Government assistance, but in spite of this 'Ali Mesar defeated them and Dud was killed. Now Mas'ud continued the struggle with the help of his Rizeygat allies; but the Mahdi was upon the country, and it was 'Ali Mesar, who first made effective contact with him, who finally succeeded in defeating Mas'ud. Faris Ṣaluḥa of the Metanin had gone to El Obeid to state his case, but he too was thwarted by the events of the Mahdiya.

There was a great exodus of Humr to Omdurman when the Mahdiya was established, and the Humr were among the 'Baggara Horse' in many of the battles. Today Humr are Mahdists to a man, but at the beginning there was some resistance. An anti-Mahdist faction in the tribe was led by Menawwir Habila (Awlad Kamil, Dar Umm Sheyba Zerga section). It consisted of some of that section, some Kelabna and some Fayyarin,[8] and perhaps representatives of other sections as well. At first they successfully resisted raids against them by Mahdist forces, but eventually they were defeated. Menawwir was killed, and the remnants spent the Mahdiya among the Dinka swamps.

[8] See Henderson, op. cit., p. 69.

These episodes, sketchy though our information about them is, give some indication of the nature of leadership and alliances. They suggest that the notion of leadership was always present, but also that there were few occasions when a leader effectively led the tribe as a whole. 'Ali bu Gurun and Faris Ṣaluḥa may have been successful for short periods. Much of the fighting during the last century appears to have been occasioned by rivalry between the Metanin and Awlad Serur for tribal leadership. Jubarat and Salamat allied themselves now with one, now with another. During this period Metanin and Awlad Serur are said to have entered a raiding alliance against the other two on one occasion; it may be possible to see in this a fusion of 'true' Felaita against the Salamat and Jubarat strangers.

But we are not led to believe that the 'Ajaira involved themselves in this struggle for leadership, at least at the early stage. We hear of conflict within the 'Ajaira: at one time one section of Awlad Kamil allied themselves with the Rizeygat, who had recently been hostile and who still occupied land on the Regeba Umm Bioro that had once belonged to Humr. Together they attacked another section of Awlad Kamil. Later the major issue of the acceptance of Mahdism divided the tribe in such a way that members of the same lineages were on different sides.[9] But there is no evidence of conflict between the two major sections, except indirectly and doubtfully; perhaps when 'Ali Mesar was recognized as head of the 'River Humr' (in Henderson's words), his followers were 'Ajaira, while the Felaita continued to follow Faris Ṣaluḥa; but this is mere conjecture. What is clear is that Felaita (Metanin and Awlad Serur) were in conflict among themselves in the early period for tribal leadership, and that the 'Ajaira (two sections of Awlad Kamil) were in conflict among themselves at the later period for tribal leadership. We are told, however, of 'Ajaira and Felaita, or parts of them, uniting against outsiders. This occurred under 'Ali bu Gurun; on another occasion a man of the Mezaghna, on hearing of the death of a Seruri at the hands of Awlad Ḥimeyd, another Baggara tribe, said 'The Felaita shall never mourn when the 'Ajaira are content', and gathered 'Ajaira to help the Felaita avenge themselves. And there are suggestions that 'Ajaira and Felaita combined against raids of Rizeygat and later of Messiriya Zurg.

[9] Henderson (loc. cit.) mentions that among the anti-Mahdist militants were Fayyarin (i.e. of the same omodiya as the man who led the Humr Mahdists to Omdurman—reference on same page) and Kelabna, the major lineage of A. Kamil to which the Mahdist 'Ali Mesar belonged.

TRIBAL POLITICS SINCE THE REOCCUPATION

In the nineteenth century, administration, if it can be said to have existed at all, was casual, unsystematic, and sporadic: yet it was starting to make itself felt, and recognition by the authorities became a matter of concern to some of the later aspirants to tribal leadership. Positive acts of administration seem to have been few, and did not include acts of a kind that would have required representative authorities for component sections of the tribe. The positive actions we know of are the appointment, or recognition, of men as nazirs of the tribe or part of it; the attempt by Zubeyr Pasha to raise tribute of a thousand head of cattle; occasional attempts by the El Obeid authorities to raise tribute; and the order by Gordon Pasha, in 1879, that the Baggara might loot and drive out the slaving Jellaba. An administrative organization was unnecessary.

One avowed intention of the Reoccupation was the establishment of a stable administration. Representative authorities and rational systems of legal and fiscal organization were a necessary part of this. The administration appointed officers through whom they could reach the tribe.

The main source for this period, the *Sudan Intelligence Reports*, does not give a connected account of the establishment of administration and the appointment of the first officials. The first mention is for September 1901, when Bimbashi Townsend, who had been appointed Inspector of Western Kordofan, based on Nahud, reported that 'Muhammad Ali Gulla, Nazir of the Humr tribe, came in; he has a dispute with one Hamid Yasin as to which of the two is nazir of the Fellaita section'. In January 1902 the Governor of Kordofan reported that 'Ali Julla was nominally nazir of all the Humr (above, p. 103). Then in 1903 the Governor of Kordofan visited Humr country, 'where he personally collected their tribute and appointed Ali Gula [Julla] as Nazir of the tribe and one Hag wad Yahob [El Ḥaj Ya'gub] was appointed Nazir of the Humr Fellaita'.[10] Sheikhs were recognized as described in the last chapter. Thus from the beginning the tribe had two nazirs, that of the 'Ajaira being nominally at least the nazir for the whole tribe as well. Henderson pointed out that the ancient claim of the Metanin (Felaita), for leadership of the whole tribe could 'no longer be regarded seriously with the Ajaira in a two-thirds

[10] *S.I.R.* 86, 90. 104. But according to another report in the Kordofan provincial files El Ḥaj Ya'gub was the third of the Felaita nazirs, having been preceded by Sheyn Ḥamdi and Ḥamid Yasin, both of the Metanin (the latter based his claim on his close kinship with Faris Ṣaluḥa). Both were quickly replaced.

majority, and when Ali Mesar waived his claim on grounds of old age and illness, there was no bar to the appointment of Ali el Julla'.[11]

'Ali Julla is an important figure in Humr politics: he was the first nazir appointed by the Condominium and he and his descendants have ruled the 'Ajaira ever since. Henderson says it was he whom 'Ali

'ALI JULLA
Nazir of 'Ajaira
Nazir of Humr

- NIMR
  Nazir of 'Ajaira
  - BABO
    Nazir of 'Ajaira
    Nazir Umum of Humr
    Nazir Umum of Humr, Messiriya and Ngok Dinka
    Senator
  - 'ALI
    Nazir of 'Ajaira
    Member of Parliament
- MEKKI
  Court President, Abyad
  Omda/Court President, Muglad town

EL ḤAJ AJBER
Nazir of Felaita

- SEREYR
  Omda of Jubarat
  Court President, Keylak
  Court President, Abyad
  Nazir of Felaita
  - NUR EL DIN
    Court President, Keylak
  - ?
    Court President, Keylak
- ṢUBEYR
  Omda of Jubarat
- ABṲ JABR
  Executive Officer, Muglad

FIG. 15. The ruling families of 'Ajaira and Felaita with some of the posts their leading members have held in Dar Humr.

Mesar sent in the first instance to make contact with the Mahdi. Before this he had acted as a guide on some of Gordon's journeys and in return had received money and slaves.[12] At Omdurman during the Mahdiya he was appointed an attendant of the Khalifa; here he gained

[11] Henderson, op. cit., p. 70. The Intelligence Reports show Henderson's statement that 'Ali Julla was not appointed until 1905 to be mistaken.

[12] 'Ali Julla, 'The defeat of Hicks Pasha', p. 123. He claims to have received 45 slaves. It may be that the sudden access of wealth from Gordon's hands laid the ground for the influence that 'Ali Julla and his family have subsequently had in the tribe.

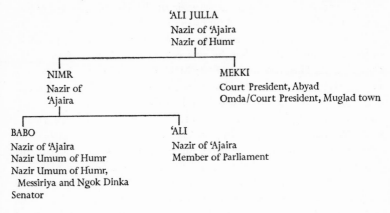

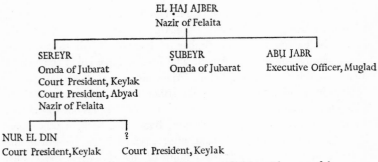

the friendship of Slatin Bey, who, as Governor of Darfur under the Turkiya, had been imprisoned in Omdurman. Slatin escaped, and returned later to Sudan with the Reoccupation forces in the capacity of Director of Military Intelligence. By this time 'Ali Julla had been taken prisoner after the final defeat of the Khalifa in 1899. Slatin recommended his appointment as nazir of the Humr, and he became at the same time nazir of the 'Ajaira section.

El Ḥaj Ya'gub, appointed nazir of the Felaita in 1903, lasted in office only until 1907, when he was replaced by Mekki Ḥasab (also called Mekki Ḥasoba), again of the Metanin, who lost his job in 1914 for 'falsifying a divorce'.[13] His replacement was Aris Mahe, again of the Metanin. In 1920 Aris was found to have accepted a £20 bribe; and this discovery marked the end of the Metanin control of the Felaita nazirate. The Intelligence Report states: 'It was obvious that the stronger personalities of the tribe, finding it impossible to get themselves elected, had decided to avoid the still greater evil of inclusion with the Ajaira . . . by choosing as nazir a man whom they considered would be powerless to interfere with their own activities.' The 'stronger personalities' who had been candidates were Adim Yusuf, of the Ziyud, a former lineage of the Metanin, and Shweyn el Ḍeyf, omda of the Metanin. Instead, they put up El Ḥaj Ajber, omda of the Jubarat.

Far from being a weak man, El Ḥaj Ajber created for his own family among the Felaita a position similar to that which 'Ali Julla created for his family among the 'Ajaira. The former have ruled the Felaita since 1920, the latter have ruled the 'Ajaira since 1901. Both nazirs have relatives in positions of power in the tribe. 'Ali Julla himself ruled the 'Ajaira until about 1915, when he was removed[14] in favour of his son, Nimr, who died in 1924. Nimr's son, Babo, has been in office ever since; first as nazir of the 'Ajaira, after 1938 as Nazir Umum of the Humr, and after 1942 as Nazir Umum of the Messiriya, the Humr, and the Ngok Dinka. He was also a national Senator for a short period. After Babo became Nazir Umum, his half-brother 'Ali Nimr became nazir of the 'Ajaira. For a short time he was a member of Parliament. His father's brother, Mekki 'Ali Julla, was a court president until he became omda, with a court, over the settled people of Muglad town and surrounding districts. Some others of his immediate kin live a settled life in the town of Muglad, one of them holding the office of 'guarantor' at the cattle market.

[13] Kn. P. CR/66/E.13, p. 237.

[14] He was described in administrative reports as being a 'notorious eater of his people'.

By 1945 Nazir El Ḥaj Ajber of the Felaita was aging. His son Sereyr had already been a court president at Abyad and was now acting unofficially as deputy nazir. The Metanin unsuccessfully fielded a candidate to regain the nazirate. In confirming the appointment of Sereyr to the nazirate the administration remarked that the Metanin candidate (the son of Shweyn el Ḍeyf, and the then omda of the Metanin) 'is not of any such superior qualities as to warrant dropping the house of El Haj Ajber'.[15] Sereyr is still nazir; his brother is omda of the Jubarat; Nur el Din, the son of Sereyr, was court president at Keylak until he joined the Game Department of the Sudan Government and his place as court president was taken by a younger brother. Another brother of Sereyr, Abu Jabr, became executive officer of the tribe, stationed at Muglad, until he was later promoted in Sudan Government service to a post in another province.[16]

The Reoccupation had a profound effect on Humr leadership in two respects. First, it recognized the existence of two main sections ('sub-tribes' or even 'tribes', as many of the reports called them)[17] and, on the grounds of administrative convenience and stability, allotted a permanent nazirate to each. It thus created power positions which had to be continually filled, and the function of the offices was to exercise administrative control over specific groups of people. It picked out agnatic divisions and gave them a rigidity and value they had not had before; and for administrative purposes these became the only divisions recognized. In the last century, tribesmen allowed a few men for short periods to have power; now, men chosen by the consent of the majority received Government backing and would continue to do so while they remained in the Government's favour.

Secondly, the Government, while saying that it did not necessarily hold to the hereditary principle in nazirates, showed a preference, so long as there were suitable men in the family concerned, to replace office-bearers by kinsmen. This, combined with the establishment in 1938 of the 'Nazir Umum', has created a rivalry of some bitterness between the family of El Ḥaj Ajber and the family of 'Ali Julla, which matches the wider expression of rivalry between the Felaita and the 'Ajaira as a whole.

[15] Kn. P. CR/66/E.43.

[16] The last two were the only Humr with whom I could converse in English.

[17] For a short time, after 1910, 'Ajaira and Felaita even belonged to different administrative districts of Kordofan province, the Felaita being joined up with the western Nuba.

This rivalry is apparent in some of the episodes which have aroused tribal interest since the late 1930s.

1. *The court at Abyad.* The first of these affairs arose over the appointment of Mekki 'Ali Julla, the present omda and court president of the settled population of Muglad, to a court presidency at Lake Abyad. This court is in the depths of Felaita country, in the south-east corner of Dar Humr; Mekki was a son of 'Ali Julla and father's

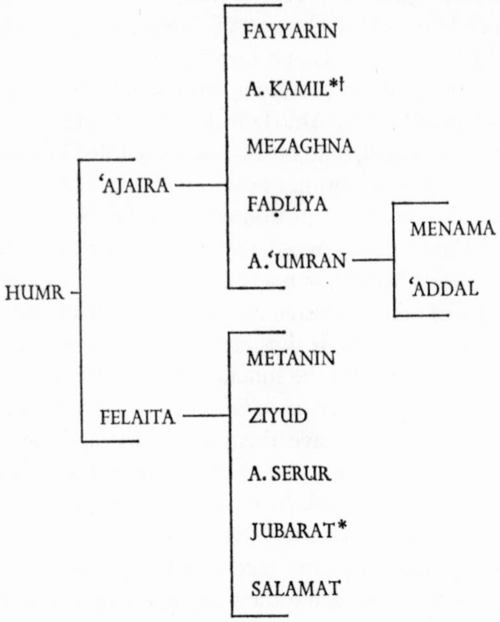

FIG. 16. The division of the Humr into omodiyas, illustrating recent historical episodes.

* Location of nazirs' families.
† Location of Nazir Umum.

brother of Nazir Babo, who, together with the District Commissioner, and with the agreement of Nazir El Ḥaj of the Felaita, announced the appointment. While Nazir El Ḥaj was always a moderating influence, his son and deputy, Sereyr, was more aggressive in upholding what he saw as the proper rights of the Felaita. Accordingly he viewed the appointment with disfavour and succeeded in gathering the Felaita omdas to confront Nazir Babo at Muglad. Nazir Babo, at that time Nazir Umum of the Humr, replied that arrangements had already been made with the Felaita nazir, and that the affair was closed.

The District Commissioner answered in like fashion when they approached him. Mekki's tenure of office at Abyad court was marked by continual accusations on the part of the Felaita and counter-accusations on the part of Mekki and his followers. After a short time another British official, attracted by the trouble at Abyad, declared that it was a bad thing for an 'Ajaira man to have a court in Felaita country; and the court was temporarily closed.

2. *The alleged black market.* The Second World War affected the Humr largely by the introduction of rationing of tea, sugar, and cloth. The arrangement for distributing the rations was that Nazir Babo should share the goods out to the omodiyas according to the ratios laid down for the distribution of blood-money coming from outside the tribe.[18] Since everything passed through the hands of Nazir Babo, the situation provided scope for accusations that not all of the material was distributed and that, in short, he ran a black market.[19] The Felaita congregated in the Babanusa; they beat the *khadim*, the drum call to gather the people in an emergency. I did not discover the end of this affair, although one consequence was that the District Commissioner got the active Sereyr made nazir, and El Ḥaj went into an honoured retirement. In doing this, the D.C. was answering a demand from the Felaita for aggressive representation and a forceful counter to the family of the 'Ajaira nazirs.

3. *The court at Keylak.* When Sereyr was established as nazir of the Felaita, he is said to have persuaded the Felaita omdas to swear on the Koran that they would accept his son Nur el Din as his unofficial deputy. The court presidency at Keylak had to be filled, and Nazir Babo went there to discuss an appointment. The Felaita omdas put up the name of Nur el Din; but Nazir Babo refused the suggestion, saying it did not come from the people. On his way back to Muglad he met 'Isa Shweyn (the brother of Musa Shweyn, the Metanin omda), and gave him assurance of his support if 'Isa had sufficient following to be able to claim the court presidency. 'Isa began an intrigue against Sereyr and the omdas over rationing: he said that of the rationed goods delivered to the Felaita, about £50 worth from each omodiya was sold illegally. The Felaita omdas responded that they were only doing what

[18] *Diat el soff*, see p. 102.

[19] In these episodes I am reporting not proven facts but simply allegations, the interpretation of events upon which a political group based aggressive action. In this particular case the allegation is hardly unexpected, in view of the way the Humr consider that those in authority act, the rivalry between the two families, and the scarcity of these highly valued goods in wartime. This mode of political action, which Humr call the *fitna*, will be discussed later.

the 'Ajaira omdas were doing: and so the intrigue rebounded. The District Commissioner heard about all this; he jailed 'Isa for three months for false accusation.[20] Meanwhile the Ziyud, the Jubarat, and the Salamat supported Nur el Din, while the Metanin were against him and Awlad Serur remained undecided. But the District Commissioner re-entered the affair, addressed the men of Awlad Serur, and told them that if Nur el Din were appointed to Keylak he would re-open the Abyad court; in saying this he had his eye fixed significantly on the Seruri notable, El Riḥeyd Dirhan. This brought Awlad Serur round; Nur el Din and El Riḥeyd both received court presidencies. The Metanin alone remained discontented; but this was by now expected.

4. *The revolt of Awlad 'Umran.* The only occasion when parties came close to a show of force was an affair mainly within the 'Ajaira, but Awlad 'Umran are said to have had the silent support of the Felaita in their aspirations. Every year or so a cattle census is organized by the administration for the purpose of bringing tax lists up to date. On this occasion Nazir Babo accused two sheikhs of Awlad 'Umran of hiding cattle from the enumerators. He sent out local police to check. Awlad 'Umran said they had no more; Nazir Babo responded that the police were going anyway; and if they found more, what would Awlad 'Umran do? Awlad 'Umran replied that Nazir Babo could 'eat' them. The police found thirty more cattle; they were seized, sold at an auction, and the cash went to the tribal treasury. Awlad 'Umran gathered, beat the *khadim*; youths galloped to and fro, very excited, and a man was speared to death in the tumult. The notables swore on the Koran that they would not 'cross the wadi' (i.e. migrate south over the Wadi el Ghalla), thus threatening starvation for their herds, until the nazirate in Awlad Kamil was finished. Meanwhile Nazir Babo was told of the threats, and the *khadim* was beaten in Muglad. It was harvest time, with most of the 'Ajaira in or near their gardens. Soon Fayyarin, Awlad Kamil, Mezaghna, and Faḍliya all came into Muglad in what informants described as a most impressive crowd. The omodiyas gathered around courtyards in the town which their omdas used. News arrived that Awlad 'Umran were coming in force to kill Babo. Old women danced the *fanjfanj* in honour of war and vengeance. Nazir Babo's massive support was disturbed temporarily when the crowds were gathered at his house, for one of the Fayyarin of Awlad

[20] There were many other accusations and counter-accusations at the same time; it is impossible to tell now which, if any, were true, or which 'Isa was jailed for.

Kimeyl section, which had years before left Awlad Kamil because of a grudge, proclaimed 'we do not want the Mezaghna and the Faḍliya, we and Awlad Kamil ourselves can defend Babo'. The Mezaghna and the Faḍliya created a furore and walked out to go back to their camps; Mekki 'Ali Julla called them back, said that the Fayyari who had spoken was a dog, and persuaded them to stay. Babo declared that his support without them was nothing. He sent word to Awlad 'Umran that he had the Government behind him. They waited: Awlad 'Umran did not come, and the affair fizzled out. Later the breach was mended. Babo called a great meeting of the 'Ajaira, without Awlad 'Umran; they decided that after all Awlad 'Umran were their brothers, and that Babo should make restitution to them of the money realized at the auction, which should be delivered to the original owners; and reconciliation was made in the traditional manner.

The 'silent backing' of the Felaita, so 'Ajaira told me, arose from their hope of being able to exploit the confusion which would result from the march on Muglad. They would seize cattle; they would try hard to seize the nazirate. 'For the Felaita are our enemies', 'Ajaira said.

5. *The Legislative Assembly.* When the Legislative Assembly opened in Khartoum a member was required from the district covered by Dar Messiriya Rural Council. The Felaita gathered and, the Metanin dissenting, decided to propose Abu Jabr, the educated brother of their nazir, and executive officer at Muglad. They would ask Nazir Babo not to stand; the Felaita would not vote for him, but together 'Ajaira and Felaita would demolish any candidate the Messiriya Zurg might put up. Nazir Babo would not agree, and the Felaita then tried to enlist the support of the Metanin. At first they refused, stung by the possibility of even more power going to the Jubarat. Their omda Musa Shweyn said that he was prepared to go and live anywhere, but he did not consider himself to belong to the Felaita. Adim Yusuf, the omda of the Ziyud who had led the deputation to Nazir Babo, then declared that Babo had insulted them all by saying that the Felaita were too few to get what they wanted. This brought Musa and the Metanin over to him; they swore that from that day on they were Felaita. Later, when it was shown that Abu Jabr was too young to stand, he had to withdraw. The Felaita then approached Awlad 'Umran, who had fielded a candidate, promising their support: this was shortly after their revolt. But somehow El Ḥaj exerted his moderating influence again, and persuaded everyone to vote for Babo. Nazir Sereyr made a stipulation that when the next political office arose he

himself should stand; but Babo managed affairs adroitly, and it was Babo who later became Senator.

6. *The Parliamentary elections.* In 1954 the first Parliamentary elections took place in the Sudan. Ibrahim 'Ali Julla, Nazir Babo's uncle, was announced as a candidate, while Nazir Sereyr put up Nur el Din, his son, who was court president at Keylak.[21] In order to understand the course of events, we have to appreciate the links which the Humr in general and Babo's family in particular have with the Mahdist movement. We have seen (p. 135) that 'Ali Mesar, through his kinsman 'Ali Julla (also of the Awlad Kamil, Kelabna section), was the first in the tribe to make contact with the Mahdi; that most of the tribe went to Omdurman as Ansar, or followers, in active support of the Mahdi and his successor the Khalifa. On their return to Dar Humr, the tribe continued to hold fast to the Mahdist way of religion; many made pilgrimages to Aba Island on the Nile, where the Mahdi's posthumous son, Sayed 'Abd el Raḥman, became the leader of the movement, and this was almost equivalent in religious value to the Mecca pilgrimage. Sayed 'Abd el Raḥman won the favour of the British rulers; he was knighted. Gradually the movement, from being religious, turned politico-religious; the followers of the Umma party are largely Ansar, the followers of the Mahdist sect. At the time of the elections they stood for Sudanese independence and friendship with Britain, while their main opponents at first favoured union, and later friendship, with Egypt. In his work in Khartoum Babo became a personal friend of many of the leading Mahdists, and eventually married into the family. The descendants of the Mahdi are wealthy; great farm owners, much of their income arises from the profits of pump-irrigated cotton. They own palaces in Khartoum and Omdurman and entertain on a lavish scale. But to the Humr their greatest quality is that of *baraka*, holiness, deriving from their connexion with the original Mahdi.

Nazir Babo could thus use his links with the movement and with Khartoum. Since Ngok Dinka were in the same constituency and their support was known to be split, the outcome of the election was uncertain. Nazir Babo's uncle Ibrahim withdrew his candidature, and his father-in-law, Sayed El Faḍil Maḥmud, a grandson of the first Mahdi and a resident of Omdurman, stood instead. Sayed El Faḍil visited the

[21] There were three other candidates: two minor figures—one of the Fayyarin and one of A. Kamil, Dar Umm Sheyba Zerga lineage, both of whom were expected to have votes only from their minor lineages; and a merchant (not a Humrawi) in Muglad town, who would attract the votes only of his fellows. The first four candidates were all Mahdists of the Umma political party, the followers of Sayed 'Abd el Raḥman el Mahdi.

tribe; people gazed on him with awe, knelt and kissed his clothing. Nazir Sereyr of the Felaita was nonplussed; it is said that he answered by offering to exchange Nur el Din's candidature in the election for the presidency of a new court shortly to be established at Nyama; but Babo, seeing the effect that Sayed El Faḍil had on his people, refused. Sayed El Faḍil won the election, his support consisting, apart from the 'Ajaira, of one of the Dinka factions and, so it is reported, the Metanin omodiya of the Felaita. But the fear of divine displeasure against those who did not support the Mahdi's kinsman was not enough to prevent a solid block of votes for Nur el Din.

7. *The court at Nyama.* A court was established at Nyama in 1955. Nyama lies upon the line to the east of which the Felaita and to the west of which the 'Ajaira have traditional migratory routes and camp sites. The area around Nyama, the Firshai, had been used by both sections as dry-season pasturage. The omodiyas which used it most (Ziyud and Awlad 'Umran respectively) could point to landmarks to prove their association with the place—old tombs of holy men of their groups. In the late 1940s a man from Awlad 'Umran started, with great success, to plant cotton there. Within a few years Nyama became one of the biggest cotton centres of Dar Humr, and was attracting planters from most omodiyas of the tribe. The final decision to appoint a man of Awlad 'Umran as court president was eventually made on the ground that it was one of their number who had opened the place up for cotton and had thus attracted enough people to the area to make the establishment of a court worth while. In terms of Humr custom the problem posed was unanswerable, for no one group has a greater right to any place than any other group. In forcing the tribe to find an answer, the administration furthered the association of group with locality. A similar argument exists between the Jubarat and the Salamat, of whom the former have control of Keylak court. Normally Jubarat camp to the south and Salamat to the north of the lake. Salamat claim that it was they who cleared Keylak of enemies many generations ago, and that therefore they have a special right to it; and they demand the court presidency.

POWER, ALLIANCES, AND ADMINISTRATIVE ACTION

The administrative processes which impinged most on the tribe during the Condominium were taxation, cattle census and inoculation, the administration of justice, the maintenance of public order, and the appointment of successive officers. The kind of administration which then existed made it convenient for administrators to have stable groups to work through and to deal with them through appointed officers. The establishment of leaders over identifiable and relatively stable groups was especially important for these tasks, since the tribe was nomadic and locality alone could not serve as a basis for administration. Already, bounded and recognizable groups existed, and many men put forward their claims for recognition as spokesmen for groups of agnates—groups of the kind over which informal leadership had been exerted in the past. The Government found on taking control of the tribe that it consisted of related lineages. 'Ajaira and Felaita have remained as they were at the time and so have the *bedanas* which became omodiyas; but the Government made some adjustments by allowing lineages which were big and wealthy enough, and under forceful spokesmen, to be granted omdaships.[22] Thereupon it anchored these groups. Nazirs and omdas are here to stay; they hold positions over the units through which the administration works. As we shall see, the administration has left considerable latitude at the lower levels of tribal segmentation, but at the higher levels the arrangements of parts is stable. The administration helped stabilization of another kind by conniving at a hereditary principle for the nazirates; the same principle has often been applied to the omdaships as well.

While 'Ajaira and Felaita have retained the same composition, events have shown that these names do not coincide with groups that unite in political action. Humr speak of them as if they were political units. The names carry, however, the sense of 'the 'Ajaira less dissident members', and 'the Felaita less dissident members'. Administratively they are more accurate. It is the same with omodiyas. If it is said 'Awlad Kamil had their cattle inoculated yesterday', then Awlad Kamil had, in accordance with administrative arrangements; but the statement which I heard, 'the Felaita backed Nur el Din as Parliamentary candidate', is true only so long as we regard the Metanin as a dissident section that did not, in this event, participate.

The brotherhood of the closest does not entirely explain alliances. In Humr dogma an incorporated stranger is no less a brother than is a blood kinsman. Our term 'agnate' assumes this, since it assumes the equal value of biological and putative kinship. On the agnatic-segmentary model, a question which involves the two major segments of a

[22] Another characteristic of the 'new' omodiyas is that all could point to an origin separate from that of the group in which they had been incorporated. All except Faḍliya and Mezaghna were strangers; Faḍliya were genealogically distinguished from A. 'Umran, and Mezaghna from A. Kamil.

unit aligns their respective members as allies. For Humr, one such question is the leadership of the tribe, which brings 'the Felaita' into a conflict of rivalry with 'the 'Ajaira', as Humr themselves say. But the Felaita do not act in unison, for to the Metanin the leadership of the tribe has been (except for the occasion in the episode of the Legislative Assembly) of less importance than the leadership of the Felaita. That is to say, a quarrel within the Felaita has continued to be operative when a wider quarrel, between 'Ajaira and Felaita, was being actively pursued, and the former took precedence as far as the Metanin were concerned.

When Awlad 'Umran attacked the nazirate the situation was more complex, because what they were attacking was a family which held both overall power in the tribe and power within the 'Ajaira; but the threats were made against the person of the Nazir Umum. Here it was irrelevant to Awlad 'Umran that the Felaita were rivals for the Nazir Umum's power; and they did not behave as if they felt obliged to keep 'Ajaira ranks consolidated against Felaita attacks. Awlad 'Umran and the Metanin have both been rebels, against 'Ajaira and Felaita respectively, over the question of leadership. Other similar examples of the failure of the sections to align themselves in the manner of agnatic 'fission and fusion' are evident in others of the episodes mentioned.

I suggested that the brief alliance of Metanin and Awlad Serur (p. 130) might be seen as a reflection of a different method of arranging the Felaita lineages: an alliance of the 'real' against the 'stranger' Felaita. Among the 'Ajaira it is perhaps possible to interpret the revolt of Awlad 'Umran as an alliance of the descendants of Idris Ka'b against those of Muḥammad Kheyr; but I reserve until later the discussion of the relation between the various modes of segmentation of the tribe.

The confused accounts of the last century give us little to go on for an understanding of the changes in forms of alliance which have been wrought by the new administrative system. Accordingly I would rather not draw firm conclusions about it. *A priori*, however, the establishment of permanent positions, some of them lucrative and all of them involving an access to power by the successful candidate, ought to intensify the rivalry among these groups which can put forward candidates for a position. For the office of omda, in particular, we shall find this evident. The new administration brought with it not only a formalism at certain levels which the old system lacked; it also introduced a number of new elements into political life. A dissident section wishing to attack a nazir has to contend not only with a nazir and his backers, but also with the national administration, which puts him there and keeps him there as long as it conveniently can. The entrenched position of the two great families and the fact that the Government always backs them for administrative convenience mean that rival sections have to go to great lengths to try and discredit them, particularly in the eyes of the administration. Although bribery or running black markets of rationed goods are items which, if my analysis in Chapter 8 is correct, need not bring their perpetrators disrespect from fellow-Humr, they are used in order to bring the nazirs into disrepute with the national administration, which holds the final power.

I think we may also read into Government action an interest in intensifying the sense of unity of the groups which have been stabilized by being made into administrative units, and an attempt to create a balance of power between the two main sections of the tribe. This is perhaps a necessary response, on administrative grounds, to a situation which was of the administration's own making. Humr told me that in the period 1924 to 1938 the relationship between 'Ajaira and Felaita, as personified by their nazirs, was very happy. Babo and El Ḥaj were equals; at court cases involving litigants from each section they sat side by side. The creation of the overall nazirate, which was doubtless simplified for the administration because Babo with his towering personality was the obvious candidate and 'Ajaira outnumbered Felaita, was the start of the intense rivalry. When Felaita began to appear discontented, the administration chose not to rely further on El Ḥaj's moderation, but to replace him by his aggressive son, who would be able to further Felaita interests in the face of 'Ajaira ascendancy. The episode of the court at Keylak, described above, is particularly instructive. It showed the District Commissioner favouring the appointment of a man of the nazir's family to a court presidency; it showed his willingness to bury certain facts which might have damaged both the nazirates; and it punished a man of a lineage hostile to its own nazir. Apparently, the nazirates as established had become so convenient to the administration that it would go to great lengths to support them.

A further consequence of the arrival of stable administration was that now it was no longer possible, at the higher levels, entirely to divorce places from people. In general, Humr custom demands that, individually owned agricultural land apart, no person or group of persons should have specific rights to land in Dar Humr; that, as they now express it, the land belongs to the Government and is open for exploitation by any member of any group. Leadership in the past was independent of local considerations. A leader controlled not a stretch of land with people on it but a lineage or an alliance of people, wherever they might be. But the problem of locality became important when it was decided to establish courts in various parts of the country in addition to the courts of the nazirs in Muglad: for a large part of the year the nazirs' courts were too far from the tribe for convenience and efficiency, and although the nazirs did hear lawsuits on tour, it was impossible for them to cover all the districts in use in the dry season. Local courts were established[23] to act during seasons of the year when there were people in the vicinity. These courts were tied to places; they required the appointment of court presidents, and the problem arose of deciding from which omodiya or main section of the tribe it was appropriate to appoint presidents to courts in these places.

Apart from the court of Grimti, which lies squarely in the country which the Fayyarin occupy in the dry season, the establishment of these courts has caused dispute. Humr regard the presidencies as jobs which are highly respectable, and a salary is attached. They see it as appropriate that the Grimti court should be in the hands of the Fayyarin. The Abyad court is in land usually occupied by Awlad Serur in summer, but many members of other omodiyas (mostly Felaita) have cotton gardens there. Sereyr was a court president there before he got the nazirate: then he went to Keylak court, while Mekki 'Ali Julla of Babo's family was appointed at Abyad. This appointment resulted in the episode of the court at Abyad (described above), and the District Commissioner announced that it was unsuitable to have someone from the 'Ajaira in office over Felaita: a Seruri was appointed in his place.

An important and permanent local association is that of the 'Ajaira with Muglad town. Muglad was established as the administrative centre for the Humr in the early years of the Condominium; there had been no town there before. It lies, surrounded by 'Ajaira gardens, in the north-west part of the Muglad. Nearly all the Felaita gardens are eastwards, along the Wadi el Ghalla. Muglad remained the chief town of Dar Humr until El Fula was built, in traditional Felaita country, in the early 1950s to become the administrative capital for the Dar Messiriya Rural Council; Muglad still remained the capital of the Humr, the home of the Nazir Umum, and the biggest market in the country. The very fact of Muglad's position was a cause of Felaita discontent;

[23] Local courts for Humr exist at Keylak, Abyad, Nyama, and Grimti.

for Felaita who had business with the administration or who came to market were there as visitors, while 'Ajaira were at home. Consequently, with the rise of El Fula the Felaita nazir made it his own headquarters and associated it closely with his group, in order to have a place of business to match that of the 'Ajaira.

The establishment by the administration of power positions at the top levels of an agnatic lineage system has meant a rigid structure, a growing association of lineage with place, and an intensive rivalry for the new positions available. At the lower levels, in the structure and politics of the omodiya, where administrative influence is slighter, the system is more complex and more fluid.

10

THE OMODIYA

THE OMODIYA AS A LINEAGE

THE omodiya is the smallest lineage which has been 'frozen' for administrative purposes. This treatment has enhanced its importance. The omodiyas of today correspond largely, though not entirely, to groups which the Condominium administration first recognized. Although people now discuss the nineteenth-century groups as if they were the same as the present omodiyas, it would not be safe to infer that in the nineteenth century these units were any more distinctive and autonomous than groups of other sizes, because people may discuss the past by extrapolating from the present. At any rate the appointment of omdas to control and represent omodiyas increased rather than decreased the degree of permanence and identity of these units.

Omodiyas are large enough to allow of much internal political activity. This chapter and the next deal respectively with groupings and processes involved in it.

It is possible to see the component parts of an omodiya arranged in a variety of ways, but again, within the omodiya, there is a widely accepted dogmatic arrangement of parts. As the tribe is divided into two main sections, and each of these main sections is divided into omodiyas, according to the dogmatic mode, so further the omodiyas are divided into major lineages, these into minor lineages, and these into surras; in a few cases there are 'medium' lineages as well. This mode, in which each lineage has an independence and a status equal to its collaterals, and in which collaterals are socially equidistant from one another, is the standard, dogmatic form in which lineage relationships are expressed. A second kind of grouping is based on the knowledge that some lineages are and others are not descended from the omodiya founder. A third kind of grouping, using a more detailed genealogy, states that among collaterals some are closer than others. These modes are analogous to those already discussed for the larger groups. In addition, within the omodiya the officials, the tribute sheikhs, have followings which do not necessarily correspond to any of the above; and finally political action and blood-money co-operation may bring people together in still another way.

While administrative action has had the effect of stabilizing the two main sections of the tribe and the omodiyas, it has not been responsible for stabilizing any of the smaller groups; yet the standard form of segmentation there seems to be just as 'dogmatic' as it is at higher levels, and certainly has an important place in the Humr scheme of political values. It may be that the arrangement for the payment and receipt of blood-money have involved the need for some stability at this level of the kind which the administration later created for the larger groups.

The Mezaghna omodiya has the sections that are shown in the Appendix, p. 216. Humr often inquire of one another about the composition of their lineages, and they get answers in the form 'the Mezaghna are three'. Similarly, one of the major lineages, Dar Abu Timani, has five sections, and one of the minor lineages, Awlad Salamy, has seven surras, as the diagram shows. But further inquiry reveals some sections to be 'strangers' and others to be especially closely related to one another, although to outsiders they are described as equidistant. The reason given for additional closeness may be that one group, dogmatically represented as an equal collateral, had split off from another, or that a female link of importance is present in addition to the male link. In the Mezaghna omodiya a strengthening female link is claimed between 'Ariya and Dar Bakheyt major lineages, while the surra 'Iyal Ganiṣ is supposed to have split off from 'Iyal Rigeyby, and 'Iyal Bulola later from 'Iyal Ganiṣ.

These facts were very troublesome to discover, and it was not until half-way through my second year that I hit upon the appropriate question to elicit them: 'If 'Iyal Ganiṣ died out, who would take their property?' For it is especially in relation to residual property rights that Humr regard the grouping of collaterals as important. In brief, collateral lineages which are regarded as being equal share the property in equal measure; but if one is closer than others this one has all the residual rights. Thus 'Iyal Ganiṣ and 'Iyal Bulola have reciprocal residual rights which exclude claims by all others. If 'Iyal Rigeyby died out, 'Iyal Ganiṣ and 'Iyal Bulola would share the property equally. 'Iyal Rigeyby would take the property if both 'Iyal Ganiṣ and 'Iyal Bulola died out. The other surras of Awlad Salamy minor lineage would benefit only on the dying out of all these three.[1] Other links

[1] This close relationship between certain parts of A. Salamy had practical significance when blood-money was finally distributed following the death of a man of I. Rigeyby. See Appendix 5.

within the minor lineage are between 'Iyal Belebbo and 'Iyal Jabir, and between 'Iyal Beyyen and 'Iyal Damura.

All this contradicts the projection of the lineage as a close-knit band of allies with each collateral segment of equal status. In fact the seven surras of Awlad Salamy are grouped, in this mode, into three lots. Similar considerations apply to the arrangement of larger lineages; for instance, Dar Abu Timani major lineage consists of five lineages when reckoned in the dogmatic mode, but in another mode it consists of three groups. It is important to note that both the equality and the inequality of component parts of a whole are ideas which have simultaneous currency.

THE TRIBUTE SHEIKHS

Within omodiyas the representative office-holders, apart from omdas, are the tribute sheikhs. Since the early days of Condominium administration their role has altered and they they have increased in number. They were originally responsible for the collection of 'tribute' or tax money from their lineages. With the establishment of omdas intermediate between them and the nazirs, sheikhs had control of small groups and they became more numerous. They proliferated more during the Second World War. Humr see this increase in connexion with rationing. The final division of rationed goods was in the hands of sheikhs, and smaller groups of people were interested to have sheikhs of their own, in order to benefit from any weakness in the system of distribution which could exploited. The Mezaghna had one sheikh in 1905; they had three, one for each major lineage, on the first appointment of omdas; later the number increased to six, and during the War it rose to fourteen, where it now stands.

The administration does not concern itself with fixing or approving the number of sheikhs;[2] it is concerned only that every tribesman should be the responsibility of one sheikh as far as his payment of tax and his whereabouts are concerned. The administration is not interested in the number of followers which any sheikh has, and does not lay down who his followers should be. Sheikhs' followings vary in number from less than ten to many hundreds. Sometimes the following consists of all the members of a sheikh's surra or minor lineage, while other sheikhs have followers who together do not constitute a single lineage. Members of a single surra may follow two different sheikhs;

[2] The appointment of a nazir has to be ratified by Khartoum and that of an omda by El Obeid; appointment of a sheikh needs only the nazir's confirmation.

two minor lineages may group together behind one sheikh. There is often a regrouping. Some followers of one sheikh can break away and elect a sheikh of their own. If a sheikh resigns or dies there may be no one suitable or willing within his following to take the job, and his followers may register in the meantime with one or more others. There is much irregularity in the pattern of sheikhs' followings, and much change over the years.

A sheikh has little security in office. His main task, the collection of tax money, is unpopular, and is unlikely to be wholly successful. His reward is ten per cent. of the tax due but only if he succeeds in collecting it all. There is a head tax for active men, 'spear-bearers' (*shail harba*), and also a poll tax on cattle, sheep, goats, and horses. A sheikh is involved in continual argument with his tax-payers over the number of cattle which are registered in their names, and hence over the amount of tax to be paid. Since few sheikhs or tax-payers can write, and since tax money is paid in irregular instalments throughout the year, the confusion of debts is considerable. Nor is this all; while the official duty of a sheikh is to collect tax, in the eyes of Humr he has the worthier obligation of lending out the tax money he has collected. Every few weeks he takes money to the tribal treasury, but if he has some in his pocket and refuses a loan he is neglecting his prime duty towards his followers. With the borrowed money men buy livestock; they drive them to a distant market and hope to come back with a profit. Often these debts remain unsettled for one reason or another. In consequence, towards April, the time of the annual reckoning, a sheikh may well see difficulties ahead and use tax money in the same way, buying cattle and trading them, to answer his commitments. He may succeed; but he may not, and accordingly may find himself in official trouble. His closest kinsmen, to avoid the possibility of his going to jail, rally and contribute cattle to pay debts, but if this impoverishes the family then the sheikh will not be in a position to do the job in the next year; he must be rich to start with as a reasonable assurance against the failure of the trading ventures of his followers and himself. A new sheikh is congratulated to his face, but behind his back men commiserate.

A man who is offered a sheikhship has the final choice in his own hands. He is unlikely to refuse the offer, although sometimes kin, especially if they are poor, may put pressure on him to do so because they realize that their wealth is in jeopardy. Apart from the threat of impoverishment, the work is hard and exasperating: a sheikh is said to count spear-bearers in his sleep. But an invitation to a sheikhship is a suggestion that a man has qualities which distinguish him from his fellows; it would lead to the widespread knowledge of his name in his own omodiya, among the nazirs, and in the tribal administration; and it is a first step towards higher office such as court presidency, omdaship, or council membership.[3] A man who retires from a successful period of sheikhship does so as a respected person, and the administration looks upon him as a 'notable'. The people regarded as leaders of most lineages are men who have at one time been sheikhs, and most omdas have worked their way through a period of sheikhship before being appointed. It appears difficult to become an omda without either being the son of a previous omda or having been a sheikh. Some have been both.

Apart from the tax duties, a sheikh assists the omda in many ways, for instance by trying to locate people wanted by police or administration. He has the duty of mustering his people on administrative occasions like cattle census and inoculation. He has the main burden of collecting and distributing blood-money. And sometimes, in omodiya affairs, he acts as a spokesman for his followers towards the administration; when administrative officers are trying to assess omodiya views on the appointment of an omda, each sheikh is regarded as having as many voices as he has followers. As his duties bring him into frequent contact with his omda, his nazir, and the administrative and district officers, he becomes accustomed to discussing and negotiating with them, and gains experience in the kind of business he would encounter if he rose to higher office.

LEADERS OF INTERMEDIATE LINEAGES

While sheikhs alone have official recognition, there are other leaders within omodiyas who are rallying points and main spokesmen for lineage policies. In a minor lineage the leader is likely to be the most influential surra leader in it, and so on up the scale. Such a leader is not deliberately chosen; rather he emerges through recognition of his general qualities. Typically these positions are held by men who were once sheikhs, or who still are sheikhs.

The intermediate lineages do not act corporately in day-to-day affairs, and the role of a leader is not such as to give continuous demonstration of his ascendancy. But men become established as influential, and there is a tendency, when one speaks of a certain lineage,

[3] These higher but less exacting offices are described as 'seats', the word used being *kursi*, chair.

to identify it with a certain man. Yet his lineage fellows can take him or leave him, and there are nearly always some dissidents. However, the identification of these positions with lineages indicates again the ideal of lineage unity and segmentation. The leaders are most active when disputes arise, and in particular their support or criticism of the omda carries much weight with their followers.

THE COURSE OF DISPUTES

The most serious disputes within omodiyas are those involving homicide, but various other quarrels continually arise and have to be resolved. An argument between two men of the same surra can be settled by the quiet and persuasive discussion, around the camp fire, of elders and other senior men admitted to the secret that two surra members are quarrelling. But the more distant the disputants are within the surra, the more difficult it is for settlement to be reached in this way. If the matter is taken to court to be 'finally' settled, it may not in fact finish there, because the very act of taking a surra brother to court is an additional breach of brotherhood which has to be settled in its turn. If a settlement fails, a variety of courses is open.

One solution was that reached by the dissident section of 'Iyal Ganiṣ after the marriage dispute (p. 78); they camped separately to avoid sharing the same tree and entertaining the same guests, but they still kept up day-to-day visiting and for the most part moved together. This was not serious. Other solutions are seen in the various possible herding arrangements (pp. 69–71). Another step would be to transfer allegiance to another sheikh.[4] A more drastic move would be to keep far away, camping alone or with another surra. The final possibility would be to forswear brotherhood with their own group and join another.

If the disputants are of different surras the possibilities of action are of the same general kind. Responsible men of the lineages come together with mediators to try and arrange for the sides to accept a compromise. If the estrangement is serious, however, the two sections involved enter a relation with one another known as *muwagafa*.[5] This involves withholding courtesy visits, although the avoidance may be confined to the senior members while the juniors and the women remain outwardly unaffected. But there is a chance of trouble

[4] Members of the splinter camp at I. Ganiṣ followed a different sheikh; but I could not discover if they did so as a result of the various marriage disputes, or if they had had the arrangement before.

[5] From the root *wagaf*, to stop.

arising at dances, and youths may make a point of not going to girls' tents in the hostile camps. In spite of the estrangement any co-operation which the sections had before over the payment and receipt of blood-money may still stand, or stand with some modifications: it need not be annulled completely. It may be that one or other of the parties will not continue to recognize the informal leader of the lineage which includes them both.

At a more serious stage of dispute a relationship called *mugaṭa'a*[6] comes into being, and here blood-money co-operation is brought to an end. The section breaks its brotherhood with its former allies and contracts a fresh alliance with others. It can do this while remaining where it is and moving in its former trails; more radically, it can move to another part of the country—to a place associated with another lineage, omodiya, or even tribe—and then disregard its former ties. This institution is partly responsible for the groups of greatly varied origin which compose political sections among the Humr.

In either event, sooner or later attempts are made to restore brotherhood. After some years of *mugaṭa'a*, mediators try and bring the aggrieved section back. With *muwagafa*, mediators are interested in trying to put an end to the situation. In both cases there has been a breach in the ideal of the brotherhood of the closest. They may succeed, they may fail. Success is followed by a ceremonial peace-making, called *murḍa*, in which one of the parties admits guilt and humbly requests to be readmitted to the brotherhood of the other. The new pact is sealed by recitation of the opening verse of the Koran. The aggrieved party usually names a price, in cash or cattle, for the peace; later this is likely to be reduced, or to be declared unnecessary.

An affair which arose in the Dar Umm Sheyba section of Awlad Kamil may serve as an example of a dispute between two men in collateral medium lineages. An adulterer of Dar Umm Sheyba Zerga medium lineage went to the wife of a man in Dar Umm Sheyba Ḥamra medium lineage. Because of the social distance between the two parties, the argument did not concern them alone but involved the whole of the two medium lineages. A meeting was arranged through intermediaries: elders of a number of surras of the Zerga lineage went to the husband's camp, where they found elders of a number of sections of the Ḥamra lineage. The hosts of the occasion gave a feast, for which they slaughtered two bulls. The adulterer's party admitted their guilt; they offered an out-of-court indemnity of £6, begged that the youth should not be taken to court, and promised that he would never again

[6] From the root *gaṭa'*, to cut.

speak to the girl. The husband's people thanked them for their re-assertion of brotherhood, which, they said, 'they would never exchange for money'; and they 'killed' a half of the indemnity, accepting £3, and restored brotherly relations.[7] Here the breach was restored by admission of guilt and a nominal payment for peace, the breach apparently taking place along agnatic lines, and the restoration bringing about the original condition of brotherhood between members of the two collateral lineages. While the matter lay at first between cuckold and adulterer, their social distance made it an affair between two lineages, and it became a political issue. The result could have been either a breach between the two lineages or a reaffirmation of their brotherhood. In the event, it was the latter. Settlement was easy with the offer of an out-of-court compensation. This was a sign that the lineages recognized that they were still brothers in spite of the misdemeanour; that their general relation was still one of kindness and generosity—a state which they call *mehanny*.[8] No doubt the easy settlement depended on more general relations at the time between the two lineages; the affair could have been made the excuse for a total breach of relations.

In a more serious case among Awlad Kamil, a dispute over the omdaship led to the departure of one of the major lineages from their usual camping grounds and migration trails. Dar Mota lineage had held the omdaship for a short time, and when, as a result of an intrigue, they lost it, they broke away in disgust, cancelled their blood-money alliances, and made a new contract of alliance with the Fayyarin omodiya, their neighbours to the west. Here contact was not entirely broken; Dar Mota still belonged to the 'Ajaira, remained under the same nazir (a man of Awlad Kamil), litigated in the same courts, and marketed at the same markets as the rest of Awlad Kamil; but they moved and camped a few miles west of their former position. Many years later all the other lineages of Awlad Kamil, and not merely the lineage which now admitted its responsibility for driving them away, combined to entice Dar Mota back among them. At the peace ceremony the price of peace was fixed at £60, but Dar Mota, the recipients, eventually returned half of this money.

[7] Had the case been taken to court, the adulterer would have been fined £12, and the plaintiff would have seen nothing of it.

[8] An important word in Humr politics. *Hanun*, from the same stem, means 'kind'. The opposite word is *jafa'*, which is a state of grudge. Their use came out clearly when Humr were talking about the recent proliferation of sheikhs. In the old days, they said, Arabs were *hanunin*, they were prepared to go share and share alike. But today it is a matter of *jafa'*, each group going its own way and trying to get every advantage for itself.

A much graver affair, which arose in the early years of the century, had a different outcome. Two groups of a large surra[9] fought when one of them failed to isolate its cattle at wells during an epidemic. Many deaths occurred at the original fight, and the fighting continued sporadically. The section most aggrieved (the section whose cattle had originally been threatened with contagion) decided to pull out. They contracted brotherhood with a section of the Rizeygat tribe and remained with them for many years. They seem, however, not to have been too well received, and later began to drift back to their original surra. Eventually they all returned and the surra regards the episode as closed and best forgotten.

In the first case the blood-money arrangements went on as before, but in the other two they were temporarily suspended. The suspension marked the very serious nature of the offences. When relations become impossible, or dangerous, the section most aggrieved goes away, as the nature of landholding and of agnation freely allows them to do. They do not always return, but when blood has cooled pressure is always brought to bear on them. What is not possible is for sections which are in a state of anger to remain near one another for any length of time.

In this section I have emphasized customary action when disputes arise. I have written in terms of lineages as wholes, since I do not have full details of these cases, and it was in terms of lineages as wholes that they were described to me. It was also in terms of lineages as wholes that mediators tried to heal breaches in the ideal brotherhood between collateral lineages. But the detailed case given in the next chapter will indicate that the political reality is rather different.

BLOOD-MONEY

Relations between groups within omodiya or lineage are stated in formal terms by agreement or refusal to co-operate in the payment and receipt of blood-money. The principle was put squarely when I was asked: 'Is he your brother who doesn't pay blood-money with you?' Finer shades of relationship are expressed by variations in the methods of payment and distribution. While some of the factors which go to determine the state of political relations are homicide, injury, and ensuing behaviour, others refer to disputes of a different nature. An occasion giving rise to blood-money is also an occasion for assessing whether in all respects the degree of brotherhood of allied groups

[9] I had to promise not to name it.

matches up to the ideal. The practical brotherhood of supposed brothers is put to the test, and the verdict is expressed in the degree of co-operation in blood-money decided upon.

Because they express nuances of political relationships, blood-money arrangements are complex and variable, and these relationships, within the omodiya especially, cannot be appreciated without knowledge of the possible variations.

Humr distinguish between compensation paid as the result of an injury and compensation paid as the result of a death.[10] There is an 'official' rate of payment for injuries of all kinds which is enforced when cases reach court, but omodiyas have much lower traditional rates of their own to which they adhere in out-of-court settlements, which are usual. Some omodiyas have slightly different scales from one lineage to another. When problems arise about the correct rates for one of the many possible injuries, elders are asked to define the 'custom of the caravan',[11] the implication being that those who usually move together usually share the same scales; they move together because they are close kin, and close kin should belong to a group which co-operates in blood-money. I deal no further with compensation for injury except to note that, save for very small payments, the money is collected by the same groups and distributed in the same way as *dia* payments proper;[12] and to mention that, whereas half *dia* is paid on account of a dead woman, the same compensation is paid whether the injured person is a woman or a man.[13]

In the past there was an alternative means of settlement, a form of distraint called *khamy*. Howell says that 'other segments of the group would combine against the culprit and his more immediate kinsmen

[10] Although both are commonly called *dia*, compensation for injury is sometimes (and more correctly, I was told) called *ta'wiḍ*.

[11] *Adat el ḍa'iny*.

[12] In the case of very small payments, such as compensation for the loss of a finger joint, only the injured man receives, and the range of payers may be much reduced.

[13] In a useful noted collected by A. C. Beaton, 'Notes on Baggara Law' (gathered in 1947 at Abyei from senior Humr informants and available in the Kordofan Province files), the following 'official' rates were given, such as a Humr court would award: loss of arm, 30 cattle; complete finger, 10; finger joint, 3½; hand, 15; leg, 30; eye, 20; tooth, 1 (*jeḍa'a*); hearing of one ear, 30; ear, 5; part of ear, 1 (*raba'ya*); complete loss of any of the senses, 60, as for death. For damages causing disfigurement and not impairing use, amounts are less.

In contrast, according to Mezaghna informants the scales in operation in that omodiya—their 'custom of the caravan'—include: arm, 7; finger, 2; leg, 7; eye, 8; tooth, 1 (*jeḍa'a*). If the limb still works no compensation is paid.

The payment for a death is invariable at 60 head for a man and 30 head for a woman.

and compel them to forfeit all their possessions . . . which were handed to the kinsmen of the deceased'; he adds, 'I doubt whether the khama was often applied.'[14] Beaton reported that 'neutral elders . . . would, in pre-Mahdia times, take possession of all the property of the killer and his close relatives and hand it over to the close relatives of the dead man, who would divide it among the "houses" comprising the clan [i.e. *khashm beyt*].'[15] My own informants told me that the killer's camp, fearing vengeance, would settle with all its possessions as guests upon some strangers. Mediators would seize the killer's family property, and the hosts would allow this as a means of safeguarding the lives of their guests. The mediators would then try to persuade the dead man's kin to accept the property as compensation.

Humr said that this was an alternative to blood-money during the Mahdiya and at other times when cattle were scarce. Beaton and Howell do not mention shortage of cattle; but I doubt if Humr honour would be satisfied with anything less valuable than cattle, and it is unlikely that *khamy* was practised at times when cattle were available.[16]

With the exception of intertribal cases, all blood-money negotiations are of the same general form and open to the same kinds of variation. Intertribal transactions are the only ones in which the range of participants and the primary sharing are conventionally invariable: the range is the whole tribe, the primary sharing is among omodiyas.[17] But the way in which each omodiya then deals with its share varies according to the principles which apply in intra-tribal transactions. These are flexible, and no permanent units exist for payment on receipt,[18] each case being considered on its merits.

The responsibility for payment rests on the killer, but his kinsmen help him out, and those who especially do so are his extended family and, if his extended family is poor, the rest of the surra, with whom indeed a special responsibility lies. By custom the killer and his immediate kin pay a third of the blood-money. The remaining two-thirds

[14] Howell, MS, p. 45. [15] Beaton, op. cit.

[16] W. Lloyd, an early administrator, adapted the custom for his own ends. Reporting on a patrol in Dar Humr in November 1905 he wrote: 'We camped at Shamber and Sheikh Eylyan abu Shanta of the A. Serur came in. Last year he bolted when I arrived. He now explained that he had done so as in 1903 he had had to pay all his tribe's [lineage's] tribute, but when he heard I took it by Kham el beyt [*khamy*] he went off and paid it at Talodi.' *S.I.R.*, Dec. 1905.

[17] See above, p. 102.

[18] Beaton stated that 'the payment of blood money is not a tribal but a clan (khashm el beyt) responsibility' (op. cit.). The implication that the omodiya or major or minor lineage is a stable unit for co-operation is incorrect, although it is true to say that the main paying or receiving unit on any occasion is never larger than the omodiya.

are paid by those who are willing to co-operate on the occasion. A surra should thus be in effective alliance with others, but it always retains the responsibility which goes with the dogma of shared blood: it is to the surra that the saying 'blood cannot be cut' applies.[19] A man can leave because of a dispute, take his cattle, and become an effective member of another surra, but his original one still has to help him with a killer's share. His new allies will share with him only in respect of the remainder.

Co-operation in payment and receipt is founded on alliances of two main kinds, called *'aṣala* and *kitab*; these words mean respectively 'origin' and 'book'. Those bound by *'aṣala* are so bound through common agnatic ancestry, and although this strictly comprises the whole of the tribe, common origin further back than omodiya ancestor is neglected for this purpose. The *kitab* alliances are so called because Humr make them by swearing on the Koran.[20] A Book alliance usually implies an original absence of *'aṣala*, but can be used to strengthen or reassert alliances of Origin. Members of one omodiya belong to one alliance of Origin, unless they happen to have broken it.

Different kinds of Book alliance exist. Firstly, a man can move elsewhere alone and, while retaining his 'blood' with his old surra, make an alliance in a different lineage or omodiya. Secondly, a surra can move and, breaking its old alliance of Origin, depend for help solely on a new Book alliance. Thirdly, while retaining its alliance of Origin a lineage can have a Book alliance with a lineage of another omodiya, which then shares in payment and receipt. Fourthly, a lineage can swear on the Book to maintain an alliance of Origin. With the first two types a Book alliance can turn into an alliance of Origin, by virtue of the common ancestry which comes to be assumed. This is the situation in which 'stranger' groups eventually find themselves.

Because alliances of Origin are supplemented by Book alliances groups which co-operate in paying blood-money overlap; and because alliances of both kinds are often cut, changed, and reasserted, there are continual changes in alliance patterns, and varying overlaps, and few transactions involve a predictable group of people. Commonly a minor lineage seeks Book allies outside the omodiya, to relieve the heavy obligations if one of its men should kill.[21]

[19] *El damm ma bengaṭṭi'.*

[20] The oath has the form 'children for children, wealth for wealth' (*'iyal be 'iyal, mal be mal*).

[21] A. Salamy minor lineage of the Mezaghna had such alliances with the Faḍliya omodiya, and with the Kelabna major lineage of A. Kamil; of any share which A. Salamy paid or received, the Book allies paid or received one-third,

The arrangements for paying and receiving blood-money vary in their details with the state of the relationships of allied groups. Humr recognize two opposite states, which they call *mehanny* and *jafa'* (see p. 156). With the former, shares are allotted equally to everyone, regardless of the number of sub-groups in the alliance: with the latter, each sub-group has an equal share, whatever its strength in terms of payers. To share alike throughout is more brotherly than to divide first by the number of component sub-groups, for no sub-group, with few members, will have more to pay in proportion to the number of its payers: all co-operate to equalize each payer's burden. Thus the group in which the share is finally divided among individual payers is one that, for the time being, is in intimate brotherhood. In the Humr-Messiriya transaction (above, p. 102) Howell noted that four omodiyas divided their share straight away among individual payers, while the others made prior division of one share to each major lineage or close blood-money alliance inside it. Each omodiya dealt with its share in terms of current political relations.

Other variations which exist between omodiyas are differing 'customs of the caravan' and do not indicate political distance. For example, shares in some omodiyas are finally divided among 'spear-bearers', each adult male having a share, while in others they are finally divided among '*iyal rajl*, brothers whose father had died.[22] The latter, which Humr regard as the more equitable method, is the one commonly used. Differences also occur in the amount to be paid by the killer and his close kin, and the amount to be received by the dead man's kin.[23]

For killings within the tribe the blood-money is set at sixty head. These are made up of eleven cows and one bull of each grade from *maḍmun* to *bikr*.[24] The third which the killer and his extended family pay is called the 'spearhead' or the 'share of the blood'.[25] The remainder constitutes the 'share of the many' or 'share of the caravan'.[26] The

[22] These are respectively '*ajaj*, short for '*ajaj fog el ẓol*; and *wald el rajl*, short for '*ajaj fog wald el rajl*. '*Ajaj* means a dust storm; in the first phrase the dust falls on every man (*ẓol*), and in the second on every '*iyal rajl*.

[23] Among the Faḍliya the killer pays only a cow and a bull. Jubarat and Salamat give six head from every *dia* to their nazir, and Salamat give one head to their omda.

[24] *Maḍmuna*, *jeḍa'a*, *teniya*, *raba'ya*, *bikr*. The total value is in the range of three to four hundred pounds.

[25] Respectively *sinn el harba* and '*ud el damm*.

[26] Respectively '*ud el ketiry* and '*ud el ḍa'iny*. For the implication of 'caravan', see p. 158.

and vice versa. As these were individual contracts no agreement operated between the Faḍliya and the Kelabna.

two-thirds which go to the close kin of the dead man are also called the 'share of the blood' (but not the 'spearhead').[27] One head is set aside to feed the intermediaries who inspect the beasts as they are handed over.[28]

A feature of Humr blood-money is that, where killer and killed belong to the same omodiya, there are usually people who are due to pay and due to receive in the same transaction. The machinery, complicated because of the illiteracy of the payers, collectors, and distributors, is still brought into action; political debates take place, and a form of alliance is set, if only for a short time.

SHIFTING ALLIANCES IN THE MEZAGHNA OMODIYA

A record of changes in blood-money arrangements in the Mezaghna omodiya, over a period of about ten years, shows the flexibility of the system. These changes are related to others in the internal relations of the omodiya which are described in the next chapter. It has not been possible to correlate the two series exactly: a blood-money transaction is long drawn out; before it is completed other events have altered the situation; and negotiations over successive affairs of blood overlap. Nevertheless, some correlation does emerge.

Mezaghna say that in the old days they all paid together (*ḍarabo jemi'*). Perhaps they did; the sheikhs have certainly proliferated, and a separate sheikh can indicate political separation. But there have been constant factors among the changes. One of these is the co-operation of Dar Bakheyt and 'Ariya major lineages to pay and receive in fixed proportions; another is the division of the five minor lineages of Dar Abu Timani into three groups, which likewise co-operate and enter negotiations about blood payments as three distinct units.

My earliest record is of a time when a man of 'Iyal Ma'aty (Jumal el Din Zerga lineage) killed a man of Abu Ḥejer (Abu Ghadir lineage—both 'Ariya).[29] On this occasion Dar Abu Timani did not contribute,

[27] Until recently this share was one-third, but it was altered by a decision of the Rural Council.

[28] They can refuse a mangy beast, but once accepted there is no need to replace it if it should die.

The total amount of blood-money is handed over in kind. The spearhead payers provide animals; those paying small amounts provide cash with which other animals are bought, from market or from camps as convenient; intermediaries supervise the transfer in a specially built thorn enclosure; those receiving the share of the blood get cattle; recipients of smaller amounts get shares of the proceeds from the remaining cattle, which are sold, generally in the market.

[29] See pp. 166 and 216 for Mezaghna lineages and main alliances.

and the share of the many was to be paid by 'Ariya and Dar Bakheyt in the proportion of three to one.[30] If the Mezaghna as a whole had been in a situation of *mehanny*, Dar Abu Timani, as one of three lineages of the Mezaghna, would have paid a third, or possibly a half, if we consider the small lineage of Dar Bakheyt to be in permanent alliance with the 'Ariya. Soon another killing took place among the 'Ariya and was dealt with similarly. Then a man of the Terakana killed a man of Awlad Salamy—a killing which was the start of the feud within Dar Abu Timani described in the next chapter. Since Dar Abu Timani had taken no part in the blood payments following the 'Ariya killings, 'Ariya and Dar Bakheyt were unwilling to take part in this one; but Nazir Babo suggested, and the leader of the 'Ariya agreed, that 'Ariya and Dar Bakheyt should together pay one-third, and Dar Abu Timani two-thirds, of the share of the many. Later, as an act of repentance for not having undertaken what they felt to be their full commitment in the Terakana killing, the 'Ariya gave twelve head of cattle to be distributed among Dar Abu Timani. Then, when the Mezaghna received their share of the extra-tribal blood-money from the Messiriya, they divided it at once, by virtue of these good relations, among all '*iyal rajl* of the omodiya without prior division by lineages.

But the situation did not last. 'Ariya and Dar Bakheyt broke again with Dar Abu Timani, although Jumal el Din Zerga, a minor lineage of the 'Ariya, retained friendship. When a man of Awlad Salamy had his arm broken by a man of Awlad Mumin, those who paid were solely Dar Abu Timani, the share of the many being at once divided equally among all '*iyal rajl*. But then Jumal el Din Zerga lineage of the 'Ariya contracted a Book alliance with Awlad Salamy. Thus, when a man of 'Iyal Bulola surra (Awlad Salamy) broke the leg of his wife (of Awlad Kamil omodiya), Jumal el Din Zerga helped to pay. But the payers were not the whole of Dar Abu Timani: the vengeance situation between Awlad Salamy and the Terakana was sharpening, and Awlad Salamy paid alone. Obviously the distance apart of the parties concerned does not affect the range of payers and receivers.

The distinction between agnatic groups and blood-money cooperators emerges clearly from a case which arose during the period when 'Ariya and Dar Bakheyt had broken with Dar Abu Timani; when Jumal el Din Zerga and 'Iyal Basshar of the 'Ariya both had

[30] Proportions of division and receipt, as originally decided, are not always carried into practice. Appendix 5 gives details of one transaction which shows how the situation alters in the course of a case.

Book alliances with Awlad Salamy; and when Jumal el Din Zerga had broken with the rest of the 'Ariya, except 'Iyal Basshar. A man of Jumal el Din Zerga broke the finger of a man of Beni Helba. The finger was assessed at a *raba'ya* cow and a *teniya* cow, whose market values that day were £8 and £7 respectively. Of the £15, £5 was paid as spear-head, and the remaining £10 was paid in shares of 5½ piastres by all the *'iyal rajl* of Jumal el Din Zerga, 'Iyal Basshar, and Awlad Salamy. This was a case which potentially involved two major lineages, but the payment and receipt brought in only small segments of them. Awlad Salamy, although they belonged to the injured major lineage, paid but did not receive, the only recipients being Beni Helba, and Awlad Mumin with whom they are normally allied.

Deaths and injuries leading to compensation are very frequent, and at most times there are three or four cases within one omodiya awaiting completion. Humr are thus almost constantly faced with the need to come to political decisions, for the settlement of these cases depends upon people co-operating in paying and receiving, and such co-operation depends in turn upon a political decision. The decision follows an assessment of relations within the omodiya, so that payment and receipt can be shared by people who are satisfied that their colleagues in the transaction are, at the time, brotherly enough to co-operate with. In relation to these decisions the leaders of intermediate lineages have an important part in influencing, and acting as focal points for, lineage opinion. As the next chapter will show, affairs of blood play their part in the power politics of the omodiya and in rivalry for the omdaship, in which the leaders of intermediate lineages may themselves have a direct interest.

11

RECENT POWER RELATIONS IN ONE OMODIYA

THE account of recent political events in one omodiya, which is the subject of this chapter, shows how many of the elements of political life among the Humr which have been isolated in previous chapters interact in a single situation.

MEZAGHNA GROUPS

The Mezaghna, a medium-sized omodiya moving in the middle of 'Ajaira country, had rather fewer cattle than some of the other omodiyas because they bore the brunt of serious epidemics in the late 1940s. This comparative poverty applies also to the kin of the omda, Ḥurgaṣ Merida of 'Iyal Ganiṣ, whose family and camp I have described. Ḥurgaṣ's father and grandfather were much wealthier. Umm Beddy, the grandfather, was a man of great influence, and except for a short period, the leadership of Awlad Salamy, of Dar Abu Timani, and of the Mezaghna has remained in the hands of this one line. Ḥurgaṣ could not have achieved his position with his own present wealth; he owes it to the wealth of his ancestors. He has been omda since 1927, an exceptionally long tenure, and in the course of it he has deflected many violent intrigues away from himself.[1]

The omda has an official position over all the Mezaghna, friend and foe alike. The Mezaghna conceive themselves as a lineage, and their dogmatic mode of segmentation is included in Appendix 7. As is the case elsewhere among the Humr, this dogmatic mode is the one with reference to which they explain themselves to outsiders, each person being concerned to convince his hearer that the unit he belongs to, surra, lineage, or omodiya, is one in which members dwell in harmonious and undifferentiated brotherhood. The deception is deliberate:

[1] For two years it belonged to I. Rigeyby, the closely related surra within A. Salamy. Ḥurgaṣ was still omda in 1965.

they know that in everyday political relations the picture is very different. In taking stock of Mezaghna politics we have to show this and to describe how alliances and differentiation in fact take place.

Among Dar Abu Timani lineage, only two minor lineages, Awlad Salamy and Dar Ḥantor, are held to be descended from the founder. The name Abu Timani means 'father of twins'; the twins were the ancestors of these two minor lineages; there were, it is said, no other children. The other minor lineages are strangers. Nevertheless they are all members of Dar Abu Timani, which Humr understand as being nothing other than the name of a lineage. Within Awlad Salamy the

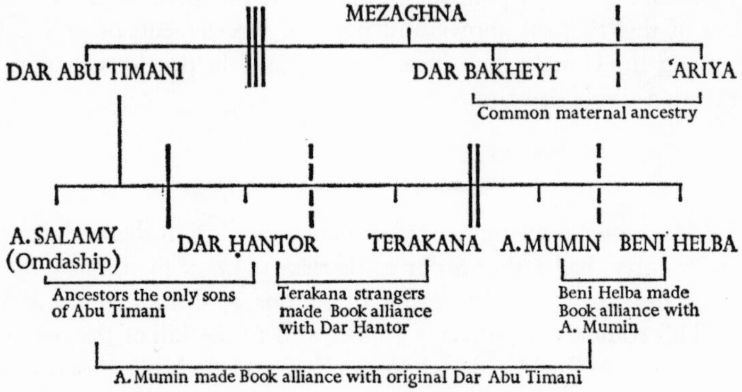

FIG. 17. Some alliances within the Mezaghna omodiya.

surras 'Iyal Jabir and 'Iyal Belebbo are not descended from Salamy, although they and others commonly say that they are: I think they were once 'Ariya. To all intents and purposes, it is as if they were of the Dar Abu Timani lineage. The dogmatic lineage neglects the fact of strangerhood. Yet there is differentiation of collaterals within it, and this comes out in action.

Let us take the situation of blood-money receipt. If blood-money comes from outside the tribe, the Mezaghna as a constituent omodiya get a share which they can dispose of as they see fit. This share may first be divided into three, one to each major lineage. Each major lineage may then further subdivide its share; Dar Abu Timani, for example, might divide into five lots, of which Awlad Salamy, as a constituent minor lineage, would get one. Then Awlad Salamy could further subdivide its share into seven lots, one lot for each surra. This method of sharing is theoretically possible. It could be used if the omodiya as a whole, as well as constituent parts of major and minor lineages, were at the time in a state of *jafa'*;[2] and the theoretical possibility of this method does reflect the theoretically equal status of subsections within one section. But the making and breaking of alliances and the recognition or non-recognition of kinship can lead to different ways of sharing.

Of the three major lineages Dar Abu Timani is the largest; it is followed in size by the 'Ariya, while Dar Bakheyt is comparatively small. The ancestors of the 'Ariya and of Dar Bakheyt are said to have been related through their mothers as well as through their fathers; this gives them a closer genealogical connexion to one another than to Dar Abu Timani. Politically they have tended to remain together and speak with one voice against Dar Abu Timani.[3] This claim of additional kinship may, of course, simply be a response to the *de facto* alliance between them. This alliance shows itself clearly, since the 'Ariya and Dar Bakheyt stand as a unit against Dar Abu Timani in blood-money transactions: money received by the omodiya may be divided primarily not into three shares, one for each major lineage, but into two shares, one for each unit which usually co-operates in affairs of blood.[4]

In a similar fashion the five minor lineages of Dar Abu Timani often become three divisions. Awlad Salamy, who have the omdaship, are by themselves, although their closest genealogical relationship is with Dar Ḥantor. These stand with the Terakana, who, long ago, came and made brotherhood with them on the Book. Awlad Mumin stand with Beni Helba, who came as strangers and made a Book alliance with them. Awlad Mumin themselves, when they had earlier come as strangers, had made a Book alliance with what was then Dar Abu Timani. Now blood-money coming to the major lineage may be divided primarily into three, one share for each of these allied groups. Again, Awlad Salamy, Dar Ḥantor, and the Terakana stand together against Awlad Mumin and Beni Helba, and in some respects this major lineage of five minor lineages divides into two parts: for example, the two Baramka clubs of the lineage follow this division. Fig. 17 illustrates these modes of alliance within the omodiya down to the level of the minor lineage.

Lastly, within Awlad Salamy the seven surras are grouped into three lots. 'Iyal Jabir and 'Iyal Belebbo are together; they were once all 'Iyal Jabir, but 'Iyal Belebbo split off following an accidental homicide

[2] Above, p. 156.

[3] 'Ariya and Dar Bakheyt generally camp eastwards of Dar Abu Timani. This is most noticeable on the Bahr: gardens are intermingled.

[4] Lewis's convenient term 'dia-paying group' applies to a more permanent alliance among Somali, so I have not used it (*A Pastoral Democracy*, p. 6).

during a hunt.[5] 'Iyal Ganiṣ, 'Iyal Rigeyby, and 'Iyal Bulola were one surra until recent times, but now they are three. 'Iyal Damura and 'Iyal Beyyen stand together, having once formed a single surra. Although 'Iyal Ganiṣ, 'Iyal Rigeyby, and 'Iyal Bulola form a unit for residual rights in property, 'Iyal Bulola, as will appear, are enemies of 'Iyal Ganiṣ and the omda personally.[6] From the lowest to the highest parts of the tribal structure close genealogical or agnatic kinship does not necessarily imply close political alliance. Indeed, it would be a mistake to assume that any particular kind of relationship between lineages constituted a sure basis for alliance of a lasting kind.

The present distribution of Mezaghna sheikhs partly tallies, and partly does not, with the alliances so far mentioned. Before omdas were appointed in 1911 there were three sheikhs, one for each major lineage. Then, up to the Second World War, there were six: one for Awlad Salamy, one for Dar Ḥantor and the Terakana, one for Awlad Mumin and Beni Helba—three in Dar Abu Timani. In addition, there was one for Dar Bakheyt, while the 'Ariya had two, one for Jumal el Din and one for Abu Ghadir. Now, the fourteen sheikhs are divided as follows. Awlad Salamy have three: one for 'Iyal Belebbo and 'Iyal Jabir; one for 'Iyal Beyyen, 'Iyal Damura, and 'Iyal Rigeyby; and one for 'Iyal Bulola. 'Iyal Ganiṣ, who hold the omdaship, are subject partly to the sheikh of 'Iyal Beyyen and partly to that of 'Iyal Belebbo. Dar Ḥantor and the Terakana share a sheikh between them; the present sheikh belongs to Dar Ḥantor, though his predecessor belonged to the Terakana. Awlad Mumin and Beni Helba have two sheikhs between them, both belonging to Awlad Mumin; each sheikh has followers from both lineages. Dar Bakheyt has a sheikh for each minor lineage. The 'Ariya have many; two in Jumal el Din and five in Abu Ghadir. The latter are divided in this way: 'Iyal Basshar and 'Iyal Abu Ḥejer each have their own, 'Iyal Sileyman share one with half of 'Iyal Didan, and the other half of 'Iyal Didan share one with half of 'Iyal Aginda. The other half of 'Iyal Aginda has its own sheikh. During my stay 'Iyal Didan were unsuccessfully trying to agree on a sheikh of their own.

Since the duties of a sheikh go beyond purely administrative

[5] The use of force within a surra is most shameful; this accident, which seems to have happened about the turn of the century, had a correspondingly important social significance.

[6] An important gap in my field material was caused by my inability to elicit clear statements about the ways in which surras split up, or the period at which they had done so. I could sometimes learn the cause of the split, but without detail, without date, and without genealogical information. I can only assume that the factions of a surra, like the inhabitants of the two camps of I. Ganiṣ, do not necessarily coincide with agnatic segments within it.

matters and include the collection and distribution of blood-money, it is not surprising that there is some correspondence between the following of sheikhs and people who are in semi-permanent alliance (of which agreement to co-operate in blood-money payment and distribution is a usual feature). Sharing of sheikhs by Awlad Mumin and Beni Helba on the one hand, and by Dar Ḥantor and the Terakana on the other, is in line with the traditional alliances. Those surras of Awlad Salamy which are linked by following the same sheikhs mostly have elements in common which distinguish them from other surras of the lineage: ʻIyal Belebbo and its offshoot ʻIyal Jabir, ʻIyal Beyyen and its offshoot ʻIyal Damura. ʻIyal Bulola, the surra which broke from ʻIyal Ganiṣ under its present leader Ndalo, is in rivalry for the omdaship and is a very independent member of Awlad Salamy: it has Ndalo as its own private sheikh. ʻIyal Ganiṣ is at present split into two residential camps, but it is closely linked by patrilineal descent with ʻIyal Rigeyby (who also pay to the sheikh of ʻIyal Beyyen) and, by marriage, to ʻIyal Belebbo. The only man with wealth enough in ʻIyal Ganiṣ to be a sheikh is Ḥurgaṣ himself, and he has other duties to perform.

The sheikhs apart, Dar Abu Timani contained a number of men generally regarded as spokesmen: lineage leaders. Ḥurgaṣ himself held Awlad Salamy with the exception of ʻIyal Bulola, who listened to their sheikh Ndalo. Boya el Zeyn of ʻIyal Rigeyby also had a powerful voice in Awlad Salamy. He was the son of a previous omda and the admitted deputy of Ḥurgaṣ; he was wealthy, and his brother was wealthy, and he had a line of talk which attracted people by its sterling common sense and its adherence to the manliest of Humr virtues. He supported the omda loyally. A man called Fiḍeyly, a former sheikh, was leader of the Terakana, and for the most part Dar Ḥantor also listened to him. Another former sheikh was leader of Beni Helba, and for the most part Awlad Mumin also listened to him. While to outsiders Ḥurgaṣ was representative of, and spokesmen for, Awlad Salamy, Dar Abu Timani, and the whole of the Mezaghna, in fact he was beset by enemies. Of those spokesmen which I have mentioned only Boya, during my field period, actively supported him as omda, but even he harboured a personal grudge. Among the ʻAriya, Shigeyfa, a former sheikh and the father of the present sheikh of Abu Ghadir, was a dominant character; another, ʻIsa ʻUlm of ʻIyal Sileyman, gained adherents from his enormous wealth; both were hostile. But Jumal el Din Zerga lineage had a ʻnotableʼ, an old man and a former sheikh, who was now member for the Mezaghna on the local council; he remained friendly with Ḥurgaṣ, with whose support he had won the position, and his lineage continued to share blood-money responsibilities with Awlad Salamy after the rest of the 'Ariya had withdrawn.

INTRIGUE AND THE OMDASHIP

The general method of intrigue (*fitna*) which has been described amongst the nazirs finds its place also amongst contenders for the omdaship. Indeed, the prospect of landing an enemy in jail, by dint of one's own spying, or general suspicions, through information given to the nazir or police, is employed even by cattleman against cattleman; but the institution comes to fullest blossom in attempts to have an omda removed from office. It has been most successful amongst Awlad Kamil, who have at least four ex-omdas alive. Attacks have been made in other omodiyas, some successful and some not; Ḥurgaṣ of the Mezaghna and his father have had a full share of them. No doubt Ḥurgaṣ's affinal relationship with the Nazir Umum[7] has helped to keep him in office in the face of savage attacks; no doubt, as well, his own magnetic personality has played its part here. For two years I watched him using, with the utmost skill, his charm and volubility and generosity on those he had to attract, and his thrift and authority on those upon whom he could rely, exploiting the potential of his resources and his personality in the way that would bring the greatest political reward.

In the next section I relate the course of a blood feud which was the main event of the Mezaghna during my stay with them. In order to understand the course of events which follows a killing, it is quite insufficient to describe the death, the vengeance, the agreement to compensate with blood-money, and the final peace-making, as an independent sequence of events. For with the involvement in negotiations of the omda, a man in a position of power, and with the extension of the quarrel to include the members of the whole omodiya, all with their own opinions, opportunities are laid open for individuals to exploit the situation and settle scores of their own. And typically, with this killing in the Mezaghna the tenure of the omda himself came into question. Thus, inevitably, when the affairs reached a conclusion the debate turned upon the personality of the omda and the appropriateness of his behaviour. What started as a crime of passion took on the public character of a struggle for a high position of power. Thus we have to consider the events in relation to the Mezaghna power structure and

[7] Ḥurgaṣ's eldest son, Nimr, treasurer to the local council, married Nazir Babo's daughter.

the personalities involved in it. There is nothing mechanical about the course of a feud and its settlement.

Since the Mezaghna omdaship began, successive omdas, all of Awlad Salamy, have been under attack from other lineages: the Terakana, Awlad Mumin, the ʻAriya of Abu Ghadir, the ʻAriya of ʻIyal Sileyman, and even by ʻIyal Bulola of Awlad Salamy itself. While friendships shift, a fairly constant hostility has been directed against the omda from the ʻAriya; and a continual tendency towards hostility has been shown by the ʻAriya, generally with the backing of Dar Bakheyt, against Dar Abu Timani as a whole. In the days when there were few sheikhs Shigeyfa Wenesa was sheikh of Abu Ghadir section of the ʻAriya. Although he is still sheikh officially, in fact his son Aḥmed Shigeyfa does most of the work. In the 1920s Shigeyfa used to turn out to elephant hunts with great followings of horsemen, thus outdoing the omda. About 1927 he was instrumental, it is said, in having the father of the present omda removed from office by reporting to the authorities an alleged offence in connexion with the sale of ivory. Instead of being himself installed, as he had hoped, he saw the young Ḥurgaṣ, the son of the previous omda, enter office. After a while Ḥurgaṣ and Shigeyfa proceeded to patch up a friendship. Shigeyfa spent much of his time at L. Abyad cultivating cotton. From here he used to return on short visits to his ʻAriya and surpass the omda in generosity and hospitality. His camp under his son Aḥmed generally moved near the Ganiṣ camp, and friendship grew up between them; it went through many vicissitudes, but when I first went to the Humr in 1952 they appeared to be on very good terms. But the most serious ʻAriya attack on the omdaship was shortly to follow.

A former sheikh of the Beni Helba, an old man and their present leader, worked up a quarrel over the ownership of a small strip of garden land; this has now, after about twenty years, developed into an argument over the omdaship. He persuaded his people during the course of the argument to refer to themselves not as Mezaghna but as Beni Helba.[8] In this argument, Awlad Mumin stood with them.

Then, as the result of a homicide involving Awlad Salamy and the Terakana, the traditional friendship of these two groups was broken, and as matters went from bad to worse the sheikh of the Terakana declared in court that he would no longer follow Ḥurgaṣ. In this, Dar

[8] A very definite slight. The ʻBeni Helbaʼ are a Baggara tribe in their own right whom this lineage left to join the Mezaghna. By calling themselves Beni Helba instead of Mezaghna they stressed their stranger status: the reverse of the more usual insult by which a man states that a group to which he does not belong is a stranger group.

Ḥantor stood with the Terakana. The relationship was one of *muwagafa* with a threat of *mugaṭa'a*.

Finally 'Iyal Bulola, recently established as an autonomous surra by splitting from 'Iyal Ganiṣ, started an intrigue against the omda. Its young leader Ndalo, who had made himself a sheikh with only eight tax-payers, became a successful merchant in Abyei, leaving his brother to look after his substantial herd in the forest. Being a fearless talker, he managed to make the Mezaghna respect his 'mouth', which means that people feared that he would be ready to inform on them about illicit activities, actual or invented. His attack consisted in reporting to the authorities that a member of the omda's surra had been poaching giraffe, implying that the omda had been protecting him for kinship's sake. The poacher was fined heavily and his horse confiscated, but Ḥurgaṣ survived in office.[9]

In 1954 the 'Ariya suddenly returned to the attack. The camps of 'Iyal Ganiṣ and 'Iyal Basshar had been together throughout the summer, and when the rains began Aḥmed Shigeyfa joined those members of 'Iyal Ganiṣ who were cultivating cotton near Abyei. At this time some omdas, including Ḥurgaṣ, were told to find and register those Fellata nomads who were in their areas and get tax money from them.[10] Aḥmed Shigeyfa accused the omda of having seized sheep in excess of the number required to be sold for tax, and of having transported them by secret paths to a market. (Many similar attacks were made in other omodiyas at the same time.) The visiting magistrate dismissed the case for lack of proper evidence after it had dragged on for many weeks. When this failed, the 'Ariya accused the omda of having given away stray cattle as presents rather than handing them to the Government pen for strays. This failed. They then accused him of having shot a gazelle (he had a shotgun licence, which permits the shooting of birds but not animals). In this case a small fine was imposed; but the man who brought the charge had hoped that at least the gun, an important status symbol, would be confiscated. As a last resort they claimed to have a list of people in the omda's minor lineage who were in possession of unlicensed guns, but this failed too, because on the day

[9] After I left the field there was a *rapprochement* between Ḥurgaṣ and Ndalo. When Ḥurgaṣ heard that Ndalo intended to stand as Senator at the end of Nazir Babo's term, he lobbied to have him elected, even visiting the Felaita omdas to this end. Ndalo was a Senator for a short time before 1958. The advantage to the omda was that for much of the year Senators reside in Khartoum.

[10] Fellata: nomadic cattlemen from N. Nigeria who wander in unfrequented paths throughout much of N. Sudan; they usually avoid payment of taxes, and create discord by using Humr wells and eating much of the grass upon which Humr depend in their migrations.

the list was produced, police raided the camps and found nothing. This great onslaught had no success. But the method of attack can be fruitful, for when a common informer lays a complaint the police are bound to investigate.[11]

This prolonged attack by one part of an omodiya on another, within the family, as the Humr considered, caused great distress to members of other omodiyas. It was the topic of discussion wherever people met at camp fire or market-place during the rains of 1954. Strangers would approach Mezaghna men, express their sympathy, and complain that the expected mediators, in this case the Faḍliya, were not intervening. In their movements the Faḍliya often intermingle with the Mezaghna, and they are in close friendship with them; yet they belong to a different 'family'. The opinion was widely held that it should be the positive duty of the Faḍliya to try and mediate between the two sections, or to try to make the 'Ariya act less immoderately. Some Mezaghna unsuccessfully attempted mediation. The omda's 'Ariya allies in Jumal el Din Zerga lineage, instead of attempting to moderate their kin, simply stayed and kept company with Ḥurgaṣ. A group of Awlad Kamil, who also move with the Mezaghna, ineffectively tried to make a truce. The battle was still raging when I left Muglad in early 1955. But a reconciliation at the hands of interested friends is the normal first step in bringing peace.

This was the course of Mezaghna power politics which both influenced and was affected by the blood feud which I now describe.

THE COURSE OF A BLOOD FEUD

A young man called Ḍaḥiya of 'Iyal Rigeyby surra had laid claim to his patrilineal cousin, El Nunayi, a girl who was also his mother's brother's daughter. During 1948 a youth of the Terakana, called 'Abd el Raḥman, was a regular visitor to the girl's tent at night. One evening Ḍaḥiya spoke to 'Isa, the son of Nur el Din, who was also of 'Iyal Rigeyby and a close cousin to himself and to El Nunayi. The girl's father had agreed to marry her to Ḍaḥiya, but, I was told, her mother had her own ideas and allowed 'Abd el Raḥman access to the tent. One night Ḍaḥiya and 'Isa heard the 'Abd el Raḥman and El Nunayi

[11] It is noteworthy, from the point of view of nazirs' influence, that this attack began on the day that Nazir Babo left for Khartoum: Nazir 'Ali was also out of the country. On the same day a feud that had been dormant for some time among the Ziyud broke out again with some ferocity. Humr mentioned the coincidence to me, and suggested that it was better to indulge in these 'shameful' matters in the absence of the 'big people'.

were together in the forest, and went out armed with sticks. On finding them, Ḍaḥiya challenged 'Abd el Raḥman by saying: 'Don't run away.' 'Abd el Raḥman drew his knife,[12] killed 'Isa, and stabbed Ḍaḥiya in the stomach. El Nunayi ran off to her tent and remained quiet, but Ḍaḥiya managed to crawl to the tent of Boya, the surra leader. Boya's wife awoke first, wakened her husband, but tried to restrain him; however, he went out and found Ḍaḥiya. Then the news spread. The Mezaghna had gathered in the Muglad for cattle inoculation, and were all encamped within an area about three miles square; and mediators soon came, at first members of Awlad Mumin and Beni Helba, 'Ariya and Dar Bakheyt, followed later by Faḍliya and Awlad Kamil.

It is the mediators' duty[13] to prevent immediate reprisals. To this end they tied to trees those likely to take vengeance—brothers and fathers' brothers of the victims, as well as Boya the surra leader. They removed 'Iyal Rigeyby from the camp. They sent to Muglad, some twelve miles away, for police, who soon arrived in numbers and as a precaution took to jail those who had been tied up. Ḍaḥiya went to hospital and recovered. 'Abd el Raḥman was tried a month later and received a sentence of seven years, the court having decided that Ḍaḥiya had acted provocatively. Public opinion regarded the seven years' jail as adequate recompense for Ḍaḥiya's wounds; and blood-money, sixty head of cattle, was to be paid for 'Isa's death. The cattle were handed over during the following dry season. The prisoners were released one by one under oath to keep the peace.

By Humr custom the payment of blood-money is enough to compound for a death. No sooner do negotiations start than the whole matter is taken out of the hands of the families concerned and enters the hands of larger groups. Those who negotiate are the leaders, and other representatives, of the two lineages concerned. Thus here it was Ḥurgaṣ, the omda, in his capacity as leader of Awlad Salamy, on the one hand, and Fiḍeyly, former sheikh, in his capacity as leader of the Terakana, on the other, both with others of their lineages. The negotiations were difficult, but eventually blood-money was paid.

The payment failed to assuage the dead man's kin. Two years passed. During the rains of 1950 there was a shortage of grain in Dinka country, and, amongst others, some Terakana went south to barter grain for cattle. Muḥammad, a close relative of 'Isa, saw here

[12] All Humr wear dagger-like knives strapped to the upper arm under their smocks.

[13] The word I translate as mediators is *ajawid*. For fuller definition see p. 184.

his opportunity. With a party he went to Dinka country and set an ambush for the returning Terakana. He speared to death a kinsman of 'Abd el Raḥman. Dinka police arrested Muḥammad's party, except for one man who rushed to Muglad and warned Awlad Salamy that they might expect vengeance on them. The news went about; Terakana were tied to trees; police moved the camp of 'Iyal Rigeyby to the middle of Awlad Kamil omodiya. This was not an ordinary killing, but one which had broken the peace-making bond of blood-money and which thus demanded unusual measures. Muḥammad was tried and sentenced to death; he calmly told the judge: 'Since my brother was killed I have lived only for vengeance by the spear. You can do with me what you want.' The judge pressed him to appeal, but the appeal failed. Because he was hanged the Terakana did not ask for blood-money; but the affair was not over, for the circumstances of the vengeance suggested that the Terakana would probably kill a man. It would not be over until Awlad Salamy came to the Terakana, admitted their guilt, and supplicated for peace.

The event shook the Mezaghna profoundly. Between Awlad Salamy and the Terakana, and to a lesser extent Dar Ḥantor, the relationship became one of *muwagafa*, a direct consequence here of the fact that a state of vengeance existed between them.[14] Normal visiting was cut out. Precautions were taken by people of consequence not to choose their routes near camps of the other side, and camps of the two lineages no longer moved and pitched near one another. But, still, if someone died in the ordinary way, the opposite parties would come, each man at his own convenience, and sit for some time with the bereaved people, for failure to do this would have marked the hostility between the two sections as being for ever irreconcilable. There was no more courting between members of the two lineages. If visitors from each were guests at the same camp, the host would take care not to have them feed from the same dish. But affinal relationships were honoured as usual; a few economic transactions took place in the market; there was contact over administrative matters; co-operation in payment and distribution of blood-money resulting from other events continued; and the affair hardly affected the women, who would commiserate with one another over the breach in the long-standing brotherhood and between close kin.

Up to about 1954 little happened to alter the position, but it was realized that the slightest additional friction might have serious

[14] *Beynathum tar* is another stock description of a political relationship: 'there is vengeance between them'.

consequences. In that year two events occurred which almost led to further serious trouble.[15]

A member of 'Iyal Belebbo surra (Awlad Salamy) had been sentenced for poaching giraffe; he was in prison, and his horse had been confiscated. The Government auctions animals thus seized, and Dawud of the Terakana, who had married into Awlad Salamy and was the nazir's nominee as guarantor of the peace between the two lineages of the dispute, bought the horse back for twenty-three pounds. He was expected to sell it to its old owner's brother; but one day in March he rode up to the Belebbo camp, and said he would not sell because Nazir 'Ali had told him not to. The argument raged through the day, and Belebbo girls bringing food made it quite clear that they intended to get the horse back.[16] Later Dawud offered to sell it for twenty-seven pounds. 'Iyal Belebbo accepted the offer, but at the same time noted the implicit hostility, for a brother-in-law of Awlad Salamy, and a guarantor of the peace, was making capital out of the misfortunes of his kinsmen, and that at a time when the horse's rightful owner was in jail.

The second occurrence took place in June of the same year, at the time of the northward migration. It happened that 'Abbad, a youth of Awlad Salamy ('Iyal Damura), and Ibrahim, a youth of the Terakana, visited the same girl of Awlad Mumin on the same night. Ibrahim gave her cloth, and demanded a pound from 'Abbad.[17] The mother realized the danger and told 'Abbad to leave. He went out, the girl followed, and finally Ibrahim. The two men went off together, leaving the girl behind. Then it seems that 'Abbad snatched Ibrahim's knife, they fought, and 'Abbad claimed he made Ibrahim flee. 'Abbad went to his own camp, taking the knife with him. Later the mother's father of the girl, the ex-sheikh of Beni Helba, managed to make a sort of peace and

[15] Although I was living with A. Salamy it was some months before I learned of the situation. The omda had gone out of his way to introduce me to many people of the Mezaghna, and this included the sheikh of the Terakana, who had given us hospitality. Only later, when I knew of the feud, was the non-arrival explained of a baggage bull for which the omda had bargained with the sheikh of the Terakana on my behalf: the sheikh had wished to put the omda in an embarrassing position towards his guest.

[16] This fine horse was one of the best giraffe hunters in Dar Humr. It greatly enhanced the prestige of I. Belebbo, whose men were already known for their manliness (particularly in terms of horsemanship and prowess in the chase). By Humr standards the horse was worth about £40; but the auction had taken place at Abyemnom, which is peopled mainly by Dinka, and it had gone cheaply. The nazir intervened because he thought that reselling to the original owner went against the spirit of the confiscation.

[17] Thus challenging him to have in his pocket the amount of money 'Abbad had spent on cloth for the girl; a customary procedure between rival suitors. The winner can then boast 'ana faitak', I surpass you. The girl should take the winner.

have the knife returned. But 'Abbad boasted to Awlad Salamy of having made Ibrahim flee, and in spreading the story he referred to him not by the name Ibrahim, but as 'the son of Fiḍeyly', the leader of the Terakana; and the girls of Awlad Salamy started to mock the son of Fiḍeyly in song.

A month later, when the camps reached the Muglad, another youth of the Terakana, called Nur, sought the girl in marriage. He had the agreement of her parents, but the girl did not want him. He went one night to her tent and she refused to have anything to do with him; when he was there, 'Abbad arrived. Nur went out, but instead of making off he went round the tent and entered by the doorway, climbed straight over the bed, and went out again beneath the tent wall at the back.[18] 'Abbad went after him; they had a fight in which Nur was bitten on the face and had a tooth nearly knocked out.

The affair reached court. Nur was the plaintiff; it was rumoured that Nazir 'Ali had persuaded him to complain in order to give the relationship between Awlad Salamy and the Terakana an airing. 'Abbad received a six months' jail sentence for his fight with Ibrahim, and a £2 fine (which he refused to pay) or a month in jail for his fight with Nur; he would also have to pay compensation of a *jeḍa'a* cow if Nur's tooth should come out. The sentence was severe for two reasons. First, before the sentence was given, 'Abbad repeated in front of the assessors that Ibrahim had been afraid of him and run away. The court thought not only that this was insulting to them, but also that it was a deliberate provocation of the hostility between the two lineages. So the sentence was exemplary. The court also ordered the girls of Awlad Salamy to stop singing about Ibrahim, otherwise they would go to jail.[19]

Ibrahim's father, Sheikh Fiḍeyly, was present. After the sentence he gave a long speech in which he claimed that Ḥurgaṣ was unsuitable as an omda, for he was permitting the state of vengeance to continue, he had not approached the Terakana to admit the guilt of Awlad Salamy as a prelude to peace-making, and he had done nothing to prevent further trouble, but had indeed connived at the girls'

[18] The customary mode of entry and exit for suitors is beneath the bark of the tent wall at the back, where there is much less chance of being seen by men in camp. To do anything else is also a lapse in manners, for the women are as interested as the suitors in keeping the visits secret. Nur, no doubt on purpose, aggravated the situation by conspicuously flouting this custom.

[19] It was made quite clear that they were not attacking the Humr custom which allows slanderous songs; they were only forbidding them in this inflammatory situation.

singing.[20] Fiḍeyly threatened to leave the Mezaghna, and everyone knew that if he left, the Terakana and probably Dar Ḥantor would all leave together.

Nevertheless, at this time there were indications of improved relationships. Two of the Terakana who were married to women of 'Iyal Ganiṣ and who had often lived in the Ganiṣ camps in the past now returned. The 'Ariya attack and the Fellata sheep trial were in progress. Further, word went about that a new court presidency was to be established and that the authorities might favour giving the post to a man of Dar Abu Timani if this major lineage should show a united front.[21] Circumstances were more in favour of a settlement, and as soon as the omda was reassured by winning the Fellata sheep case, he was ready to listen to the strong advice from his lineage fellows to reach agreement with the Terakana. Indeed, they had long been giving such advice, but it required the extra incentives to make the omda move.

Before the approach could be made the omda had to make peace among his own Awlad Salamy, because of the personal grudge which Boya had towards him. Boya was the leader of 'Iyal Rigeyby, the surra involved in the homicides and genealogically closest to 'Iyal Ganiṣ. In the past the two surras had always moved and camped together in friendship. Boya was, next to Ḥurgaṣ, the most influential man of Awlad Salamy. When the omda was away it was he who entertained those guests who would normally go to the omda, and he had incurred heavy outlays on meat, tea, and sugar. The omda, whose resources were not unlimited, had been obliged to expend most of his wealth, for political reasons, on hospitality to more distant members of the omodiya and to strangers; and consequently he had to conserve his resources with respect to Boya and others, trusting that the bonds of close kinship would be enough to keep them loyal. Boya was satisfied with Ḥurgaṣ as omda and would have none other; but his grudge was that he had received scant recognition for this moral and economic support. They had not been on speaking terms, although the relations between the surras were unaffected. Now when the 'Ariya attacked, Boya spent most of his time in Muglad, away from his cattle, to keep Ḥurgaṣ

[20] In fact, when Ḥurgaṣ heard of the fight between 'Abbad and Ibrahim, he rode to the place (a two-day journey) immediately in his concern to find a settlement. It is true that during the previous year Fiḍeyly had deviously tried to make Ḥurgaṣ come to him and beg for peace; that he failed is said to have been due largely to intrigue by the leader of Beni Helba, who profited by the continuing breach in the A. Salamy/Dar Ḥantor/Terakana group.

[21] I interpret this rumour as an attempt, perhaps on the nazir's part, to influence relations within Dar Abu Timani. Inquiries later failed to disclose any plans for a new court to which the rumour might have referred.

PLATE IV

Omda Hurgaṣ with his elders on the way to peace-making ceremony

(*Facing p.* 179)

company through his difficult days. In order to approach the Terakana in strength, Ḥurgaṣ had first to heal his personal breach with Boya.[22]

In the rainy season in the Babanusa the camps of Boya and Ḥurgaṣ were within a mile of one another. Ḥurgaṣ sent word that he was coming, and, in company with most of the men of 'Iyal Ganiṣ and some mediators from other Awlad Salamy surras and the Faḍliya, went to make peace. He supplicated for it and admitted his guilt, the mediators supported his plea, and Boya accepted his protestation of brotherhood. The meeting ended with a recitation of the opening of the Koran. Thereupon Boya and the omda decided to make overtures to the Terakana, and they sent Dawud, the affine, to the Terakana to arrange a day for the meeting.

In October the whole of the Mezaghna were encamped within an area about three miles square. The Terakana at once agreed to meet, and with their Dar Ḥantor allies made preparations in a large thicket to receive and feed the visitors. They were the hosts on this occasion. Dar Ḥantor and Terakana slaughtered two bulls and provided grain. In the thicket, each alliance sat separately; Terakana and Dar Ḥantor together, Awlad Mumin and Beni Helba together, Awlad Salamy together, 'Ariya and Dar Bakheyt together.[23] 'Iyal Bulola were not represented; and some men of the 'Ariya, Jumal el Din Zerga lineage, sat with Awlad Salamy.

On this day many political issues were decided among the Mezaghna. The normal methods of political disputation were observed. It would require a better linguist than myself to discover how a consensus can be reached by a large group of men facing inwards upon one another in a tightly packed circle, each man shouting his opinion in order to make it heard above all the others, and simultaneously emphasizing his points by moving stick or spear vigorously up and down. The group breaks up, the voices dying away if a consensus has been found, the shouting continuing if it has not.[24] Most of these discussions were

[22] He did not attempt to heal the breach with I. Bulola: perhaps because they consisted of only eight tax-payers, or perhaps simply because he realised it would have been impossible.

[23] Nazir Babo used this occasion to introduce to the Mezaghna his prospective member of Parliament, his father-in-law from Omdurman. The morning was more in the form of a reception, in which the common devotion of all present to the cause and aura of Mahdism was in marked contrast to the divisions, otherwise present during the day, among the Mezaghna.

[24] Howell (MS., p. 64) quotes Sir Douglas Newbold: 'I have myself attended many Messiria . . . meetings for the appointment of omdas and they are notorious for clamorous discussions. . . . I am a believer in democracy, but not the Baggara brand of democracy.'

on the subject of minor cases of blood-money which were under negotiation, for it is through them, and through decisions to join or not to join with others in payment and receipt, that political relations most commonly find their expression.

After the midday meal Awlad Salamy moved nervously and diffidently to the trees where the Terakana and Dar Ḥantor were sitting. The three lineages arranged themselves in a large circle, the adversaries facing one another, with Fiḍeyly and Ḥurgaṣ close together in the centre. Mediators, who now by the nature of the case and their interest in good relations among the Mezaghna would support the omda's supplication for peace, sat with Awlad Salamy. Awlad Salamy had asked Mekki 'Ali Julla to be chairman: he, as a court president and kinsman of Nazir Babo, was acceptable to the other side also. Although he was chairman, he sat (on the only deck-chair, brought in his lorry from Muglad) among Awlad Salamy.

No one talked, and quietly the chairman asked Awlad Salamy elders to speak in turn. First the leader of 'Iyal Damura said, addressing the Terakana: 'First of all when the wound was upon us[25] you came and made reconciliation; then the wound was upon you; and now with our coming here all we want is brotherhood, and if you make it we shall be thankful.'[26](A)

All the speeches were short, and attended with complete silence. The next speaker, the leader of 'Iyal Jabir, said: 'When blood fell among us you came and made reconciliation; when it fell among you, we did not come to you, we were very wrong and we know our error. Our arm is clean broken. We shall never again (?)see these sons of ours. Then let you and us be brothers. We have spread out our smocks before you.[27] We know our blemish. Do this for us.'(B)

An elder of Rigeyby surra said the same, and then Boya, the leader of Rigeyby, the surra most closely involved, said: 'I am the owner of the blood, but when the wound was on us you came and you knew me, and when the wound was on you I did not come to you and make reconciliation. I am very wrong. Without you, we do not want brotherhood at all. We want manliness, and there is no manliness for us without you among us. If you deny us your brotherhood, we shall not deny you ours.'(C)

The omda was next to speak, but he did so very quietly, and both

[25] i.e., at the time of the first killing.

[26] Immediately after the meeting, members of I. Ganiṣ repeated the speeches to me verbatim. I add these in transliterated Arabic in Appendix 6, as examples of Baggara political idiom. Letters after the speeches refer to the Arabic texts in the appendix.

[27] i.e. for you to place our mistakes upon them.

myself and the people with whom I later discussed the proceedings were unable to reproduce what he said. One person did think, however, that he said much the same as those who had spoken before. He seemed anxious all day and found the whole affair a great strain.

Then the leader of the Terakana rose up (the others had all spoken sitting). He looked angry and in contrast to the previous speakers his voice was harsh and loud. He said: 'I am angry with the omda; when blood fell among you he kept deceiving me. He said come to me[28] at such and such a place, then said no, the water was bad. I said, when we camp at Umm Bireysy I'll come to you; he said no, the birds are eating my millet gardens. Omda, where will I come to you? Come to me at Umm Tebeddir, he said. Is that genuine? Yes, that's genuine. I put on my best clothes and collected my people. I am coming I said, and he said no I'm moving camp. The omda's talk, you cannot lay hold of it. Then what's your opinion, omda? He said come to me at Bieyṭy. Again he said come to me at Abu Ḥejel. [They met.] There were few of us; myself [and a few others he mentioned]. I asked him where the sons of El Zeyn[29] were. He said I know their opinion. I asked him where the sons of Nur el Din[30] were. He said I know their opinion. I accepted this, and we made a reconciliation.[31] We spent the dry season, and in the early rains came back here to the Muglad. When the people were coming up through the Goz, blood fell again. After that, I wanted the omda to come to me. [He did not.] I don't want your brotherhood at all.'(D)

The next Turkani spoke as follows: 'My words are addressed to Ḥurgaṣ sitting there. I made reconciliation with Ḥurgaṣ but when blood was spilt among my people Ḥurgaṣ did not come and make reconciliation with me. The omda has done nothing but deceive me. And I haven't run away. But the only people who have listened to me are the 'Ariya. Since you don't want my brotherhood, I don't want yours.'(E) And another Turkani said that the omda's brotherhood was 'brotherhood of deception only'.

After this it was the turn of the mediators. The sheikh of Jumal el Din Zerga of the 'Ariya, who retained the alliance with Awlad Salamy after the rest of the 'Ariya had broken it, and who was sitting with Awlad Salamy, spoke thus: 'What I have seen here [in Dar Humr] is that if there is a killing, the two sides break off their relationships for

[28] In order to make reconciliation and in this case arrange for the payment of blood-money.

[29] i.e. Boya's influential extended family.

[30] i.e. the brothers of the dead man.

[31] By the payment of blood-money.

a long time, but in the end they make reconciliation. This is not an invention of ours but it is a custom of our grandfathers. In the old days when something happened by night [i.e. a homicide, which arises mainly over women and at night] the matter did not go to court, but they settled the thing between themselves. Then our time came, and courts came and every little thing they take to the district office. Now we elders are like the great men of olden times. The people who came after us have become very bad, the youngsters do not listen to tradition. In the presence of us elders, you have to agree completely to reconciliation. Am I not from the 'Ariya? Today I have left the 'Ariya and I'm sitting with you. Here and now you must say the *Fatḥa*.'[32](F)

This elder was a man with a great sense of social responsibility, and had been the Mezaghna representative in the Rural Council. His speech of regret at the passing of his wise generation, however, was simply a sign that he himself had passed that age at which a youth likes to boast 'I'm better than you, I've killed a man'.[33]

The omda of Awlad Kamil was present and tried a bit more persuasion on the Terakana: 'All your talk about the omda is true. But Ḥurgaṣ knows his wrong; he won't be beaten with a stick; it is better to blame him than to beat him. But if the omda behaves in this way again then we elders shall be on your side. But now listen to what we say: be brothers.' (G)

A notable of Awlad Kamil gave a specific example of the patching up of a feud in his omodiya: 'Look, there was an affair with us once, but now Dar Nala and 'Iyal Ghashim have become brothers. I who am talking to you became their sheikh. You all know 'Iyal Ghashim, and their killing was a tougher matter than yours, and people were in jail for ten years. But we became brothers. Since Allah created the Arabs, men have killed their brothers and made it up with them. Omda, you are in error. Admit your guilt and finish the matter off'.(H)

After another example from the Jubarat by a Jubari notable, the chairman turned to the Terakana and addressed them: 'Look, your talk in this place before the elders and mediators is not fitting. When we go to our camps, we shall pass judgement on the omda and say that the Terakana blood was spilt, but that it passed over his head and he refused to come to terms; and you Terakana, I am with you because what you say of the omda is true. The omda won't be beaten and won't be

[32] The opening of the Koran.

[33] i.e. in vengeance. But in the ideology of men of their twenties vengeance here implies not only vengeance for a killing but vengeance for any slight. The phrase is '*Ana faitak, ana katalta ẓol*'.

The end of the feud: saying the opening of the Koran

(*Facing p.* 183)

slaughtered, and continuous blame like this is not good. Now we have all come, look at the thicket full of people on your behalf. Make peace. Listen to what I and the elders are saying.'(I)

One of the Terakana replied, and after a fiery start, ended with: 'Very well, after two days leave the omdaship and seventy pounds here before us', offering brotherhood at a price. The elders quietened the buzz of excitement that now arose, and explained that the omdaship was in the hands of no one but the nazir. Then Dawud, the Turkani in-law of Awlad Salamy, said: 'My words to you are these. See how we are all sitting here together, there can be nothing sweeter than this. And your talk about the omdaship and of the seventy pounds—the omdaship is not Ḥurgaṣ's, it belongs to the Government. No, simply reconcile yourselves without further fuss.'(J) But Sheikh Fiḍeyly was still fighting: he said that Dawud had spent the rains with the omda at the cotton gardens in the south, and that they had come to terms already.

Awlad Salamy took up the offer, and soon the wealthy members of 'Iyal Rigeyby were on their feet and swearing by the divorce of their wives to offer cattle to the value demanded and more. Some Terakana were still objecting, but one of them arose and said: 'Quiet, everybody, quiet. Quiet, you Terakana. Look, see how we are sitting together, what could be better than this. Say the *Fatḥa* and make no more talk.' (K) And the *Fatḥa* was said.

The next day, representatives of Dar Ḥantor told Awlad Salamy that they had decided to take only one *teniya* cow, worth £10, which would be divided—£6 to the Terakana and £4 to Dar Ḥantor; but that Dar Ḥantor had subsequently refused even this, and so £6 should be paid to the Terakana. On the next Thursday, market day, Awlad Salamy met the Terakana in Muglad with £6 provided by three members of 'Iyal Rigeyby. The Terakana refused to take it. They had demanded a price of peace, and, in consideration of their genuine desire for brotherhood, had now 'killed' every piastre of it.

When this peace was accomplished, the political alignment of the Mezaghna was as follows: Awlad Salamy, Dar Ḥantor and Terakana, and Jumal el Din Zerga were together; Awlad Mumin and Beni Helba; and Dar Bakheyt with the remainder of the 'Ariya. Bulola, under Ndalo, were by themselves. During the 'Ariya attacks on the omdaship Shigeyfa, Ndalo, and the sheikh of Awlad Mumin were said to be making common cause. Dar Bakheyt, although still allied with the 'Ariya, were said to be a restraining influence on them. Perhaps for this reason, the first thing that the newly reaffirmed alliance in Dar Abu Timani did was to have a man from Dar Bakheyt chosen as the member of the Rural Council for Mezaghna affairs, on the retirement of Ndalo from that post.

There were also signs of a change of heart in the splinter camp of 'Iyal Ganiṣ. During the 'Fellata' trials most of them had stood by Ḥurgaṣ in Muglad, but there was bad feeling between the two camps; for one thing, a member of the main camp threw a spear at (and missed) a member of the splinter camp whom he found with his wife;[34] and for another, a member of the main camp was complaining bitterly about the treatment meted out to his sister and his niece by the member of the splinter camp to whom his niece had been betrothed. But when the 'Ariya began their attack, it was a young man from the splinter camp who showed the most indignation at it. The domestic squabbles, though serious, were not enough to make the splinter camp withdraw their political support from the omda.

In the quarrel between the Terakana and Awlad Salamy, political groups took over immediately after the first death and continued to try and regulate it right through. To begin with, their attempt failed when payment of blood-money did not have the customary effect of preventing a reprisal. Personalities entered again later, for normally the leader of the guilty lineage (here Ḥurgaṣ) should have begged for peace sooner than he did. He was a stubborn man with a high and very personal sense of honour; and as he held back, on account of minor disputes within the major quarrel, from offering to buy peace, the sheikh of the Terakana heaped greater calumnies on his head, and as a result Ḥurgaṣ became the more offended, and prevaricated the more. But in the end continual pressure from neutrals, elders, and the men of Awlad Salamy persuaded him, and exterior factors persuaded him even more strongly, to admit the guilt of his lineage and press for peace.

The people whom I have called elders and mediators, the *ajawid*, played a very important part throughout. The activities which they had in common in the affair were aimed at the prevention of further bloodshed and the restoration of brotherhood and political alliance. In the beginning they tied up the men who would be most likely to go off immediately and commit an act of vengeance. When it came to the peace-making, the *ajawid* were not really neutrals, because they were on the side of the omda—in fact it was the omda who had invited them; their aim was not primarily to find a middle way but to ensure peace between the contending parties. In fact they are not neutrals at all. They are identified with the side which is seeking peace rather than the side

[34] Although he may have suspected, he had not known in the dark that the man was a surra fellow. Suspicions were confirmed only later.

which would continue vengeance. Thus, however old they may happen to be, in affairs in which they are not themselves involved, they take the part of moderates to curb hot-headedness: they proclaim the virtue of patience rather than that of vengeance, of humility rather than righteous indignation. Accordingly it seems that their role here goes rather beyond that of the 'stranger' or 'outsider' in many anthropological accounts.[35] For they take an *active* part in forestalling likely vengeance by tying the possible avengers to trees and informing the police about the situation; and they are supposed to be active rather than passive agents in bringing about reconciliation. For example, the indignation over the absence of the Faḍliya (p. 173) assumed that these men, great friends of, yet agnatically apart from, the Mezaghna, were failing in their duty by not taking deliberate steps to bring the parties together. The stranger is something more than a suitable intermediary whom contending parties invite to help them compound their difficulties. In short, there are two regular stages on the road to peace. The first is that discussion of the affair is removed from the hands of the families most immediately concerned and is made a matter for the representatives of the lineages to which the contenders belong; and secondly, the mediators come, at times voluntarily, at times commandeered, to put over the value of brotherhood and general peace on a plane above the value of vengeance and continuing grudge—both attitudes being among the Humr highly acceptable in different circumstances. Perhaps 'moderator' would best describe the role of these men.

It would appear also that the peace-making ceremony itself enhances the role of the mediators and of the values which they represent. Awlad Salamy were very doubtful from the outset about the result of the ceremony, and after the first speech by Sheikh Fiḍeyly no one thought there would be a successful conclusion. Nevertheless, I believe that Fiḍeyly's speech was simply a pose of anger and hostility, and that those who eventually are willing to sell peace for a price like to make it appear that they do so only because of the dignity of the occasion and the presence of serious and responsible elders and mediators, and out of respect to them.[36] Their actual desire for peace was

[35] The emotional atmosphere of the whole meeting, particularly following Fiḍeyly's speech, was very tense.

[36] Cf. Evans-Pritchard on the Nuer leopard-skin chief (*The Nuer*, Chap. V) and Frankenberg on the role of the 'stranger' in a Welsh village (*Village on the Border*, *passim*).

After the meeting one sceptic said that the Terakana and Dar Ḥantor could hardly have refused to make peace. Had they refused, on a later occasion they would have been obliged to slaughter two more bulls.

confirmed later by their refusal to 'eat' the £70 which Awlad Salamy were prepared to pay them for it.

When affairs reach the stage that the Terakana–Awlad Salamy dispute had reached in the rains of 1954, two courses are open to prevent the continuation of a running sore within the wider lineage. One course is for the lineages to keep their camps and migration routes at a distance, so that in effect no contact remains between the adversaries; or to break the brotherhood, and for the aggrieved party—here the Terakana—to go off and make alliance elsewhere. Fiḍeyly threatened this; had he gone, all the Terakana and possibly Dar Ḥantor would have followed him. The other course is to make peace in a solemn ceremony, as actually happened. What Humr see as unworkable is to continue for any length of time in the kind of relationship in which these two lineages found themselves over five or six years. The matter is solved by ending the quarrel, or else by moving so that contact becomes unlikely.

The outcome of this feud has to be seen in the light of the context of Mezaghna power relations generally. The event which made the men of Awlad Salamy apply pressure to Ḥurgaṣ was the continuing bitter attack by the 'Ariya on his omdaship, a matter which Awlad Salamy regarded as their own personal prerogative.[37] The event which finally persuaded Ḥurgaṣ to swallow his pride, to approach his kinsmen, and his junior, Boya, with expressions of guilt and humility, was the rumour that Dar Abu Timani, if they were united, might be offered a court presidency. This strengthening of his own immediate lineage was Ḥurgaṣ's first step in attempting a *rapprochement* with the Terakana and Dar Ḥantor. Fiḍeyly had been waiting for Ḥurgaṣ to approach him and sue for peace: without this, Fiḍeyly and his followers could never come to terms with Ḥurgaṣ, for to everyone the situation was clear—Ḥurgaṣ was the leader of the offending lineage in the dispute, so Ḥurgaṣ had to go on his knees and beg. Fiḍeyly's angry speeches reflected his long-lasting frustration and made the pact more telling when it was finally concluded. The newly sealed alliance later on the same day approached Awlad Mumin and Beni Helba; but attempts at a peace between them ended in a babble of rage from both sides. Dar Abu Timani was still riven—but the sides were now reduced to the primary divisions within it, Awlad Mumin and Beni Helba standing together against Awlad Salamy, the Terakana, and Dar Ḥantor.

[37] As Boya said: 'The omdaship—what matters is not the name the omda gets, but the honour which it brings to his kinsmen.'

12

POWER AND THE AGNATIC SEGMENTARY MODEL

CONCLUSION

OUR review of political behaviour has shown the Humr to possess many features of stateless, agnatic-segmentary societies, yet we can hardly place them squarely in this category. They are now, so to speak, less stateless than they were: some of the floating power positions of the previous century have become stabilized, and there are signs of dynastic development. The agnatic-segmentary attributes, while present, do not operate systematically. The episodes point to the incompatibility of stabilized power and the agnatic-segmentary model, and it is to this problem that my concluding remarks apply.

Before an external administration imposed them, the society had no stable offices. Their introduction necessarily implied radical change: for while the exercise of *uninstituted* power seems quite compatible with an agnatic-segmentary system, such a system would appear to require the absence of *instituted* power positions, for the following reason. The system comprises sets of lineages, the components of each set being not only collateral in accepted dogma, but also equal in political status, the balance between them being 'sustained by a distribution of like, but competitive, interests among homologous segments'[1] at all levels of segmentation; as Barnes remarked, the 'particular characteristic of lineage systems which significantly distinguishes them from the fixed social divisions of many states' is that 'segmentation goes on continually'; and because of this continuous process, 'the system is governed by the same principles at all levels'.[2] In such a system, if personal power positions exist, then so long as their distribution is flexible the sovereignty of each segment and sub-segment can be asserted by a refusal to follow a super-ordinate leader, and by the adoption of a leader of its own. But establishment of stable offices at some

[1] Fortes and Evans-Pritchard, *African Political Systems*, p. 14. The contrast is between the model there presented and contemporary Humr practice.

[2] Barnes, *Politics in a Changing Society*, p. 49.

levels must then break this continuity, and the system cannot remain governed by the same principle at all levels. When, as among the Humr, high-level offices are established and have to remain filled, the autonomy of the lower segments is weakened. The system is coterminous with the society; and seen from the aspect of collateral segments the instituted offices mean that one segment, through the officer, has formal authority over others. The balance of parts, which is supposed to let the system function and persist, is lost.

From an early stage of fieldwork it was plain that the agnatic segmentary model did not wholly explain past and existing divisions and alliances. I tried to build a picture of the political system from the data of observed or narrated political events, and to avoid forcing facts into an agnatic mould. M. G. Smith rightly pointed out that 'lineages have been taken as institutions *sui generis* and the tendency has developed to define political organization in segmentary societies in terms of lineage organization, *instead of the other way about*'.[3] This remark comes from a passage aimed at finding a meaning of 'political organization' that would be valid for societies of any type. The Humr themselves made it hard for me to follow the implied injunction, because their 'dogmatic mode' of segmentation, which is their own agnatic segmentary model, colours most events, and their interpretation of most events. It tends to lead the investigator astray.

To define Humr political organization 'in terms of lineage organization' would be misleading. While an appropriate lineage morphology is present, and while there undoubtedly exists a political morality—the 'brotherhood of the closest'—derived from the dogmatic mode, nevertheless political action often disregards it. Humr sometimes act in accordance with it, but more often it remains an ideal, a blueprint to them of what their society *ought* to be like and which they—mediators and others—bear in mind at times of crisis. They are not, and they realize that they are not, organized in terms of it in their everyday political relations.

It is clear that the 'dogmatic mode' does not explain but stands as a part, and only a part, of Humr political reality. We have to cut it down size and gauge the role of this enduring model in the whole political process.

An agnatic model implies comparatively stable lineage segments which are potentially durable as political units. Their segmentary attribute logically means that, to be effective, each group is demarcated in terms of some interests from collaterals, and shares with them other interests on the basis of which they unite in action from time to time.

[3] Smith, 'On segmentary lineage systems', p. 59, italics added.

Such a model loses explanatory power if it is shown that other groupings, differently based on other interests, cut across lineage segments. The 'peace in the feud' depends not so much on a balance between lineage segments as on the fact that these have little real autonomy, their individual members being so swayed by other diverging interests with cognates, affines, and neighbours that they have little time for the single-minded pursuit of the interests of their lineages.[4]

With the Humr, an additional factor impairs the efficacy that the agnatic segmentary model might have. This is power. While the power structure has changed, the presence of some men with more power than others has been constant. Power among the Humr derives largely from wealth and strength of personality. Before the Condominium, Humr had a horse, cow, and slave culture in which the ability to attract and lead men to raid slaves and to defend themselves against cattle raids brought material advantage to all concerned. Bravery and manly qualities were at a premium. From time to time fights broke out for the command of followings. The temporary ascendancy of a man and through him of his lineage was a recognized fact; this leader was allowed the exercise of power by his followers, but his leadership was ephemeral and the size of following changed.

The new administration altered the power structure by its very existence, and in particular by establishing offices over the tribe as a whole, over its two main sections, and eventually over omodiyas. These positions gave some men a measure of ascriptive authority over people who might never have followed them otherwise. As the positions become established so did rivalry for them in the institution of the intrigue or *fitna*. In the absence of a 'royal family' with generations of social approval behind it, a position is open to any johnny-come-lately with the wealth, personality, and inclination to command a following; only strong Government support enabled the two families of nazirates to entrench themselves. A Humrawi holds no man or line to be specially fitted for office; broadly, though not exclusively, he sees as unfit the omda or nazir who belongs to a line other than his own. Rivals are not the possible candidates from one family only, but from the whole group of which the officer to be replaced is representative. Thus the field of competition is wide; rebellion in the local form of intrigue is prevalent, and the turnover of omdas shows how effective it can be.

In the old days political association under leaders was an answer to various challenges, for warfare and enemy raids were of common occurrence, while slave-raiding and elephant-hunting were profitable

[4] Gluckman, *Custom and Conflict in Africa*, Chapter I.

pursuits that needed numbers, leadership, and organization. But now these reasons for leaders have little strength. What kind of interests now compel men to follow leaders and to associate politically?

Many studies of segmentary societies have stressed the significance of local loyalties, based in interests in common territory, and have shown how these become identified with the loyalties of agnatic segments. The defence of, and the right to exploit, their own territory are among the factors creating bonds of community interest. But the Humr lack local communities. None of their segments has rights in land; there is only casual association, through frequent usage, with stretches of territory. No Humrawi uses force against other Humr encroaching on the place he is at. There are no internal boundaries. They do not compete with one another for land as an economic resource. They regard the land they live on as Government property which the Government lets the tribe, as a whole, exploit. The free grazing is used without friction by segments however far they may be from their usual areas. There is a moral obligation not to fight over surface water; well water can be tapped readily over most of the dry-season area. There is little conflict over privately owned gardens. The traditional areas associated with the larger sections are not so different from one another as to lead to competition for superior stretches; and the very variable and sporadic water in the Babanusa during the early rains creates over a succession of years a community rather than a division of interest among the tribe as a whole.

Wealth or class differences are another possible economic ground for political action which can be excluded. In the past especially, but also today, variations through time of one family's stock prevented the rise of classes distinguished by differences in wealth. It is true that the descendants of former slaves are distinguishable by their status, and most have poverty in common, but they do not combine; rather, each family sees its security in vertical attachment to its former masters.

Political action must accordingly have other grounds. Analysis of the various kinds of segmentation and alliance in being—the 'dogmatic mode', 'genealogical mode', and the 'alliances'—will perhaps suggest what these grounds may be. The dogmatic mode exists as a kind of political philosophy in the idiom of agnatic kinship. Apart from that it has the appearance of being effective in a number of ways as an organizing principle. We have seen it apparently at work in the geographical distribution of the larger segments,[5] in the leadership of intermediate lineages,[6] in the paths which men tread in seeking power[7] in extra-

[5] p. 26. [6] p. 153. [7] p. 110.

tribal blood-money transactions,[8] and in the frequencies of close and distant marriage partnerships.[9] But often enough this mode has only the appearance of being the basis of action.[10] Humr say a lineage acts in concert, but this simply means that most of its members do, or that its most famous men and his followers do.[11] It does not mean that all of them necessarily do. The end of the Mezaghna feud showed this very clearly. The omda wanted to rally his major lineage, and he set about trying to achieve this in a manner consistent with the agnatic segmentary model, by first rallying his minor lineage. Although 'Iyal Bulola continued to stand apart, it was nevertheless Awlad Salamy that approached the Terakana and Dar Ḥantor. Again, in the dispute of the 'Ariya against Dar Abu Timani, the 'Ariya were without Jumal el Din Zerga, who were, in fact, with the enemy, and Dar Abu Timani were without 'Iyal Bulola, Awlad Mumin, and Beni Helba.[12]

The most drastic changes in the dogmatic mode occurred with the introduction of a new power structure. Some major lineages had their status raised to omodiyas.[13] Alterations of other kinds sometimes occur with the displacement of a sub-segment from one segment to another.[14] This is, in itself, quite in line with what is known as agnation, where genuine and fictitious links are of equal value. But here, genealogy does not 'prove' the dogmatic arrangement, or follow it when it changes. Instead, there is a separate mode of segmentation, more surely based on genealogy, which exists concurrently with it and differs from it.

The genealogical awareness that some groups are and some are not descended from Ḥeymir comes out symbolically (cattle brands);[15] and in conversation the facts are a confidence enjoyably related by 'true' Humr. The knowledge can be used, as by the Metanin against the Jubarat, or in opposite fashion by Beni Helba against Awlad Salamy, to underline existing hostility;[16] but where friendship obtains (Metanin and Ziyud) the distinction has no value. At surra and minor lineage level the genealogical mode does not distinguish strangers but does distinguish linked segments,[17] with effects on some final blood-money distributions[18] and on residual property rights.[19]

These co-existent modes are ideal patterns which are sometimes, at least partially, translated into action. The empirical picture, however, is above all one of 'alliances' which continually emerge in different patterns. These patterns find expression in blood-money arrangements, and agreements about them are made or reviewed every time men are

[8] p. 102. [9] p. 87. [10] p. 157. [11] p. 143. [12] p. 173.
[13] p. 108. [14] p. 12. [15] p. 99. [16] p. 171. [17] p. 150.
[18] p. 210. [19] p. 150.

killed or wounded; on these occasions the patterns of co-operation and non-co-operation are public declarations of political attitudes. Examples have shown how many nuances a single blood-money transaction can express. Resulting alliances can be far from the dogmatic mode, although some basis in it is usually discernable. Now these changing alliances are central to political activity; they are established after long discussions where everything affecting the relations of the agnatic segments has been considered, and the result is an interpretation of the political condition of each segment, at all levels, for the time being.

Alliances are continually changing. Why, despite the ideological strength of the dogmatic mode, do they not conform to it? If alliances are usually at variance with the dogmatic mode, why is the latter so strongly emphasized? The agnatic-segmentary model does not have the necessary flexibility to be a model for political action. It is, of course, not entirely rigid; but its limitations are particularly evident when we consider the stabilized power positions. We have seen from examples how this kind of power leads to political action which negates the fission–fusion aspect of the model. Thus, the Metanin may consider it worth while to continue attacking the nazir of the Felaita even while the latter is involved in attacking the 'Ajaira over the question of the Nazir-Umumship.[20] Again, Jumal el Din Zerga lineage found advantage in allying themselves with Awlad Salamy, whom the rest of the 'Ariya were attacking over the omdaship, one reason being that the sheikh of Jumal el Din Zerga had already found a political office with the omda's help.[21] In other words, the expectation which the facts of instituted power bring forth conflict with expectations deriving from the agnatic-segmentary process. The intrusion of power, and its derivative patronage, may mean that greater advantages are to be had from close kinship with an omda than from distant kinship with a nazir. There is no reason to suppose that a segment will rally against another segment to uphold the power of the nazir when, within the nazir's own segment, there is rivalry for his office. Thus, when the Metanin eventually rallied to the Felaita, it was not in support of their nazir, but because of an insult to the Felaita as a whole.[22] With 'Iyal Bulola the existence of a power position allowed the sheikh to set himself up as a rival to the omda. He belonged to the same minor lineage within the omodiya and was officially under the omda in his administrative capacity. He rejected the omda's nominal leadership of the minor lineage;[23] this also impaired the omda's nominal leadership of the major lineage and of the omodiya as an agnatic group.

[20] p. 141. [21] p. 169. [22] p. 141. [23] p. 172.

The ideology is consistently departed from in practice, yet it persists. The dogmatic mode is the way in which Humr express their relationships to all other members and groups in the society; it creates order out of genealogical chaos and political flux. It provides each person with his own position in society in terms of a simple, clear, stable, inclusive, and universally recognized scheme. In this way it affords continuity of a kind which the shifting alliances could not supply, and in the absence of local communities, by means of which the relations of the parts could be spatially comprehended, we must regard this as a significant function. For it is the only mode which extends the concept of *khua*, brotherhood, to embrace every member of the society. The fact that leaders of intermediate lineages exist, despite their lack of function in comparison with surra leaders, omdas, and nazirs, emphasizes this, for they are potential foci of segment unanimity.

Alliances come into being for the immediate purpose of dealing with blood claims. The decisions are whether to co-operate or not, and if so to what extent. Full co-operation represents the height of goodwill. Evidence of unbrotherly behaviour leads to non-co-operation. Within the omodiya brotherly behaviour leads to or sustains co-operation, and outside the omodiya it leads to co-operation under the Book alliance, or to the position of mediator. Examples from our cases of the type of behaviour which led to non-co-operation included intrigue with a view to seizure of office, discontent with particular officers, intra-surra homicide, and the very wide category of failure of a guilty party, in a variety of disputes, to seek peace by admitting guilt. The latter can cover nearly everything, for Humr admit that men are hot-headed, that blood is liable to be shed, and that events take place which can be compounded only when guilt has been admitted. As the mediator said in the Mezaghna peace-making, 'Since Allah created the Arabs, men have killed one another and made it up with them'; and when it came to the point the blame did not attach to the original killer or to the man who committed the vengeance, but to the leader who for four years refused to proclaim the guilt of his minor lineage. This was the public verdict as given by the mediators. Vengeance is natural, even to be anticipated from youth, but it should be confined to the extended family concerned, while political leadership should rather formulate opinion like that of neutrals in whom moderation is more admirable than vengeance.

Discontent over appointment to office ranks high, as the prevalence of intrigue suggests. The 'Ariya wanted the omdaship;[24] 'Iyal Bulola

[24] p. 172.

wanted the omdaship;[25] the Terakana thought the wrong man was omda;[26] the Metanin wanted the nazirate of the Felaita;[27] Awlad 'Umran wanted the Nazir-Umumship removed from Awlad Kamil.[28] This was unbrotherly; and yet the situation is bound to be endemic where officers are so clearly associated with their own sub-segments in the officered unit. Omdas and nazirs go through no ceremony removing them from membership of their sub-segment, identifying them with the whole unit, and warranting their impartiality. In many respects they act for the whole, but kinship pressures, which have helped them achieve office, equally remind them of their special bond with their sub-segment. They are just as much unofficial leaders of their minor and major lineages as they are official leaders of their omodiyas. This is a cluster of roles which no omda can avoid; he has to look to the interests of his minor lineage and his omodiya simultaneously; there is no reason to suppose he will succeed.

The special advantage of having a close kinsman as omda is that he is a man in contact with higher authority, where advantages may be gained; he is rightly or wrongly envisaged as a protector or a buffer against higher authority's demands—or its excesses, as Humr see them. He is an element of security, and security of a kind is sought not only from omdas but from other leaders also. The tribute sheikh who can advance capital and perhaps help minimize the number of stock declared, the omda who can find jobs and speak in his nazir's ear, and the nazirs, the ultimate dispensers of patronage, are all leaders with functions of security. In choosing whom to follow, a factor such as kinship distance has to be weighed against the effectiveness of different personalities for the ends expected. In adhering to a leader, one is also adhering to a group of particularly close brothers within the all-embracing *khua* of the Humr, a group which for the time being finds security in sharing a single version of the truth about contemporary events, and in giving mutual support in affairs of blood. The group is usually a different set of people from that which the agnatic system alone would elicit; I have tried to show the effects of power on the alignments.

[25] p. 169. [26] p. 178. [27] p. 137. [28] p. 140.

APPENDIX 1

OMODIYA AREAS

THIS appendix should be read in conjunction with the map at the end of the book, which shows the rains and the dry-season areas and the main migration routes. In interpreting the map the reader is asked to understand that any omodiya boundary represents no more than the rough outline of the rains and dry-season districts within which most members of one omodiya camp in most years. The actual overlapping and intermingling is more than can be successfully suggested on a map. The migration trails shown are only some of the most usual routes taken. According to changing water situations, it may be necessary to blaze fresh trails, and caravans may zigzag instead of going direct. The motor roads which run from Muglad to Abyei and from Muglad to Keylak are often used, but as caravan routes they are not conspicuously better than the other commonly used trails; the road north-east from Muglad towards El Nahud is much better than the trails in the Babanusa, where bush is thick, but it goes in the wrong direction for most people. The omodiyas whose names are written against the trails are simply those which use the routes more than others.

Humr name camp sites after the place from which they get water. On the Bahr, a camp site takes its name from a rain pool, a watercourse, or a meadow; in the Goz, the Muglad, and the Babanusa, the names are those of rain pools. Near these waters there is always plenty of land available for camping, and one source of water can accommodate camps of many omodiyas around it. Beside Lake Keylak in summer there are usually some Jubarat, Salamat, and Metanin, as well as some Messiriya Zurg. Around Koya are Ziyud, Awlad Serur, and Awlad ʻUmran. Lau has Faḍliya, Mezaghna, and Awlad Kamil; Buk has Awlad Kamil and Fayyarin.

The omodiyas and the areas mainly associated with them are given in their accepted west-to-east order.

(1) *The Fayyarin.* These are concentrated in the dry season in the corner formed by the River Jurf (as the Humr call the Bahr el Arab) and the Kordofan–Darfur boundary. By administrative agreement they also extend westwards into Darfur and mix with the Rizeygat at Tigl and Konga el Ṭalḥa. They extend eastwards to Buk and Ghabush and also penetrate south of the River Jurf. Grimty, where recently a market and local court have been

established, is the acknowledged centre of their dry-season area. They move northwards on or near the road which runs from Grimty to Muglad. Their gardens were formerly all in the western and south-western part of the Muglad, but are now largely in the sandy country to the west, south-west, and north-west. In the rains they camp near their gardens, extending north-westwards as far as Tibbun.

(2) *Awlad Kamil.* They follow the Fayyarin to the east. In the dry season they camp north and south of the River Jurf, on the Regeba Umm Bioro and at Duwas, while east of the Muglad–Abyei road they camp at Goleh, Seidana, and Lau. They migrate northwards by various trails through the sand to their gardens; most of these are in the western portion of the Muglad, but a few lie east of the road. Awlad Kamil do not go more than twenty miles or so northwards from the Muglad in the rains, and they camp in a circumscribed territory which they share to a considerable extent in the west with Fayyarin and in the east with Mezaghna and Faḍliya. They have recently opened numerous gardens in the neighbourhood of Tibbun.

(3) *The Meẓaghna.* The dry-season centre of this omodiya is at Lau, some twelve miles east of Abyei, among permanent settlements of Ngok Dinka. They line the watercourses north of Lau, extending along the Regeba Zerga to Dubeyb. They extend also south-eastwards towards the River Jurf at Abyemnom, camping extensively on the open flood plain between the Abyemnom–Bentiu road and the river. Migrating, they share the Muglad–Abyei road with Awlad Kamil, and have their own trails in the sand east of the road. Nearly all their gardens are within two miles east and west of this road, from 'Angereyb in the Goz in the south, to Ghubeysha near Muglad town. Recently they have also cultivated by rain pools in the Babanusa lying on the same north–south axis. Their rains camps are almost due north of Muglad.

(4) *The Faḍliya.* When the Faḍliya were united with Awlad 'Umran they moved with them, but latterly they have been moving more with the Mezaghna. The dry-weather camp is at Lau and on the northern branch of the Regeba Zerga at Goleh, at Abu 'Iyeydat and eastwards to about Ḥasoba. They move north along the eastern Mezaghna and the western Awlad 'Umran trails to their gardens, most of which are south of the Wadi el Ghalla and near the Abyei road. In the rains they are usually in the eastern part of the district occupied by the Mezaghna.

(5) *Awlad 'Umran* (Menama and 'Addal). In the dry season Awlad 'Umran camp on the Regeba Zerga from Mellem eastwards, some crossing into the flood plain south of the Regeba Zerga near Abu Gurun. They are found also at Kwak and Koya, while some remain in the open meadowland (known as the *Firshai*) at Nyama. In moving, they go north-westwards through Nyama or just west of it cutting the Goz and reaching the Muglad in the south-east near Baraka. In this area and near the Wadi el Ghalla they have most of their cultivations. although in recent years they have opened up

many gardens in the Babanusa by El Gubba and El Sidr. In the rains they move north and north-east from the Muglad.

The omodiyas mentioned so far constitute the 'Ajaira section of the tribe. Just as there is no clear boundary between omodiyas, so is there no clear boundary between 'Ajaira and Felaita.

(6) *The Metanin.* The members of this omodiya are very scattered in the dry season, although many are near Koya and Kwak. Others spend the season just east of the Muglad itself, and in the cotton area of the Metanin on the Keylak-Muglad road. Some go to Keylak, and two lineages spend the season among Awlad Kamil. Metanin gardens are all in the Kijeyra district on the Wadi el Ghalla, east of the Muglad, and in the rains the Metanin camp in the Babanusa, from El Sidr north-east as far as Mumu.

(7) *The Ziyud.* Some spend the dry season at Nyama, others at Koya and on the small watercourse eastwards of this at Umm Ganzus and El Merfa'in. With the rains, they migrate through the Goz from Nyama to Fishik, just east of Awlad 'Umran; they cultivate with Awlad 'Umran and east of them, as well as near Kijeyra. In the rains they are to be found from Nimr to Mumu.

(8) *The Jubarat.* These spend the dry season at Kudungor, which is their centre. They sometimes extend south-westwards along the small watercourse running out of Keylak, but this is mostly for the purpose of catching fish. Others camp nearby at Keylak. They move north-westwards by the main Keylak road. As far as their gardens are concerned, these are quite out of the east–west order which is otherwise fairly well kept, for they are in the eastern part of the Muglad; in the rains the Jubarat move over roughly the same area as Awlad 'Umran, going no further north-east than Nimr.

(9) *Awlad Serur.* This omodiya camps in the dry season in and beyond the Ziyud area. From Koya they go southwards, hit the lower part of the Regeba Zerga at Doleybat, and follow it down as far as Umm Shebushaya, past summer camps of Rweng Dinka from Nabagaya. Others are at Nyama, while others still go to L. Abyad and to the various wells used by sedentary cotton cultivators in that area, many of whom are Awlad Serur. These return by the Keylak–Muglad road, while those from Koya go north, cross the Wadi Shelengo, and join the Keylak road just west of it. The gardens of Awlad Serur are at various places near the Wadi el Ghalla, from Baraka northwards towards El Fula. The rains area of this omodiya is a wide and indefinite one, much the same as that of the Ziyud and Metanin.

(10) *The Salamat.* Their dry-season camp sites are near their cotton gardens at Keylak and immediately to the north, and when water supplies finish there they move to Fezary in the Nuba hills among certain Nuba with whom they have close friendship. From the Keylak road, they migrate north-west to Dar el Kebira in Dar Messiriya, and thence to their gardens near El Fula and around the Humr–Messiriya border. They are the easternmost of the Humr in the rains also, for their camps are mostly around El Odaya in Dar Hamar, although one or two camps are to be found near Mumu.

APPENDIX 2

DISTRIBUTION OF CATTLE THROUGH INHERITANCE

THE cases of distribution given here all come from the surra of 'Iyal Ganiṣ, where I was on familiar enough terms to be able to discuss the details. The relatives mentioned as surviving include those who, in the particular case, would be entitled to receive part of the inheritance under Islamic law.

(1) On his death, Koshy (Fig. 5, p. 54) left much stock; he was survived by his wife, daughter, and two full brothers. I could not ascertain the total number of cattle. His wife got one *jeḍa'a* cow, his daughter got 'one or two' head, and his brothers divided the rest of the cattle between them.

(2) On the death of Ṭabeyg, son of Merida (Fig. 3, p. 51), ten head remained. Ṭabeyg left his father Merida, a wife, his mother, his brother Ḥurgaṣ the omda, and two sons, El Hunna and Ḍaḥiya. His wife received a *jeḍa'a* cow. The other nine head were divided between his two sons. His parents were offered shares, but declined to take them.

(3) Ḍaḥiya, brother of El Hunna (see case 2) died as a youth. He had no other brothers, and was unmarried, but his mother still lived. All the cattle went to his brother.

(4) Merida Umm Beddy (Fig. 3, p. 51) left few cattle. His son Ḥurgaṣ, by then omda, had many cattle at the time. His daughter Ghubeysha had cattle in her hands from the marriage of her daughter; Merida's son Ṭabeyg had died. He left also his wife El Nogo and his youngest son Sheybun. All the cattle went to Sheybun, who had none.

(5) When El Jaly (p. 63) died he left only one cow. He had a son and a daughter. The son got the cow.

(6) When Bokur (Fig. 6, p. 55) died, he left a large herd. He was survived by his son, who got all the cattle.

(7) Adim Kabbira (p. 61) died leaving two cows and a bull. His relatives were his wife, his son, and three daughters. The bull went to his wife and the two cows to his son.

(8) Ḥamid 'Ulm (Fig. 4, p. 54) died leaving two sons and four daughters. His property in livestock consisted of a mare, two cows, and a bull. Shortly after his death the mare gave birth to a young mare. This was bartered for a bull calf, which was slaughtered in sacrifice for the dead man. The bull went to the younger son, and the cow was shared between the two sons. The mare died.

TABLE 11. *Comparison between actual and legal distributions of cattle in cases* 1–10 *by percentages*

Case	*Distribution*									
(1)	*W*	*D*	*B*	*B*	*Z*					
Actual	*jeḍa'a*	one or two	50*	50*	—					
Islamic	12.5	50	15	15	7.5					
(2)	*W*	*F*	*M*	*S*	*S*					
Actual	10	—	—	45	45					
Islamic	12.5	16.6	16.6	27.1	27.1					
(3)	*M*	*B*								
Actual	—	100								
Islamic	33.3	66.7								
(4)	*W*	*S*	*S*	*D*	*D*	*D*	*D*			
Actual	—	—	100	—	—	—	—			
Islamic	12.5	21.9	21.9	10.9	10.9	10.9	10.9			
(5)	*S*	*D*								
Actual	100	—								
Islamic	66.7	33.3								
(6)	*S*									
Actual	100									
Islamic	100									
(7)	*W*	*S*	*D*	*D*	*D*					
Actual	33.3	66.7	—	—	—					
Islamic	12.5	35	17.5	17.5	17.5					
(8)	*S*	*S*	*D*	*D*	*D*	*D*				
Actual	66.7	33.3	—	—	—	—				
Islamic	25	25	12.5	12.5	12.5	12.5				
(9)	*W*	*M*	*S*	*S*	*D*	*D*	*D*	*D*		
Actual	*jeḍa'a*	—	50*	50*	—	—	—	—		
Islamic	12.5	16.2	17.8	17.8	8.9	8.9	8.9	8.9		
(10)	*W*	*W*	*B*	*B*	*B*	*Z*	*Z*	*Z*	*Z*	*D*
Actual	—	—	—	—	66.7	—	—	—	—	33.0
Islamic	6.25	6.25	7.5	7.5	7.5	3.75	3.75	3.75	3.75	50

* In cases 1 and 9, those marked at 50 per cent. shared the residue of larger herds after distribution of other named cattle.

(9) Jedid Ḍow el Nur (Fig. 6, p. 55) left a large herd. His survivors were a wife, his mother, two sons, and four daughters. The cattle were divided as follows: his wife got a *jeḍa'a* cow, and the remainder was divided equally between the two sons. His mother refused the share offered to her. The daughters got nothing.

(10) Aḥmed Ibrahim (p. 62) died leaving two cows and a bull. He left two wives, a daughter, three younger brothers, and four sisters. His daughter got a cow, and his youngest brother got a cow and a bull.

(11) El Nagy and his wife Khadijy (Fig. 3, p. 51) died in quick succession leaving an orphan baby 'Omar. In Islamic law the property of the first deceased should have been distributed before the property of the second deceased, including anything she had posthumously received from the first. Here the distribution of the ten head (husband and wife had both owned cattle) took place at the same time. The cattle were given to the husband's father to be kept in trust for the orphan; and he immediately handed them over to the orphan's mother's mother, who was looking after the child. Islamic distribution would have given 80 per cent. to the orphan, 17 per cent. to the father's father, and 2 per cent. to the mother's mother.

In Table 11 the actual distribution of cattle in these cases is tabulated and contrasted with the distribution which would have taken place if it had strictly followed Islamic law.[1] The shares in Islamic law and the shares in actual distribution have both been expressed as percentage shares and given to the nearest decimal point.

Cases 4 and 10 are particularly instructive. In case 4, under Humr custom Ḥurgaṣ and Sheybun would be the people, as sons, most likely to inherit. Ḥurgaṣ already had a herd, whereas Sheybun had nothing, and he got the cattle. In case 10 two brothers who might have received were given nothing; the eldest of these had married a rich wife and was living in her camp. The deceased had been a member of the local police; his death left a vacancy which was filled by his youngest brother, and the family felt that this was the equivalent of inheriting material goods—indeed, it amounted to the inheritance of a regular income. I was also told of one of these brothers that 'we would never have given him anything anyway; he's too stingy'.

If a case of inheritance should find its way to court, the division is made according to Islamic law as pronounced by the Islamic lawyer in court. The same happens if Humr resort to a *faghir*, a man learned in Islam, outside of court. But they prefer to settle cases of inheritance among themselves as families. They do the same over other domestic matters: cases of adultery seldom go to court, and Humr regard the out-of-court settlements as much more equitable to all concerned. A court would apply Islamic law without deviation and accordingly would fail to take into account the varying fortunes of different family members.

[1] I am grateful to Dr. Ḥasan Turabi for making this computation.

APPENDIX 3

DRUM CALLS

In some cases there are separate drum calls for each surra, while in others a whole large lineage may share the same drum call. In former years there was much jealousy over the ownership of and the right to beat out a drum call, and it is said that fights have arisen over the playing of a particular call by a man who was not entitled to do so. The drum calls are a rhythmical replica of spoken words, and the words given to match each drum call are all said to have had some origin in a particular event in the past concerning the section which owns the drum call. Many of the phrases seem now meaningless, and the transliterations may be chancy.

This appendix gives the distribution of drum calls throughout the tribe, except for the Metanin, the Jubarat, and the Menama section of Awlad 'Umran, on whose cattle brands I have no information either. I have had to rely on informants for most of the information, as a personal check of so many groups was not possible.

El Fayyarin

This omodiya has a different drum call for most surras. The A. 'Ugla surras are as follows:

Rid	has	Seyembu
Jibrin		Wazir Riff
Zibraj		Jirgeyl Dubr el Dud
Makindy		Umm Kazm
'Uthman, Shittay, and Gimray	have	'Ajuz Gum

A. Umm Hany:

Ferraj	has	Tayi Sindu
Erzag		Wazir Riff
Uḍa'a		Habbab Wald Umm Dull

A. 'Awana drum calls are as follows:

Umm Raḥma	has	Sulṭan Gal Lei Kaddab
Khuda'		?
Ḥamid		Tayi Sindu
Musa		Kheyr Sidd el Derb
Umm Ḍeyfalla		?

and A. Kimeyl el Zerga as follows:

Hambal and Hireys	have	Kelb Katal Kelb
Umm Ja'ar and Nas Kerim		'Ajuz Gum

In El Eyser section of the Fayyarin, A. Ṣaddag have the following:

Jimeyly	has	Tayi Sindu
A. 'Alama		'Ajuz Gum

and 'Iyal Ḥamdun:

El Ḥamra, Ḥamdun, and Na'im	have	Dar Ḥamdun
Nyallamte	has	Atim Bug or Kayi Durr
El Ḥaj		Jirgeyl Dubr el Dud

A. Kamil

In this omodiya, the major lineages tend to share drum calls.

All of Dar Salim	has	Wazir Riff
All of Dar Mota		Sheykh Wald Umm Dull
All of A. Kimeyl		Umm Heyny Gulti Silli
Dar Umm Sheyba Ḥamra		Tir Laga
Dar Umm Sheyba Zerga		Jengy Jull
El Barokela		Hideya Karr
All of A. Tuba		Tayi Gum
and El Kelabna		Kayi Durr

El Meẓaghna

They have only four drum calls among them.

Dar Abu Timani	has	Umm Kazm
El 'Ariya		Kuku Sidd el Derb
Dar Bakheyt:		
Umm Khyeydim		Hideya Karr Karr
Umm 'Eylyan		Allah Sidi

El Faḍliya

The distribution of drum calls is as follows:

All of Ṣabir	have	Kheyr Sidd el Derb
Among Birḍan:		
Diringil, Abu Daly, Wenesa and Kireyl		Allah Sidi
Markun and Shambol		Shibb el Goz
Sa'ur		Elfibin

A. 'Umran

The smaller lineages of the 'Addal are the units:

Abu Ḥimmeyd	has	Tir Shal Tir
Abu Isma'in		Kheyr Sidd el Derb
but Nas Ramaḍan		El Dill 'Auz el Derb
Nige'y		El Sheynat Lamman Jin
Abu Ghadeya		Ṣaleḥ Teksur Ga'id Durr
El Nowashy		Kheyr Sidd el Derb, and also Furwa Kokendey Takul el Gesh el Hey
Abu Ḥammad		Shibb el Goz el Turab el Zeyn

El Ziyud

Here the unit is the major lineage.

Umm Jemul	has	Harig Gam da Gesh el Fam
Umm Jowadat		Hideya Karr Karr
but El Faghara		Kheyr Sidd el Derb
El Ghabsha		El Tamul Jauder Beydy
El Zebada		Sheykh Wald umm Dull
A. Kucha		?
El Mahdi		Tay el Sandul (or Tayi Sindu?)
A. Ḥammad		Sheykh Wald umm Dulf
Umm Sebib:		
Ḥamra		Shibb el Goz
Zerga		Chowchow Ketir[1]

A. Serur

A. Jifir	has	Shibb el Goz el Turab da Zeyn
A. Jamma'		Wald el Dumm Ga'id Durr
Umm Khamis		Kheyr Sidd el Derb
Umm Bokoda		Kudb Kau Kau
Jerafin		Hideya Karr Karr
Umm 'Eylyan		Katalna Kelb fog el Derb

[1] Chowchow is the Dinka-Arabic word for milk, in common jocular use among the Humr.

Salamat

Most surras have their own drum call.

Deyanat	has	‘Ajuz Gum
Dude		‘Ajuz Gum except for one extended family
	which has	Kheyr Sidd el Derb
El Ma‘aly	has	Hideya Karr Karr
Musa		Tundum
Ḥamid		El Sheykhat Lamman Jin
Kirim		Tundum
Beney		Shibb el Goz
Umm Biṭṭeykh		Tundum
Ḥamid		Tayi Gum
Bokur and El Timan		Halati Gat Lei Silli
Abu Idris		Sulṭan Gal Lei Kaddab
A. Faḍl		Sheykh Wald umm Dulf

APPENDIX 4

CATTLE BRANDS

CATTLE brands, usually called simply *nar*, are marked on cattle when they are quite young. They are not used for other animals. Not all groups which have separate cattle brands have separate drum calls, and vice versa. In the list which follows, which is in no way complete, all I have tried to do is to indicate the more general cattle brands, and the reader should remember that there may, in most cases, be other differentiating brands within the smaller groups. Thus the list of brands for the omodiyas and the larger lineages is probably nearly complete, but the proliferation of them in the smaller groups is only tentative. A single animal may have many brands on it.

EL 'AJAIRA

Common to all the 'Ajaira except the Fayyarin, the Beni Helba section of the Mezaghna, and Dar Nala of the Kelabna (Awlad Kamil) is the *shelga*. This is a curve from the knee of the left hind leg round to the base of the ribs. The Fayyarin and Beni Helba do not have it because they are not 'Ajaira by descent. On the other hand, there may be other sections within the 'Ajaira who are not 'Ajaira by descent but who nevertheless use it.

Unless otherwise stated, all cattle brands are on the *left* of the animal.

El Fayyarin

The Fayyarin are in two main lineages, El Eyser and El Eymen, named from the position of their cattle brands (or vice versa): El Eymen brands are on the right, El Eyser on the left.

The Fayyarin do not use the *shelga*. They have, however, one brand which is common to all the Fayyarin, namely the *mogran*, a line from the left or right eye according to the section.

In addition to this, the sections have brands as follows:

A. 'Ugla. A. Rid have the *jerrai* on the right cheek and the *soṭ* — a long line from shoulder to knee of the right leg.
The remainder have in common the *'ogl* on the right hind leg and the *lam alif* (some on the front, others on the hind right leg). There are other minor differences.

A. Umm Hany. This khashm beyt all have *utad* on right front leg, and *damy* on right cheek.

A. 'Awana and A. Kimeyl. All have the *lam alif*, though some on front and others on hind right leg.

A. Ṣaddag. All have the *soṭ* on the (left) front leg.

A. Ḥamdun. All have the *she'by*, a single stroke, left leg.

A. Kamil

All, except Dar Nala, have the *shelga*. Lineages are distinguished variously as follows:

Dar Salim has the *rieykib*.

Dar Mota has the *soṭ* on the neck, while the surra Faḍl has, in addition, the *halaga* over the position of the liver.

Dar Umm Sheyba. Ḥamra has the *gulady* on the leg and the *kajy* over the *shelga*, with many other differences among surras.

Zerga has the *gulady* on the neck, snout, and leg, with an arc (unnamed) below the hump. Many other minor differences.

El Barokela have the '*arch* on neck and two diagonal lines on back leg.

A. Tuba all have the *soṭ* on front leg.

El Kelabna have the *korobach* front leg and shoulder. The cattle of Nazir 'Ali Nimr do not have the *korobach* but instead the *nun* on back left leg.

El Meẓaghna

They all, except for Beni Helba, have the *shelga*.

A. Salamy. I. Ganiṣ have the *jerrai* on flank and (cows only) the *taffer* across back legs.

The rest have the *rukab* in various positions.

El Terakana have the *taffer*, and the *rukab* on front leg.

Dar Ḥantor have no *taffer*, but *rukab* in same position.

A. Mumin have *matarig* on front leg.

Beni Helba do not have *shelga*, but have the *ashbur* in place of it.

El 'Ariya. Jumal el Din Ḥamra have the *girn mutawwag el derry*.

Jumal el Din Zerga have *mutrageyn* above front knee and also above the *shelga*.

Abu Ghadir have many different brands, e.g. Didan has the '*asay* on saddle; and Sileyman and Aginda have *rukab* over the *shelga*, the *durma'at* in front of left eye, and the *serima*.

Dar Bakheyt unverified.

El Faḍliya

All have the *shelga*.

Ṣabir. Rige'y have the *rukab* below the *shelga*: El Uḍa'a have the *gulada* on neck: Idris have the *ba'j* over liver; Umm Jabbar have the *rukab* in front of the *shelga*.

Birḍan. Diringil have *jerrai* above *shelga*.

Abu Daly and Kireyl	*damy* below right eye.
Wenesa	*ba'j*.
Merkun	*korobach* on front leg.
Shambol	*nahad* (*soṭ* on front leg) and the *she'by*.
Sa'ur	*nahad* and the *rukab* above it.

A. 'Umran

The 'Addal have mostly varieties of the *shelga* with little else.

Abu Ḥimmeyd. She'by have the *buru*, a very small *shelga*, and the *she'by* on the flank.

Buru have an ordinary *shelga* with *shelgat el buru* beside it.

Abu Isma'in all have *tetawwag el derry*.

Abu Ghadeya *shelga umm 'iyal*.

The remainder, Nige'y, El Nowaṣhy, and Abu Ḥammad, all have simply the *shelga*.

EL FELAITA

The brand of the Felaita is the *guna'* over the eye, but among the Felaita it is only those two omodiyas descended from Felait who have it, namely the A. Serur and Metanin.

A. Serur all have the *guna'*.

A. Jifir all have	*nushaby*.
A. Jamma'	*matrigeyn* on neck.
A. Umm Khamis	small *nahad* on shoulder.
Jerafin	*gulada*.
Umm 'Eylyan	*she'by* on shoulder.

El Ziyud

They do not have the *guna'*. All have the *soṭ* from shoulder to knee, but the surra of I. Soṭ Abu Erwe have the brand known as *soṭ abu erwe*.

El Salamat

These do not have the *guna'*. All have the *khutum*. The other brands among the omodiya are distributed as follows:

A. 'Ali. Zurg have the *she'by* on the waist, *el ḥarr* on back.

A. abu Gadeym. Musa have *je'eyby*, the *halaga* on lower neck, and the *shebbal*.

Ḥamid have *she'by* on cheek.

Jababry. Kirim have *she'by* on cheek and *'ogr* on front leg.
Beney have *el ḥarr* (single) on back, slightly to the left.
Umm Biṭṭeykh ?

A. Sa'idy. Ḥamid and Bokur have *she'by.*
El Timan have *el ḥarr* (single).

A. abu Idris have *mwalif* on neck.

A. Faḍl have *ba'j* and a diagonal cross on front of back leg.

El Jubarat

No *guna'*. The two main lineages into which the Jubarat are divided are named according to the brands which distinguish them, viz. the *she'by* and the *gulada.*

The cattle brands have to be distinguished on animals from brands made medicinally, for the most common indigenous means of dealing with cattle ailments is to brand them. The medicinal brandings are usually more coarsely done than the brands proper, and generally speaking they are quite readily distinguishable by their designs and their positions.

Key to cattle brands

'arch 
'asay three short horizontal lines
ashbur 
ba'j long vertical line on flank
buru very small *shelga*
damy two short diagonal lines
durma'at in front of eye
el ḥarr two short horizontal lines
girn mutawwag el derry curve from hind leg to udder
gulada (*gulady*) ?
guna' over eye
halaga a circle
jerrai 
je'eyby on rump
kajy ?
khutum as *serima*
korobach  (Kelabna) (Faḍliya—Merkun)
lam alif 
matarig, matrigeyn, mutrageyn two short horizontal lines
mogran line from eye
mwalif as *lam alif*
nahad as *soṭ*
nun 
nushaby short vertical stroke below ear
'ogl, 'ogr two short horizontal lines
rieykib 
rukab 
serima like a bridle across snout
she'by short vertical line ('Ajaira)  (Felaita)
shebbal a line at right angles to *khutum*
shelga 
shelgat el buru 
shelga umm 'iyal 
soṭ long line usually shoulder to knee
soṭ abu erwe 
taffer 
tetawwag el derry as *girn mutawwag el derry*
utad two short vertical lines

APPENDIX 5

DETAILS OF A BLOOD-MONEY TRANSACTION

In the main text I have given only the outlines of blood-money transactions. Here are details of payment and receipt following the killing of a man of Awlad Salamy by a man of the Terakana (see pp. 163 and 174).

One-third of the total of sixty head was to be paid as 'spearhead' by the killer and his close kin. This left forty head to be divided in the ratio 2 : 1, among the rest of Dar Abu Timani on the one hand and the 'Ariya and Dar Bakheyt on the other, according to the arrangement which the nazir had recommended. Within Dar Abu Timani, the share was to be divided into three, so that each of the traditional blood-money alliances would pay one share: Awlad Mumin and Beni Helba, Terakana and Dar Ḥantor, and Awlad Salamy. Then on the receipt of cattle, what was left after the 'share of the blood', of two-thirds, had been given out, would be divided in the same ratio. At the time Awlad Salamy had an arrangement with the Kelabna (of Awlad Kamil) whereby the latter would take a third of any share falling to them. We can thus tabulate as follows the various commitments:

Due to pay		*Head of cattle*	*Due to receive*		*Head of cattle*
SPEARHEAD			SHARE OF THE BLOOD		
Terakana		20	I. Rigeyby		40
SHARE OF THE MANY			SHARE OF THE MANY		
'Ariya and Dar Bakheyt	$\frac{1}{3}$	13	'Ariya and Dar Bakheyt	$\frac{1}{3}$	6½
A. Mumin and Beni Helba	$\frac{2}{3}$	9	A. Mumin and Beni Helba	$\frac{2}{3}$	4½
Terakana and Dar Ḥantor		9	Terakana and Dar Ḥantor		4½
A. Salamy		6	A. Salamy		3
Kelabna		3	Kelabna		1½
		60			60

But the actual payment was different. Most of the group that were due to pay were also due to receive; and only those paid who had more to pay than they had to receive. Half beasts were excluded in the final calculation; and on the advice of the nazir, 'Iyal Rigeyby, the dead man's surra, had nothing to pay, and the three beasts from Awlad Salamy as a whole would 'die in their belly'; thus also their Kelabna allies had nothing to pay. In the end the beasts which the elders received in the fence built for the purpose were as follows, and came from the sources indicated:

'Spearhead' from Terakana	20 head
'Ariya and Dar Bakheyt	6
A. Mumin and Beni Helba	4
Terakana and Dar Ḥantor	4
	34

In the distribution of this amount the brothers of the dead man, who were due for two-thirds of the blood-money of sixty head, got two-thirds of the number of cattle collected. The first division of the beasts was as follows:

(*a*)	Brothers of dead man	23 ($\frac{2}{3}$ of 34)
(*b*)	Father's brother	3
(*c*)	I. Rigeyby	2
(*d*)	A. Salamy less I. Rigeyby	5
(*e*)	Presiding elders	1
		34

Later, from share (*a*), the brothers of the dead man gave one of their animals to be divided among the rest of 'Iyal Rigeyby. In dealing with share (*c*), 'Iyal Rigeyby recognized their close genealogical links with 'Iyal Ganiṣ and 'Iyal Bulola, and they divided the value of the two head among the three surras in the proportions 2 : 1 : 1 respectively.

As a result the two brothers of the dead man, from the 22 head which they retained, had cattle to the value of about £90 between them. The father's brother had three head, worth about £13. With the beast from (*c*) and the beast from (*a*) 'Iyal Rigeyby had cattle worth about £9, from which each extended family received about 60 piastres. From the five head of cattle in (*d*) each extended family of Awlad Salamy, less 'Iyal Rigeyby, got 12 piastres. In addition to this, 'Iyal Ganiṣ and 'Iyal Bulola each got £1.75 piastres from the cow in (*c*); since 'Iyal Ganiṣ had seventeen extended families, each got 10 piastres, making a total for each family of 'Iyal Ganiṣ of 22 piastres. No one else received anything.

APPENDIX 6

SPEECHES MADE AT THE PEACE-MAKING CEREMONY BETWEEN A. SALAMY AND DAR ḤANTOR

(see pp. 180–3)

A. El ʿora wagaʿat fi nina jo roḍona, wal ʿora wagaʿat fokku untu, wa nina jiyitna di dairin ily el khua, ateseyu untu, kullina ḥamdin bea.

B. El dummi bigit fi nina jitu roḍotuna, wal ʿora bigit fiku untu, ma jinaku, nina ghalṭanin khalaṣ wa ghaliṭna nina ʿerifinna. Duraʿna ingaṣṣat tapp. El ʿiyal ṭawa dol ma benhafdu. Badeyn nina o untu negba akhwan. Ferrishna khalagna. ʿOritna nina ʿerifinna. ʿAmilu leyna.

C. Ana da sid ed dummi lakit el ʿora bigit fi ana intu ʿeriftuni, wal ʿora bigit fiku untu ma roḍeytku. Ana ghalṭan khalaṣ. Nina khua belaku untu ma dairinna, o nina dairin el merjela o merjela belaku untu mafi. Kin tebi khuitku nina khuitna ma mnaba.

D. Ana zaʿlan min Ḥurgaṣ da. El dummi bigit fiu zata, ghasshani begul taʿalni fi mehall fulan, gal el moya baṭala. Umm ḥaṭṭeyna Umm Bireysy bajik, gal kau, at teyr akalan az zerʿ. El ʿomda ajik yeyn? Tejini fi Umm Tebeddir. Kalam rasmi? Wai, kalam rasmi. Ana kiseyt, lammeyt nasi. Badur bajik, gal ley ana basir. Ana Ḥurgaṣ da kalama ma belmessik. Dom raiak shinu Ḥurgaṣ, gal tejini fil Bieyṭy. Gal tejini fi Abu Ḥejel. Fina schwir; ana, (. . . .) Sa'alta gal 'Iyal El Zeyn yeynu? Gal kalamhum ʿendi. Sa'alta gal 'Iyal Nur el Din yeynu? Gal kalamhum ʿendi. Ana khalaṣ ṣaddag fi kalam da, heya roḍḍeyta. Seyyefna. O jina hinny rushash. Dam el nas ṭalaʿo el goz dammitu wagaʿat. Del ḥasal, badur Ḥurgaṣ bejini. Khutak ma mnedura dut.

E. Ana kalami le Ḥurgaṣ el gaʿid da. Ḥurgaṣ ana roḍeyta ol dummi bigit fi ana Ḥurgas ma roḍani. O ana, Ḥurgaṣ yeghasshini ghassh sakit. O ana ma baʿrid. Masakoni ily el ʿAriya. Madamit khuti ma bedura, ana khuta ma daira.

F. Ana katal dummi hinny o nina o huma wagafna keee, aroḍḍeyna baṭṭan. Kalam da ma soweyna nina, el kalam min ed judud. Zeman el nas el kubar kin teḥassel haja fil leyl, ma leḥego el hukum, ja marra ayi ghalṭa yejibu el merkaz. Tabbo tehiṭna. Nina el kubar bigina zey nas el gebeyl el kubar. El nas el tabbo teḥt, el dugag, bigo baṭalin khalaṣ, ma besmaʿo el ḥadis. Jiyit el ajawid di, arḍo nina tapp. Ana mani 'Ari? El 'Ariya khalleyna ga'adna ma'ku. Fi bukanna da ily el Fatḥa.

G. Intu kalamku fog el 'omda kulla saḥḥe. Ol 'omda 'orta 'eriffa, ma binkattil be 'asa lakin el lom akheyr min el katl. Kin baṭṭan el 'omda roḍḍa kalam zey da, nina ma'ku. O hala tesma'u kalamna, tebgo akhwan.

H. Shufu, nina ḥassalat haja beynatna, o hala Dar Nala o Ghashim bigo akhwan. Ana el belkallim da bigit fokum sheykh. Ghashim kullaku te'rifuhum, katl dumm ashidd min dummuku untu o ḥabiso fia nas 'ashera sinin. Bigina akhwan. Min Alla ma khalag el 'Arab el nas katalo akhwanhum o roḍḍo. El 'omda, inta ghalṭan, shil lomak o roḍḍo tapp.

I. Shufu, kalamku da fi bukanna el ijwady ma bilrobben. Ol 'omda el ga'id da dam nimshi ferigna hinak benegṭa' fia, negul el 'omda ṭa'is, el Turkani dol nina dummithum waga'at, el kalam da kulla fait rasa, o aba ma roḍḍohum; o intu el Terakana ana ma'ku o kalamku fog el 'omda kulla saḥḥe. El 'omda ma binkattil o ma binḍabih, ol loman ma 'enda feidy. Jiyitna di shuf al kub' el melyan da, ily fi shanku untu. Arḍo tapp. Tesma'u kalami wa kalam el ajawid.

J. Ana kalami leyku, shufu ga'ditna di ahla minna mafi. O kalamku hil el 'omodiya da o hana es saba'eyn da, el 'omodiya mi Ḥurgaṣ, hil el ḥakuma. La, arḍu sakit bela kalam.

K. El juma' sa, sa. Usuktu el Terakana. El Nadhir shif ga'ditna di ahla minna mafi. Shilu el Fatḥa baṭṭan ma tesowa kalam.

APPENDIX 7

THE OMODIYAS AND THEIR SECTIONS

EL ʻAJAIRA

EL FAYYARIN

- El Eymen
  - A. ʻUgla
    - Rid
    - Jibrin
    - Zebraj
    - Makindy
    - ʻUthman
    - Shittay*
    - Gimray
  - A. Umm Hany
    - Ferraj
    - Erzag
    - Uḍaʻa
  - A. ʻAwana
    - Umm Raḥma
    - Khudaʻ
    - Ḥamid
    - Musa
    - Umm Ḍeyfalla
  - A. Kimeyl el Zerga+
    - Hambal
    - Hireya
    - Umm Jaʻar
    - Nas Kerim
- El Eyser
  - A. Ṣaddag
    - Jimeyly
    - A. ʻAlama
  - Ḥamdun
    - El Ḥamra
    - Ḥamdun
    - Naʻim
    - Nyallamte
    - El Ḥaj

* The surra called Shittay is composed of descendants of the Shatt people whom the Humr found in their country on arrival.

† A. Kimeyl el Zerga is a section which broke off from A. Kimeyl el Ḥamra lineage of A. Kamil.

Note: In these lists, the smallest subsections are surras and the others khashm beyts.

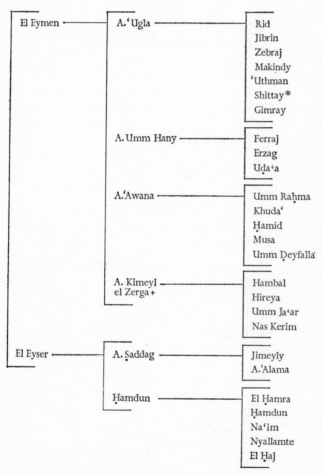

A. KAMIL

- Dar Salim
  - Ghasiby
    - Bashir
    - Kabbo
    - Hunuwa
    - Bandago
    - Wada‘talla
    - Gideyrish
  - Faḍḍala
    - Ḥamid
    - Marid
    - Jabir
    - Abgeyo
  - Bor
    - Budur
    - Idris abu Hawa
    - Ṣaliḥ
    - Abu Shenah
- Dar Mota
  - Sa‘d
    - Faḍl
      - Shidda
      - Tigga
    - Karamalla
      - Ḥamdan
      - Abu Umm Feyḍ
      - Sa‘ody
  - Umm Seyd
    - Talo
      - Sheyna
      - Ma‘la
      - Shok
    - Abu Jabra
      - Na‘m
      - Muḥammad el Yusuf
- A. Kimeyl el Ḥamra
  - Sileyman
  - Umm ‘Ajaza
  - Umm Tireymy
    - ‘Izz el Din
    - Maḥ el Din
- A. Tuba
  - Abu Diheyba
  - Ṣaluḥa
  - Faghara
  - Sefiny
  - Fakkarin

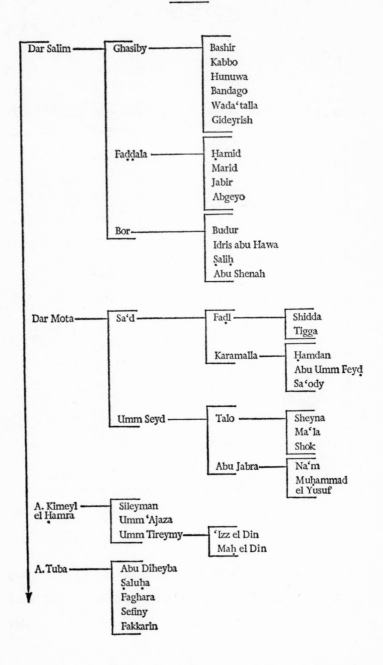

(A. Kamil continued)

- Dar Umm Sheyba
  - Ḥamra
    - Abu Sabun
      - Abu Zibeyr
      - Ḥammoda
    - Mamun
      - Abu el Naimy
      - Defi'y
      - Wanis
    - Defi'y
    - Shenab
    - Rumeyly
  - Zerga
    - Dakir
      - Habily
      - Nu'man
      - Ḥimmeydy
      - A. Salamy
      - Abu Ṣaghir
    - Jeyfil
      - Koroma
      - Habib
    - Shaily
      - 'Azoza
      - 'Aziz
    - Kelagy
      - Mungash
      - Nu'man
  - Barokela
    - Jabir
      - Miḥimmid
      - Ḥammoda
      - Roḍom
    - Atim
      - Kweys
      - 'Ali
- El Kelabna
  - Ḥarran
    - Dar Nala
    - Dar Noto
    - Dar Engeybil
  - Sileyman
    - Ghashim
      - Shimeyly
      - Abderraḥman
      - Tibbeyny
      - Ḥimmeyd
    - Dirdimy

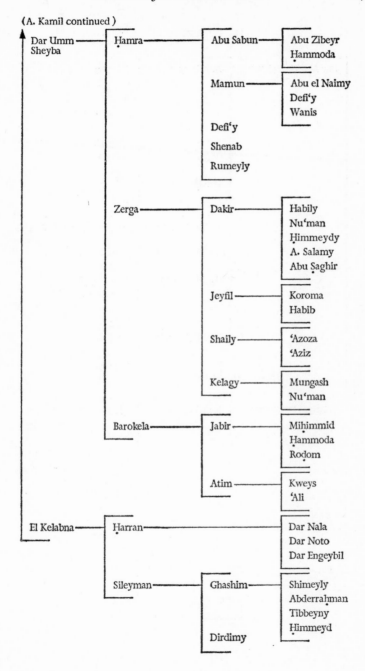

EL MEZAGHNA

- Dar Abu Timani
  - A. Salamy
    - Rigeyby
    - Ganiṣ
    - Bulola
    - Belebbo
    - Jabir
    - Damura
    - Beyyen
  - Dar Ḥantor
    - Kajbur
    - Jabir
  - El Terakana
    - Abderraḥman
      - Abu ʻAsala
      - Bushary
    - Shaibo
  - A. Mumin
    - Abu Sheygir
    - ʻIyal el Shaib
    - Derdim
  - Beni Helba
    - Gheyat
    - ʻAlaway
    - ʻAlwan
    - Gimeylat
- El ʻAriya
  - Jumal el Din
    - Ḥamra
      - Kagur
      - Khatir
    - Zerga
      - Maʻaty
      - Hady
  - Abu Ghadir
    - Abu Ḥejer
    - Basshar
    - Didan
    - Sileyman
    - Aginda
- Dar Bakheyt
  - Umm Khyeydim
  - Umm ʻEylyan
    - ʻAjuz
    - ʻAjaza

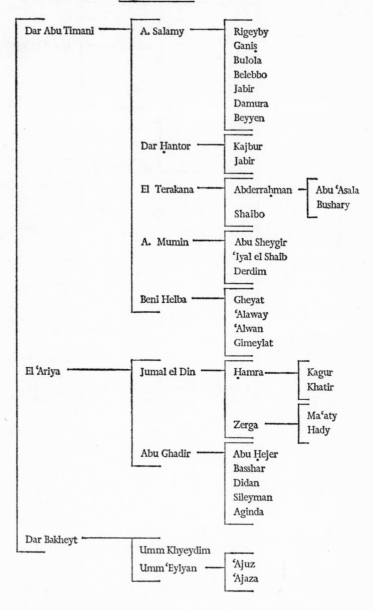

EL FAḌLIYA

- Ṣabir
  - Rigeʿy
  - El Uḍaʿa
  - Idris
  - Umm Jabbar
- Birḍan
  - Diringil
  - Abu Daly
  - Wenesa
  - Kireyl
  - Markun
  - Shambol
  - Saʿur

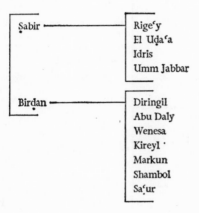

A. ʻUMRAN

- Menama
  - Umm Jod
    - A. Maʻala
    - ʻEylyan
    - Ḥammoda
    - Ḥamdalla
  - Dar Banat
    - El Sharug
    - Seytan
    - Gamar
  - Dar Zebaly
    - ʻAbdalla
    - Haniya
  - Dar Ḥeyballa
  - El Faḍliya*
- ʻAddal
  - Abu Ḥimmeyd
    - Sheʻby
    - Buru
  - Abu Ismaʻin
    - Nas Jangala
    - Nas Jammaʻ
    - Nas Abu Ḥamdy
    - Nas Ramaḍan
  - Nigeʻy
    - Umm ʻAsal
    - Umm Ḥamdun
  - Abu Ghadeya
    - Ḥamra
    - Zerga
  - El Nowashy
    - Khyeydim
    - Umm Khadm
    - Umm Jamara
  - Abu Ḥammad
    - Ṭuwal
    - Guṣar

* The surra of El Faḍliya remained with A. ʻUmran when their kinsmen broke away to form their own omodiya of El Faḍliya.

Raḥma should be added as a sixth minor lineage among the Menama.

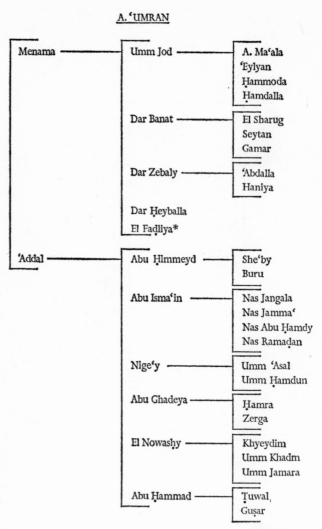

EL FELAITA

EL METANIN

A. Ziyady	Umm Juruka Bireysh Deyab Sidry
El Shamiya	Abu ʻAbdalla Abu Sogr Umm Haraby
Shebib	Ḥamid Ḥimmeyd Ḥimmeyd el Guṣar
ʻArif	ʻAli
ʻArafa	Bederon

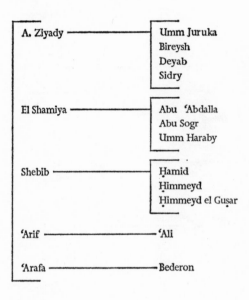

EL ZIYUD

- Umm Jemul
  - ʻIyal el Shaib
  - ʻIyal el Faghara
  - Kordaly
- Umm Jowadat
  - ʻIyal el Faghara
  - Kabberat
  - ʻIyal Soṭ Abu Erwe
  - Sileyman
  - Abu Sabun
- El Ghabsha
  - Zerga
    - Idris
  - Ḥamra
    - ʻAbd el Shafir
    - ʻAbd el Jid
- El Zebada
  - Zebeda
  - Nas el Sheykh
- A. Kucha
  - Umm Idriyas
  - Umm Baraka
- El Mahdi
  - ?
- A. Ḥammad
  - Umm Bedawy
  - ʻAbd el Ghany
  - Umm Deygir
- Umm Sebib
  - El Lezid (Hamra)
  - Ablah (Zerga)
  - Seref (Zerga)

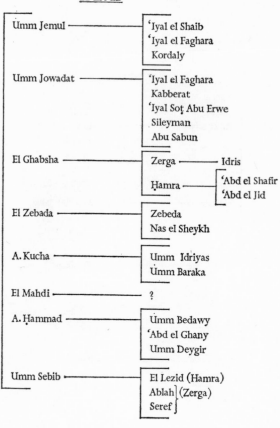

A. SERUR

- A. Jifir
  - Ḥamid
  - Baba
- A. Jamma‘
  - Amri
  - Ḥammad
  - ‘Ali
  - Suliman
- A. Umm Khamis
  - Wanis
  - Baṭran
  - Seytan
  - Ḥamid
- Umm Bokada
  - Muruwa
  - Jabbar
- Jerafin
  - El Gur‘aniya el Kubar
  - El Gur‘aniya el Dugag
- Umm ‘Eylyan
  - Jemilalla
  - Agrab
  - Jodalla

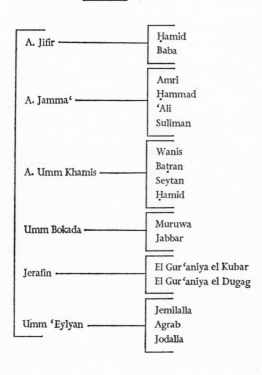

EL JUBARAT

- She'by
  - Abu Halal
  - 'Abid
  - Abu 'Id
  - Meḥsin
  - Abu Jakkak
- Gulada
  - Miḥimmid
  - Baṭran
  - Musa
  - Girfa

EL SALAMAT

- A. 'Ali
  - Zurg
    - Duda
    - Deyanat
  - Ḥumr
    - El Ma'aly
- A. Abu Gadeym
  - Musa
  - Ḥamid
- Jababry
  - Kirim
  - Beney
  - Umm Biṭṭeykh
- A. Sa'idy
  - Ḥamid
  - Bokur
  - El Timan
- Abu Idris
- A. Faḍl

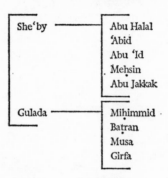

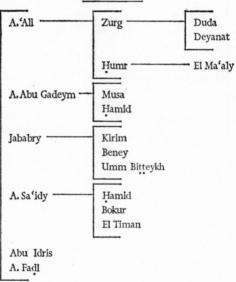

BIBLIOGRAPHY

ARBER, H. B. 'The Baramka,' *Sudan Notes and Records*, XXIII, 1 (1940), 139–50.

ASAD, T., CUNNISON, I., and HILL, L. G. 'Settlement of nomads in the Sudan: a critique of present plans'. In *Agricultural Development in the Sudan* (Proceedings of the XIIIth Annual Conference of the Sudan Philosophical Society). Khartoum, 1965.

BANTON, M. *West African City*. O.U.P., London, for International African Institute, 1957.

BARBOUR, K. M. *The Republic of the Sudan*. Athlone Press, London, 1962.

BARNES, J. A. *Politics in a Changing Society*. O.U.P., London, for Rhodes-Livingstone Institute, 1951.

BARTH, F., CUNNISON, I., and DYSON-HUDSON, N. 'The settlement of nomads as a development policy.' *Sudan Society*, II (1963) (in Arabic).

BARTH, H. *Travels and Discoveries in North and Central Africa, 1849–55*. Longmans, London, 1857–8 (5 volumes).

BEATON, A. C. 'Notes on Baggara Law'. Kordofan Provincial files, 1947.

BROWNE, W. G. *Travels in Africa, Egypt and Syria from the year 1792 to 1798*. T. Cadell Junior & W. Davies, and T. N. Longman & O. Rees, London, 1799.

CUNNISON, I. 'Giraffe hunting among the Humr tribe.' *Sudan Notes and Records*, XXXIX (1958), 49–60.

—— 'The social role of cattle,' *Sudan Journal of Veterinary Science and Animal Husbandry*, I, 1 (1960), 8–25.

—— 'The omda.' In J. CASAGRANDE (ed.), *In the Company of Man*. Harpers, New York, 1960.

—— 'Some social aspects of nomadism in a Baggara tribe.' In *Nomadism and Economic Development in the Sudan* (Proceedings of the Xth Annual Conference of the Sudan Philosophical Society). Khartoum, 1962.

—— 'Subsidiary nomadic movements of the Humr.' *The Geographical Magazine* (University of Khartoum), I (1963), 25–30.

—— 'The position of women in a Baggara tribe.' *Sudan Society*, II (1963), 24–34.

EVANS-PRITCHARD, E. E. *The Nuer*. Clarendon Press, Oxford, 1940.

—— *The Sanusi of Cyrenaica*. Clarendon Press, Oxford. 1949.

FORTES, M., and EVANS-PRITCHARD E. E. *African Political Systems*. O.U.P., London, for International African Institute, 1940.

FRANKENBERG, R. *Village on the Border*. Cohen & West, London, 1957.

GILG, J. P. 'Mobilité pastorale au Tchad occidental et central.' *Cahiers d'Etudes Africaines*, III, 4 (1963), 491–510.

GLUCKMAN, M. *Custom and Conflict in Africa*. Blackwell, Oxford, 1955.

HARRISON, M. N. *Report on a Grazing Survey of the Sudan*. Ministry of Animal Resources, Khartoum, 1955 (cyclostyled).

HENDERSON, K. D. D. 'The migration of the Messiria into S. W. Kordofan.' *Sudan Notes and Records*, XXII, 1 (1939), 49–77.

HILL, R. L. *Biographical Dictionary of the Anglo-Egyptian Sudan*. Clarendon Press, Oxford, 1951.

HOWELL, P. P. 'Some observations on the Baggara Messiria of Western Kordofan'. MS.

JULLA, 'ALI. 'The defeat of Hicks Pasha'. *Sudan Notes and Records*, VIII (1925), 119—24.

LAMPEN, G. D. 'The Baggara tribes of Darfur.' *Sudan Notes and Records*, XVI, 2 (1933), 97–118.

LEBEUF, A. M. D. *Les Populations du Tchad*. Presses Universitaires de France, Paris, 1960.

LEBEUF, J. P. 'Die Stämme zwischen Schari und Nil.' In H. A. BERNATZIK (ed.), *Afrika, Handbuch der angewandten Völkerkunde*. Schlusselverlag, Innsbruck, 1947.

LEWIS, I. M. *A Pastoral Democracy*. O.U.P., London, for International African Institute, 1962.

LLOYD, H. D. W. 'Some notes on Dar Homr.' *Geographical Journal*, XXIX (1907), 649–54.

MACMICHAEL, H. A. *The Tribes of Northern and Central Kordofan*. Cambridge University Press, 1912.

—— *A History of the Arabs in the Sudan*. Cambridge University Press, 1922 (2 volumes).

MINISTRY OF SOCIAL AFFAIRS. *First Population Census of the Sudan 1955–6*. First Interim Report.

MITCHELL, J. C. *The Kalela Dance*, Rhodes-Livingstone Paper 26 (1956).

PALLME, I. *Travels in Kordofan*. Madden, London, 1844.

REID, J. A. 'Some notes on the tribes of the White Nile Province.' *Sudan Notes and Records*, XIII, 2 (1930), 149–209.

SMITH, M. G. 'On segmentary lineage systems.' *Journal of the Royal Anthropological Institute*, LXXXVI, 2 (1956), 39–80.

EL TUNISY, MUḤAMMAD 'OMAR. *Voyage au Darfour*. Paris, 1850.

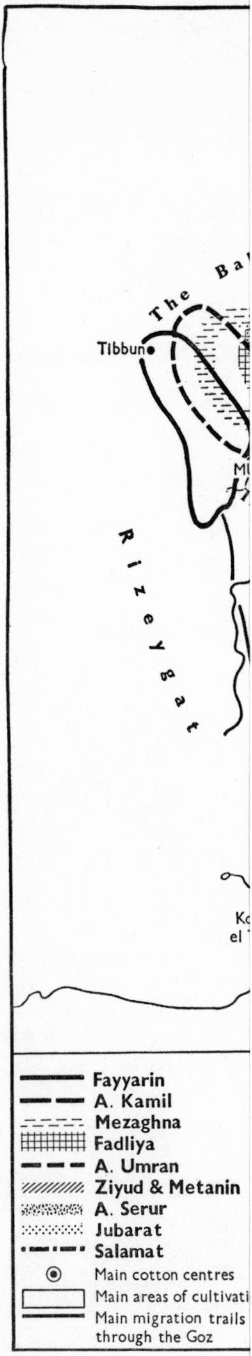
The Ba
Tibbun
Rizeygat
Fayyarin
A. Kamil
Mezaghna
Fadliya
A. Umran
Ziyud & Metanin
A. Serur
Jubarat
Salamat
Main cotton centres
Main areas of cultivati
Main migration trails
through the Goz

(Facing p. 224)

For explanation of the map see Appendix I, and p.

INDEX

Aba Island, 125, 127, 142
'Abd el Raḥman el Mahdi, Imam, 123, 142
'Abd el Wakil, 'Iyal, Fig. 7, 61f
Abu Dik Ḥamid, Fig. 5, 53ff, 61f, 79
Abu Ghadir, 'Iyal, App. 7 (216), 168f, 171, 206
Abu Ḥejer, 'Iyal, App. 7 (216), 168
Abu Jabr el Ḥaj, Fig. 15, viii, 129, 131, 137, 141
Abu Shama Ṭaha, 103, 106
Abyad, Lake, 18, 23, 171, 197
Abyei, viii, 23, 25, 172, 195
Abyemnom, 176, 196
'Addal, Fig. 1, Fig. 11, Fig. 16, App. 7 (218), 8f, 103f, 196f, 203, 207
  See also 'Umran, Awlad
Adim, 'Iyal, Fig. 5, Fig. 7, 55f, 57, 61, 79
Adim Yusuf, 102, 136, 141
adultery, 155, 200
affines, 79, 175f, 178f, 183
Aginda, 'Iyal, App. 7 (216), 168, 206
agriculture (see cultivation)
Aḥmed Shigeyfa, 171f
'Ajaira, Fig. 1, Fig. 1A, Fig. 11, Fig. 12, Fig. 14, Fig. 16, App. 7 (213ff)
  administration, 103ff
  distribution and movements, 16, 26, 195ff
  divisions, 8ff, 102ff, 111ff, 138, 213ff
  and Felaita, 8, 10, 98f, 101f, 107, 111f, 133ff, 144ff, 192
  history, 103ff, 134ff
  leadership, 98, 103, 133ff, 145
'Ajar, ancestor of the 'Ajaira, Fig. 1A, Fig. 12, 105, 112
ajawid, 174, 184f. See also mediators
'Ali bu Gurun, 28, 129f, 132
'Ali Jakkak, Fig. 6, 56f, 79
'Ali Julla, Fig. 15, 100f, 103f, 108, 134ff, 142
'Ali Mesar, 131ff, 135, 142
alliances, Book, 160, 163f, 166, 193
  changing, 97, 129ff, 145, 160, 162ff, 171ff, 191f
  cutting across agnation, 97, 113, 122ff, 145ff, 151, 155, 160, 163, 183, 191ff
  dogmatic mode as basis for, 97, 110f, 113, 168, 191, 194
  formation of, 160, 164, 193
  genealogical modes as bases for, 111, 145, 149, 157, 163ff
  and marriage, 86, 96
  influence of new political offices, vi, 145f, 192ff
  in nineteenth century, 129ff, 145
  of Origin, 160
  See also blood-money
Angol, Regeba, 78
Ansar, 142. See also Mahdism
Antila, viii
Arber, H. B., 122f
Aris Mahe, 136
'Ariya, Fig. 17, App. 7 (216), 77f, 123, 202, 206
  alliances, 162ff, 166ff, 209f
  conflict over omdaship, 101, 171ff
Asad, T., ix
'*aṣala*, 160. See also alliances of Origin; blood-money
'Aṭaya, 7, 10, 32
'Aṭiya, ancestor of the 'Aṭaya, Fig. 1A, 8, 11
Awlad or A., defined, 9
Azande, 83
'Azzaz Idris, 132

Babanusa, the, 13ff, 20f, 24f, 27, 41, 69f, 74, 78, 100, 139, 179, 190, 195ff
Babanusa town, viif, 20
bachelors, 47f, 61, 64, 67
Baggara Repeating Pattern, 16
Bagirmi, 1f
Bahr, the, 13, 18ff, 25, 64, 69, 76f, 195ff
Bahr el Arab, 18f, 131, 195f
Bahr el Ghazal Province, 25, 131
Banton, M., 126
Baramka, 122ff, 167
Barbour, K. M., 6
Barnes, J. A., 187
Barokela, Fig. 11, App. 7 (215), 99, 202, 206
Barth, F., ix, 29
Barth, H., 2, 7
Basshar, 'Iyal, App. 7 (216), 163f, 168, 172
Beaton, A. C., 158f
bedana, 8, 102, 104, 130, 132
Belebbo, 'Iyal, App. 7 (216), 63, 83, 166ff, 176
Beni Helba, Fig. 17, App. 7 (216), 6, 99f, 123, 164, 167ff, 171ff, 176, 178, 191, 205f, 209f
Berti tribe, 84, 111
Beyyen, 'Iyal, App. 7 (216), 151, 168f
black market, 139, 146
blood-money, 7, 29, 35, 39, 73, 82f, 153, 157ff
  cases, 107, 131, 155f, 162ff, 174ff, 209f
  determination of groups involved, 102, 150, 155ff, 166ff, 179f, 192f
  extra-tribal, 102f, 139, 159, 163, 166, 191
  for injuries, 158, 163f
  methods of payment and receipt, 102f, 159ff, 191, 209f
  scales of payment, 158, 161, 164, 209f
  for women, 158
Bokur, 'Iyal, Fig. 6, Fig. 7, 57, 61
Boya el Zeyn, 169, 174, 178f, 180f, 186
bribery, 107, 119, 120, 136, 146
bridewealth, 86, 92, 95
brotherhood, political, 115, 193
'brotherhood of the closest', 98, 110ff, 144
Browne, W. G., 2f
Bulola, 'Iyal, App. 7 (216), 150, 163, 168f, 171f, 179, 191ff, 210, 216

camp, composition, 25, 42, 49ff, 61ff, 65, 75ff, 80ff, 86
  economic co-operation, 66ff, 74ff
  layout, 50, 64ff, 116
  leader, 72ff
  sites, 25f, 64f, 195
  social co-operation, 71ff, 77ff
  splinter, 61, 72f, 78, 184
caravan, 65, 69, 158, 161
cash, 28f, 39f, 91f, 127, 152, 155f, 164, 209f
cattle, as blood-money, 28f, 102, 159, 161, 209f
  brands, 72, 99f, 191, 205ff
  camps, 67, 71
  and cultivation, 21f, 24, 41, 66f, 78
  and environment, 1, 13ff, 37, 85
  and followers, 28, 32f, 56f, 61, 79, 85, 114, 127, 165
  inheritance, 34f, 198ff
  loans and gifts, 33f, 83, 85
  management, 36ff, 65ff
  population, 41
  sale and purchase, 36, 39, 152
  and social change, 40
  social value, 28, 31ff, 40f
  types, 30, 36f
  uses, 28ff
  and women, 28, 30f, 34, 37ff, 61, 79, 93
  See also milk and milk products; movements, nomadic; wealth
Chad, Lake, 1, 6
Chad Republic, 4
circumcision, 34, 118
compensation, 72, 92, 158, 164, 177. See also blood-money
concubinage, 81ff

Condominium, vi, 4, 80, 103, 115, 128, 134ff, 143, 149, 151
co-operation, in cattle husbandry, 66ff, 77ff, 84f
in cultivation, 74ff
in hospitality, 71ff, 77ff, 84f
cotton, 13, 23f, 36, 38f, 53, 63, 66, 77, 143, 171, 197
Council members, 109f, 184
court presidents, 109f, 136, 139, 143, 147, 178, 186
courts, 34, 45, 109, 138ff, 146f, 154ff, 158, 177, 195, 200
local, at Abyad, 137ff, 147
at Grimti, 147
at Keylak, 137, 139f, 142, 146f
at Nyama, 143, 147
courtship, 72, 82, 91, 118, 173ff
cultivation, in relation to animal husbandry, 21f, 41, 66ff, 78
co-operation for, 22, 48f, 67f, 74ff, 123
distribution of gardens, 3, 16f, 23, 26, 75, 195ff
of household, 48f, 52
techniques, 22ff
time-table, 23f.
See also cotton; land, rights in; millet
'custom of the caravan', 158

Dajo tribe, 6f
Dakir, 'Iyal, App. 7 (215), 87, 92
Damura, 'Iyal, App. 7 (216), 100, 151, 168f, 176, 180
Dar, defined, 6
Dar Abu Timani, Fig. 17, App. 7 (216), 99f, 123, 150f, 163ff, 178, 191, 202, 209
Dar Bakheyt, Fig. 17, App. 7 (216), 123, 150, 163ff, 167ff, 179, 183, 202, 206, 209f
Dar Ḥantor, Fig. 17, App. 7 (216), 123, 166ff, 191, 206, 209f
Dar Messiriya Rural Council, viif, 109f, 141, 147, 162, 184
Dar Mota, Fig. 11, App. 7 (214), 101, 156, 202, 206
Dar Nala, App. 7 (215), 99f, 182, 205f
Dar Umm Sheyba, Fig. 11, Fig. 14, App. 7 (215), 87, 101, 132, 154, 202, 206
Darfur, 2ff, 6f, 123, 195
Dawud 'Abd el Raḥman, 176, 179, 183
Delakona Umm Beddy, Fig. 10, 52f, 82
Denga, 3, 6
dependants, economic (see maintenance of dependants)
dia (see blood-money)
Didan, 'Iyal, App. 7 (216), 168, 206
Dinka, vii, 7, 18f, 27, 29, 62f, 80ff, 102, 111, 120, 143, 174
cattle, 26, 36f, 66f
labour, 32, 40, 67, 80
disputes, 27, 72, 92f, 109, 145, 154ff, 173ff
district officers, 119ff, 126, 128, 139f, 146, 159. See also Government, central
divorce, 44, 46ff, 52ff, 63f, 72, 86, 90, 94
dress, 123f, 126
drum, 66, 72, 100
calls, 100f, 201ff
Dud Idris, 132
Dyson-Hudson, N., ix

education, 40f, 119, 162
El Dubeyb Ḥimeydan, 118
El Faḍil Maḥmud, 142f
El Fula, 13, 16, 147f, 197
El Ḥaj Ya'gub, 134, 136
El Hireyky Ṭawir, 62, 77, 79
El Hunna Ṭabeyg, Fig. 3, Fig. 6, 52, 62, 79, 198
El Ju' Kammin, Fig. 3, Fig. 10, 53, 82, 84
El Khatim Ḥeymir, 60, 62, 79
El Na'im 'Omar, 107
El Neimy Sulum, Fig. 6, 56f, 61, 91
El Nogo Kammin, Fig. 3, Fig. 10, 52f, 82, 84, 198
El Obeid, 36, 121, 125, 131f, 134
El Odaya, 131, 197

El Riheyd Dirhan, 140
elections, 110, 142f
elephant, elephant-hunting, 118, 171, 189
Evans-Pritchard, E. E., 97, 185, 187
extended family, 9, 71, 74f, 82, 85, 97f, 101
  position in camp, 65
  relation to households, 45ff, 49ff, 57f
  as part of surra, 59ff

Faḍl, ancestor of Faḍliya, 9, 105, 113
Faḍliya, Fig. 1, Fig. 11, Fig. 12, Fig. 16, App. 7 (217), 8f, 11, 103f, 140f, 203, 206
  alliances, 160
  distribution and movements, 26, 75, 77, 108, 196
  divisions, 217
  as mediators, 173f, 179, 185
  become omodiya, 105ff, 144
family, conjugal, nuclear, 45, 48, 85
Faris Ṣaluḥa, 131ff
Fayyarin, Fig. 1, Fig. 11, Fig. 14, Fig. 16, App. 7 (213), 8, 133, 201f, 205f
  alliances, 132, 140
  distribution and movements, 25f, 147, 195
  divisions, 213
  become omodiya, 108
  as strangers, 11, 102, 104, 113, 129
Felait or Felit, ancestor of the Felaita, Fig. 1A, Fig. 12, 112
Felaita, Fig. 1, Fig. 1A, Fig. 12, Fig. 13, Fig. 16, App. 7 (219ff)
  administration, 103, 105, 109, 136ff
  and 'Ajaira, 8, 10, 98f, 101f, 107, 111f, 133ff, 144ff, 192
  distribution and movements, 16, 26, 197ff
  divisions, 8ff, 112f, 219ff
  history, 129ff, 136ff
  leadership, 98, 103, 129ff, 134ff, 146
Fellata, 27, 172, 178
female links, 150, 167
feud, 94, 123, 163, 173ff, 191
Fiḍeyly, Sheikh, 169, 174, 177f, 180, 183, 185f
Firshai, the, 18, 23, 143, 196
fitna (see intrigue)
flies and insects, 13, 16ff, 25, 71
food, 30, 47, 48, 50, 66, 116f. See also milk and milk products
Fortes, M., 187
Frankenberg, R., 185
Funj, 2
Fur, 2ff, 80, 83, 123

gabily, defined, 8
Ganiṣ, 'Iyal, Fig. 7, App. 7 (216), 72, 74, 150, 165, 168f, 172, 178, 184, 198, 206, 210
  composition, 49ff, 59ff, 80ff
  co-operation in, 77ff
  marriage, 87ff
  split in (see camp, splinter)
gardens (see cultivation)
Ghashim, 'Iyal, App. 7 (215), 182
Ghereygy, 16. See also Muglad town
Ghubeysha Merida, Fig. 3, Fig. 5, Fig. 6, 52f, 83, 198
Gilg, J. P., 6
giraffe, giraffe-hunting, 18, 39, 117f, 172
Gluckman, M., ix, 189
God, 31, 39, 115
Gordon, C. G., 132, 134t
Government, central, 27, 39ff, 101, 117, 121, 143
  and Baramka, 122ff
  and Humr political organization, 97f, 103ff, 134ff, 139ff, 144ff, 149, 151, 189f
  Humr view of, 118ff, 122ff
  See also Condominium, Fur, Mahdiya, Re-occupation, Sennar, Turkiya
Goz, the, 13ff, 20ff, 27, 71, 78, 195ff
granaries, 74ff
grazing, and grasses, 15ff, 19ff, 119, 195ff
  herd, 67ff
  rights in, 25, 27, 74. See also land, rights in

guarantor of the peace, 176
guardian (*wali*), 46, 86, 89, 91ff
Gubba, 20
guests, 66, 73f
Guheyna, 1, 11
guna', 99, 207f

Habbaniya, 6, 123
Habily, 'Iyal, App. 7 (215), 87ff
Hajiz, 16
Ḥamadeyn, 'Iyal, Fig. 10, 82
Ḥamar tribe, 102
Ḥamdan, 'Iyal, Fig. 7, Fig. 8, 61f, 72, 78
Ḥamdan 'Ulm, Fig. 4, Fig. 6, Fig. 7, Fig. 8, 60f, 72, 79
Ḥamid, 'Iyal, Fig. 4, Fig. 7, 53f, 61, 79
Ḥamid el Aḥmer (see Ḥeymir)
Ḥamid Yasin, 134
Ḥamidy 'Ulm, Fig. 6, Fig. 8, 61f, 79
Ḥammad 'Abd el Jelil, 8, 182
Harrison, M. N., 3, 6, 13, 15ff, 20
Hawazma, 6f, 102, 130
hearth, men's, 64, 66, 70
Henderson, K. D. D., 1, 3, 6f, 129, 131ff
herders and herding, 66ff, 100, 119, 154
Ḥeymir, or Ḥamid el Aḥmer, ancestor of the Humr, Fig. 12, 8, 11
Ḥeymir, 'Iyal, Fig. 7, 61f
Ḥimeyd, Awlad, 6, 133
history, Baggara, 1ff
Humr, 129ff
holy men, 28, 129
homicide, 73, 154, 157, 162f, 174ff, 191ff
honey-gathering, 39
hospitality, 33, 48, 59, 69, 73, 78, 85, 101, 115, 120ff
household, 43, 45ff, 49ff, 76f.
See also maintenance of dependants; property, household; tent
Howell, P. P., 102, 113, 158f, 179
hunting, 39, 117f, 120, 124, 171f, 176, 189
Ḥurgaṣ Merida, Fig. 3, Fig. 4, Fig. 5, Fig. 6
attacks on, 63, 170ff, 177f
households of, 49ff
kinship links, 49ff, 62f, 77, 79, 91, 170
leader of extended family, 49ff, 58, 79
leader of surra, 63, 72, 77, 84, 179
leader of minor lineage, 174, 180ff
leader of major lineage, 186
omda, 49, 78f, 165, 169ff, 174, 178

Ibrahim 'Ali Julla, 142
Ibrahim, 'Iyal, Fig. 7, 61f
Idris Ka'b, Fig. 12, 145
inheritance, 58, 75, 150, 198ff
See also property, household
injury, 157f, 164, 192
intrigue, 121, 138ff, 165, 170ff, 178, 189, 193
'Isa Shweyn, 139f
'Isa 'Ulm, 169
Islam, 80. See also Mahdism
Islamic law, 34ff, 45f, 58, 198ff
Isma'in Abu Jefna, 130
'*Iyal* or I., defined, 49
'*iyal rajl* (see extended family).
In context of blood-money, 161

Jabir, 'Iyal, App. 7 (216), 83, 166f, 169, 180
jafa', 156, 161, 167
Jedid, 'Iyal, Fig. 6, Fig. 7, 56f, 61, 79
Jellaba (followers of Zubeir Pasha), 119, 132, 134
(Nubian merchants), 119
Jibril Isma'in, 130f
Jubarat, Fig. 1, Fig. 13, Fig. 16, App. 7 (222), 9, 62, 99, 105, 182, 191, 201, 208
alliances, 129ff, 133, 140f
and blood-money, 103, 107, 161
distribution and movements, 26, 75, 143, 197
leadership, 98, 136f
as strangers, 6, 11, 113, 133

Jumal el Din Zerga, App. 7 (216), 163f, 169, 173, 179, 181, 183, 191f, 206
Jurf, River (see Bahr el Arab)

Kadugli, 36, 83
Kamkara, 124
Kamil, Awlad, Fig. 1, Fig. 11, Fig. 12, Fig. 14, Fig. 16, App. 7 (214f), 8, 11, 101, 113, 155f, 160, 173, 202, 206
  distribution and movements, 26, 75, 196
  divisions, 104, 214f
  leadership, 98f, 103f, 131f
  and leadership of Humr, 98, 132f, 140f, 194
  and Mahdism, 132, 142f
Kelabna, Fig. 11, Fig. 14, App. 7 (215), 62, 101, 131, 133, 142, 160, 202, 206, 209f
Keylak, Lake, 18, 23, 25, 27, 77, 130, 143, 195, 197
Khalifa Abdullahi, the, 135f, 142
khamy, 158f
Kharif Teyman, 7
khashm beyt, defined, 9
Khitim, 'Iyal, Fig. 7, 62f
khumam, 43. See also property, household
Kibbeyry Bokur, Fig. 6, 57, 198
Kijeyra, 16, 197
Kimeyl (el Zerga), Awlad, App. 7 (213), 141, 202, 206
Kireyfan Jedid, Fig. 6, 56ff, 91
kitab, 160. See also alliances, Book.

land, rights in, 25, 27, 74, 85, 143, 146, 157, 190
leadership, 28, 32f, 42, 85, 97, 134, 144, 187, 189f
  of camps, 72f
  ephemeral nature, 98, 114f, 133, 187, 189
  of extended families, 49, 56, 58, 97f
  of major and minor lineages, 97f, 104f, 153ff, 164, 169
  of surra, 65, 72ff, 77, 97f, 153
  of tribe, 129ff
  See also nazirs; omdas; political office; sheikhs
Lebeuf, A. M. D., 6
Lebeuf, J. P., 6
Legislative Assembly, 141
Lewis, I. M., 167
Lloyd, H. D. W., 105, 159
local communities, 88, 190, 193
locality, association of group with, 24ff, 139, 143f, 147f, 190, 195ff

Ma'alia tribe, 20, 84, 111
Ma'aty, 'Iyal, App. 7 (216), 162
Macmichael, H. A., 1, 3f, 11, 113
Mahdism, 132f, 142, 179
Mahdiya, v, 4, 119, 132, 135, 142
maintenance of dependants, 34ff, 42, 45ff, 49ff, 58, 67, 79ff, 85f, 93
Malakal, 36
manliness (*merjela*), 115, 117, 126f, 189
marriage, distribution of partners, 86ff, 191
  household property in, 44f
  and non-Arab descent, 80ff
  payments, 28, 53, 86, 91f, 95
  and political relations, 77ff, 86, 94ff, 170
  preferred, 72, 86ff, 90ff, 191
  See also affines; divorce; household; maintenance of dependants
Mas'ud Idris, 132
meat, 74, 120, 127
mediators, 96, 154f, 157, 159, 173f, 181ff, 193
mehanny, 156, 161
Mekki 'Ali Julla, Fig. 15, 136, 138f, 141, 147, 180
Mekki Ḥasab (also Mekki Ḥassoba), 136
melekiya, 84
Menama, Fig. 1, Fig. 11, Fig. 13, Fig. 16, App. 7 (219), 8f, 103ff, 107f, 201. See also 'Umran, Awlad

Menawwir Habila, 132
Merida Adim, Fig. 5, 55f, 58
Merida, 'Iyal, Fig. 3, Fig. 7, 49ff, 74, 83
Merida Umm Beddy, Fig. 3, Fig. 6, Fig. 7, 49, 198
Messiriya, Fig. 1, Fig. 1A, Fig. 12, 3ff, 10, 25, 27, 131, 133, 136, 197
 blood-money with, 7, 102f, 161, 163
Metanin, Fig. 1, Fig. 12, Fig. 13, Fig. 16, App. 7 (219), 9, 11, 105, 201
 alliances, 129ff, 140ff, 144f, 191f
 and claims to leadership, 129f, 133f, 136, 194
 distribution and movements, 26, 197
 divisions, 219
Mezaghna, Fig. 1, Fig. 11, Fig. 12, Fig. 16, Fig. 17, App. 7 (216), 9, 11, 99f, 140f, 191, 202, 206
 alliances within, 150, 162ff, 165ff
 and blood-money, 107, 158, 160, 162ff, 209f
 conflict within, 101, 162ff, 165ff
 distribution and movements, 26, 75, 77, 108, 196
 divisions, 99, 123, 150f, 165ff, 216
 as part of A. Kamil, 104, 106
 sheikhs, 123, 151
migrations (historical), 4, 6, 11f
milk and milk products, 29f, 32f, 37f, 47ff, 49, 57, 67, 74, 77
millet, 3, 13, 16, 22ff, 39, 74, 76. See also cultivation
Mitchell, J. C., 126
model, agnatic-segmentary, 98, 188ff
movements, nomadic, 19ff, 78, 100, 108, 116, 129, 140, 156, 175, 186, 195ff
 kabby, *munshagh*, *ṭal'y*, *woṭy*, 22
mugaṭa'a, 155, 172
Muglad, the (area), 6, 13, 15ff, 20f, 23, 25, 27, 74ff, 78, 129, 174, 177, 195ff
Muglad town, 7f, 29, 40, 110, 125, 136, 138, 140f, 147, 175
Muḥammad el Far, ancestor of Fayyarin, 11
Muḥammad el Messir, Fig. 1A, 7f
Muḥammad Ganiṣ, Fig. 7, 59f
Muḥammad Ḥamdan, Fig. 8, 61, 77, 91
Muḥammad Kheyr, Fig. 12, 113, 145
Mumin, Awlad, Fig. 17, App. 7 (216), 63, 100, 123, 163f, 167ff, 171ff, 176, 191, 206, 209f
murḍa', 155. See also peace-making
Musa Shweyn, 137, 139, 141
muwagafa, 154f, 172, 175
Muzghan, ancestor of Mezaghna, Fig. 12, 9

Nahud, 36, 134
Nazir Umum, 94, 98, 109, 114, 136f, 145ff, 190, 192, 194
nazirs, 8, 10, 41f, 104, 120, 123, 132, 134, 144, 151, 173
 'Ali Julla (see 'Ali Julla)
 'Ali Nimr, Fig. 15, 98, 136, 173, 176f
 Babo Nimr, Fig. 15, 119, 124, 136, 138ff, 146, 163, 170, 172f, 179
 El Ḥaj Ajber, Fig. 15, 119, 136ff, 141, 146
 Nimr 'Ali (see Nimr 'Ali Julla)
 Sereyr el Ḥaj, Fig. 15, 98, 137ff, 141ff
 work of, 109
 See also Nazir Umum
Newbold, D., 179
Ndalo, Sheikh, 169, 172, 183
Nicholls, C., 122
Nimr 'Ali Julla, Fig. 15, 136
notables, 72, 153, 169
Nuba, 4, 80, 83, 102, 123, 130, 137
Nuer, 27, 117
Nur el Din Sereyr, Fig. 15, 137, 139, 142f

'Omar el Nagy, Fig. 3, 52, 200
omdas, 8, 97f, 104f, 144, 151, 153, 170, 192ff
 work of, 109
 See also Ḥurgaṣ Merida, as omda
omodiya, 8, 97, 104ff, 149ff

Omdurman, 40, 125, 132f, 135, 142
orphan, 52, 200

pagans, 80, 117
Pallme, I, 3f
Parliament, 142
peace-making, 141, 155f, 170, 179ff, 186, 193, 211f
police, 105, 153, 170, 173f
political office, achievement of, 28, 32f, 42, 85, 116f, 153
 Government recognition, 103ff, 131, 134ff, 189
 mimicry of, 122ff
 See also Council members; court presidents; nazirs; omdas; sheikhs
population, 8f
price of peace, 156, 183, 185
property, household, 29, 43ff, 95
 men's personal, 35, 47
 residual rights in, 150, 200
provider (see maintenance of dependants)

rainfall, 13ff, 27
Rashid, ancestor of Ziyud, 11
rationing, 139, 146, 151
Regeba, the, 18
Regeba Repeating Pattern, 18
Regeba Umm Bioro, 18, 25ff, 133, 196
Regeba Zerga, 18, 25, 27, 196f
Reid, J. A., 1
Re-occupation, 4, 26f, 39, 120, 127, 134ff
residence (see household)
Rigeyby, 'Iyal, App. 7 (216), 87f, 150, 165, 168f, 173ff, 209f, 216
Rizeygat, Fig. 1A, 1f, 6f, 26, 102, 125, 132f, 157, 195

Sahaly, 18, 25, 117
Salamat, Fig. 1, Fig. 13, Fig. 16, App. 7 (222), 9, 105, 143, 204, 207f
 alliances, 129ff, 133, 140
 and blood-money, 103, 161
 distribution and movements, 25ff, 99, 102, 197
 divisions, 222
Salamy, Awlad, Fig. 17, App. 7 (216), 63, 123, 206, 209f
 alliances, 160, 163, 165ff, 191f
 divisions, 150, 216
Sanusi, 97
seasons, 15ff, 19ff, 24ff, 43, 69, 195ff
segmentation, 8ff, 97ff, 111ff, 144f, 149ff, 165f, 187ff
 dogmatic mode, 10, 112, 149f, 165, 188ff, 213ff
 genealogical modes, 112, 149, 166ff, 190f
 See also alliances
Seidana, 77, 196
Seligman, C. G. and B. Z., v
Sennar, 2f, 11
Serur, Awlad, Fig. 1, Fig. 12, Fig. 13, Fig. 16, App. 7 (221)
 alliances and conflicts, 130f, 133, 140, 145
 distribution and movements, 26, 29, 147, 197
 divisions, 221
 as leaders of Humr, 129f, 133
Shatt tribe, 6
sheikhs, 72, 98, 110, 122, 149, 152f, 162, 171, 174
 distribution, 103f, 106, 151ff, 168f
 senior, 103f
 work of, 109f, 151ff, 194
shelga, 99
Sheybun Merida, Fig. 3, Fig. 10, 53, 77, 198, 200
Sheyn Ḥamdi, 134
Shigeyfa Wenesa, 169, 171, 183
Shweyn el Ḍeyf, 136f
Sileyman, 'Iyal, App. 7 (216), 168f, 171, 206
Slatin, R. von, 136
slaves and descendants, 40, 66, 80ff, 131f, 135, 189
 families, 59, 61, 80ff
 occupations, 67, 76, 80ff
Smith, M. G., 188
soil and vegetation types, 13ff
songs, 33, 117f, 123ff, 177

strangers, 6, 11f, 99, 113, 133, 144f, 150, 166, 171, 185, 191
Ṣubeyr el Ḥaj, Fig. 15, 98
sultans, 2ff, 123
surra, 9, 59ff, 86ff, 94, 97f, 114, 116, 120, 150, 160, 167ff
  summary of characteristics, 72n
surra leader, 65, 72ff, 77, 97f, 153

Ta'esha, 6
Ṭawir, 'Iyal, Fig. 7, 61f
tax, 28, 39, 72, 109f, 119, 121f, 140f, 143, 151f, 172. See also tribute
tea, 74, 119, 122ff, 139
tent, 29, 42ff, 45, 47, 49ff, 64f, 68f, 77, 102, 116, 177. See also household
Terakana, Fig. 17, App. 7 (216), 100, 123, 163, 167ff, 191, 193, 206, 209f
Townsend, Bimbashi, 134
trade, 3, 7, 28, 34, 36, 131f
transport, 23, 30, 37f, 74, 76
treasury, district, 109, 152
tree of the group (men's tree), 64, 66, 69, 73, 78, 116
tribute, 2, 4, 28, 103f, 109f, 120, 131, 134, 151. See also tax
Tuba, Awlad, Fig. 11, App. 7 (214), 101, 104, 202, 206
Tunisy, Sheikh Muḥammad 'Omar el, 2f
Turkiya, v, 4, 8, 119, 131, 159

Umm Beddy, Fig. 3, Fig. 6, Fig. 7, Fig. 10, 82, 165
Umm Una Merida, Fig. 3, Fig. 10, 52f, 77, 91
Umma party, vii, 142
'Umran, Awlad, Fig. 1, Fig. 11, Fig. 12, Fig. 14, Fig. 16, App. 7 (218), 8f, 11, 29, 77, 102, 143f, 203, 207
  conflict with A. Kamil, 132, 140f, 145, 194
  distribution and movements, 26, 108, 196f
  divisions, 104, 107, 218
  See also 'Addal, Menama
Upper Nile Province, 25, 117

vengeance, 94, 101, 115, 117, 140, 159, 163, 170, 174f, 184, 193
veterinary services, 39f

Wadai, 1ff, 6
Wadi el Ghalla, 15, 23, 75, 140, 147, 196f
warfare and raiding, 26, 102, 118, 120, 129ff, 189
water supplies, 15ff, 66, 69, 71, 74, 190, 195ff
  rights in, 25, 27
  See also wells
wealth, cattle as, 28f, 32, 38, 85
  differences in, 31, 39, 79, 85, 190
  and political office, 28, 72, 85, 118ff, 189
  and power, 28, 32, 42, 85, 118ff
  qualities thought necessary for acquiring, 31f, 39, 115, 117, 189
  and women, 31, 115f
wells, 15, 18, 25f, 69, 74, 157, 172, 190, 197
widows, 35, 46ff, 52, 61, 63f, 198ff
women, 39, 41, 47, 93, 95, 116, 123, 175
  cattle and, 31ff, 115f
  influence on public affairs, 115ff, 176
  property of, 43ff, 65, 198
  and qualities expected of men, 33f, 115, 117f, 176
  residence, 63f, 86
  See also household; maintenance of dependants; property, household

Ziyud, Fig. 1, Fig. 13, Fig. 16, App. 7 (220), 9, 29, 102, 105, 108, 136, 140f, 173, 191, 203, 207
  divisions, 220
  as strangers, 6, 11, 99, 113, 129
Zubeyr Pasha, 119, 131ff
Zurg (see Messiriya)